The Clockmakers' Library

Benjamin Lewis Vulliamy (1780–1854). Wax portrait by an unknown artist. Although Vulliamy was not the originator of the Clockmakers Company library when it was formed in 1814, he nevertheless co-operated in that year with the true founder – F. J. Barraud – and many of the earliest library acquisitions bear their joint signatures of acceptance. It is unfortunate that no likeness of F. J. Barraud is known to exist. Vulliamy was an eminent London Clockmaker who became Master of the Clockmakers Company on five occasions. (No. 1087)

The Clockmakers' Library

THE CATALOGUE OF THE BOOKS AND MANUSCRIPTS
IN THE LIBRARY OF THE
WORSHIPFUL COMPANY OF CLOCKMAKERS

Compiled by
JOHN BROMLEY

SOTHEBY PARKE BERNET PUBLICATIONS

© The Worshipful Company of Clockmakers 1977

Published by
Philip Wilson Publishers Limited
for Sotheby Parke Bernet Publications
Russell Chambers, Covent Garden, London WC2

Edition for the U.S.A.
available from
Sotheby Parke Bernet Publications
Biblio Distribution Centre
81 Adams Drive, Totowa, New Jersey 07512

ISBN 0 85667 033 2

Phototypesetting by Galleon Photosetting, Ipswich
Printed and bound in Great Britain by
The Garden City Press Ltd, Letchworth

CONTENTS

FOREWORD

by Sir Frank Francis, KCB

Besides its outstanding collection of clocks and watches, the Worshipful Company of Clockmakers has a collection of printed books and manuscript material which is likewise of intrinsic value for students of time-keeping and for historians of science. As a former Principal Librarian of the British Museum and as former Master of the Company I have a double satisfaction in assisting in the launching of the catalogue of this collection: not only does it accord with my deep professional interest in the production of good guides to specialist literature, but I am happy that the catalogue should have been prepared during my period of office.

From the horological point of view, the printed books in the Library provide a fairly complete coverage. The manuscripts are of particular interest. They include all the Court records of the Company from its inception in 1631 up to the present day and there are, in addition, many documents of great importance, including the unmatched collection of letters, drawings and essays connected with John 'Longitude' Harrison (1693–1776) and other contemporary horologists.

Every effort is made by the Company to collect and preserve the business archives of the great clock and watchmaking firms of the past as well as the present, and it is hoped that those interested in the preservation of horological documents will use their influence to ensure that further gifts and deposits are made to the Clockmakers Company for the benefit of future historians.

It is a matter of pride that the Company is able to make the whole of its collections, printed books and manuscripts as well as clocks and watches, available for consultation in Guildhall Library in the City of London, where, by courtesy of the Corporation of the City, it is most elegantly housed.

The Company is deeply indebted to Mr John Bromley for his work on the Catalogue. Mr Bromley has in the course of a lifetime's service in Guildhall Library become a leading authority on the sources of the history of London. His services to the Company were recognized by his election to the Livery in 1967.

The Company is also greatly indebted to Colonel Humphrey Quill, CBE, DSO, MVO, RM, a past Master of the Company, who has throughout placed his unique horological knowledge at Mr Bromley's disposal, and to Mr S. H. Burton, a member of the Livery, who contributed generously to the cost of publication.

Frank Francis
Master, 1974

PREFACE

The library of the Clockmakers Company was founded in 1813. An entry of 2 November 1813 in the Company's Court Minutes (Guildhall Library MS 2710/6) read as follows: 'Mr F. J. Barraud gave notice that at the next court he should move that it is expedient that this Company should possess and from time to time procure such books, pamphlets and tracts as have been written and published respecting and appertaining to the subject of the art placed under the government of this corporation.' On 10 January 1814 it was so resolved unanimously. Today the library comprises more than one thousand printed items, mainly in the field of historical horology; unique manuscript material, including the records of the Company from its incorporation in 1631; and a small collection of prints, portraits and photographs. All these are detailed in this catalogue and may be consulted in Guildhall Library where, by agreement with the Corporation of London, they are deposited.

The earliest printed catalogue of the library was published in 1830; the present catalogue is a revised version of that produced by G. H. Baillie in 1951, and incorporates accessions up to the end of September 1975. In addition, some relevant items (printed and manuscript) in Guildhall Library collections not represented in the Clockmakers Library have for convenience been included and are distinguished by asterisks. All items are incorporated in the general catalogues of Guildhall from which the respective shelf numbers may be obtained.

The form of entries in this catalogue for printed books is based on the standard formula for author entries as devised by the Anglo-American Cataloguing Code. Annotations have been kept to a minimum since this aspect is fully dealt with in Baillie's *Historical Bibliography*, of which the second volume, covering publications up to 1899, is in course of publication under the auspices of the Antiquarian Horological Society. Two indexes are supplied, one for printed books and one for manuscripts; both should be consulted. A brief list of portraits, prints and photographs is appended. It is emphasized that the collection is kept up to date, by purchase and gift, and every attempt is made to ensure that suitable items are acquired.

Colonel Humphrey Quill, CBE, DSO, MVO, RM, who encouraged me to undertake this task, has given generously of his unique knowledge of horology throughout the compilation of the catalogue. I am indebted also to my former colleagues at Guildhall: Donovan Dawe, J. L. Howgego, A. E. Hollaender and C. R. H. Cooper. The Librarian of Guildhall, Godfrey Thompson, has afforded me every facility for access to the books and documents under his control. It is a pleasant duty also to thank Mrs Joan Sarll, of Sotheby's staff, and Mr Michael Graham-Dixon, for their careful scrutiny of the text during the production stages of this volume.

Subsequent to the initiation of this catalogue two more deposits of horological material reinforce the claim of Guildhall Library to be a major source for horological research: the library of the Antiquarian Horological Society, although in part duplicating the printed works in the Clockmakers Company library, is complementary in the runs of foreign horological journals, pamphlets and illustrations that it contains; and the deposit of the extensive series of card indexes of clock and watchmakers, compiled over many years by Mr A. Osborne, comprises about 100,000 entries, largely British, together with topographical indexes.

John Bromley
Citizen and Clockmaker

LIST OF PLATES

CATALOGUE OF PRINTED BOOKS

Abbott (Francis)
1 A treatise on the management of public clocks, particularly church clocks; with hints for their improvement, and means for regulating them . . . Second edition . . . London, R. H. Moore [1838].
   43p   4 plates   20cm

Abbott (Henry G.)
2 Abbott's American watchmaker and jeweler. An encyclopedia for the horologist, jeweler, gold and silversmith . . . Illustrated with 288 engravings. Chicago, Geo. K. Hazlitt & Co., [1898].
   378p   2 fold. plates   19cm

Adams (Arthur)
3 The history of the Worshipful Company of Blacksmiths from early times until the year 1647. Being selected reproductions from the original books of the Company . . . London, privately printed, 1937.
   xiii   66p   24cm

4 **Address** to the public shewing the evils and pointing out the remedies of the present injurious system of apprenticeing boys to the watch trade . . . [*Anon.*] Coventry, J. Aston, printer, 1817.
   12p   17cm

Aked (Charles K.)
5 Electricity, magnetism and clocks. Reprinted from *Antiquarian Horology* . . . December 1971.
   18p   illus. port.   15cm

6 Famous inventor from Watten [Co. Caithness] [*Anon.*] Illustrated extract on Alexander Bain from *John O'Groats Journal*, 1960?
   Photocopy.

7 Inventor of the electric clock: Alexander Bain, Watten. Illustrated extract from *John O'Groats Journal*, 19 January 1973.
   Photocopy.
   Appended is a photocopy of a letter from Mrs Isabel Brander to Miss Bain with details of Bain and his work.

8 William Derham and *The artificial clockmaker*. Reprinted from *Antiquarian Horology*, March, June and September 1970.
   [34p]   illus. facsims.   25cm

Aked (Charles K.) and others
9 Horology in provincial and rural museums. London, Horological Antiquarian Society, 1974.
   46p   25cm
   Based on material compiled by John C. Stevens.

Allexandre (Dom Jacques)
10 Traité général des horloges . . . A Paris, chez Hippolyte Louis Guerin, 1734.
   viii   388p   25 fold. plates   3 tables   19cm

Allix (Charles Richard Peter)
11 Carriage clocks, their history and development. [London, Antique Collectors' Club, 1974.]
   vi   484p   illus. ports.   27cm

American Watch Co.
12 Souvenir catalog of the Orleans Exposition, 1884–85 . . . Bristol, Connecticut, K. Roberts, 1972.
   36p   illus.   22cm
   Facsimile reprint.

Andrade (Jules)
13 . . . Horlogerie et chronométrie . . . Paris, Librairie J. B. Baillière et fils, 1924.
   582p   23cm
   (Encyclopédie de mécanique appliquée.)

*Andrews (Herbert Caleb)**
14 A Hertfordshire worthy: John Briant, bell-founder and clockmaker, 1749–1829 . . . St Albans, East Herts Archaeological Society, 1930.
   95p   plates (inc. ports.)   24cm

Ansonia Clock Co.
15 [Catalogue of crystal regulators manufactured by the company. Boston, Mass., Brown, 1905.]
   46p   illus.   26cm
   Facsimile reprint, 1967, by the Robert G. Spence Co., of the 1905 edition in the Library of the American Clock and Watch Museum.

Antiquarian Horological Society
16 . . . Collectors' pieces, clocks and watches . . . tenth anniversary exhibition at the Science Museum, 29 May–9 August . . . [London, The Society, 1964.]
   xxii   90p   illus. plates   25cm

17 Pioneers of precision timekeeping: a symposium . . . [London, The Society, 1965.]
   117p   illus.   25cm

Antiquarian Horology and the Proceedings of the Antiquarian Horological Society
18 vol. 1 [to date] London, The Society, 1953–
   In progress.
   Published quarterly.
   With supplements.

Arnold (John)
19 An answer from John Arnold to an anonymous letter on the longitude. London, printed for T. Becket, 1782.
  24p   26cm

20 Certificates and circumstances relative to the going of Mr Arnold's chronometers. London, printed by George Bigg, 1791.
  viii 56p tables 27cm
Mainly concerns J. Arnold's chronometer watches nos 36 and 68.

Arnold (John Roger)
21 Instructions concerning Arnold's chronometers or timekeepers. [London, c 1805.]
  12p   26cm

22 Explanation of timekeepers constructed by Mr Arnold. Delivered to the Board of Longitude by Mr Arnold, 7 March 1805. [London, 1806.]
  ii 22p 3 fold. plates 26cm

23 L'art de l'horlogerie enseigné en trente leçons . . . par un ancien élève de Breguet. Paris, Audin, 1827.
  620p plates 17cm

Ashdown (Charles Henry)
24 History of the Worshipful Company of Glaziers of the City of London . . . Printed by Blades, East & Blades, London, 1918.
  iv 163p frontis. (port.) 5 plates 25cm

Asprey & Co.
25 The clockwork of the heavens; an exhibition of astronomical clocks, watches and allied scientific instruments . . . London, [Asprey,] 1973.
  92p illus. 30cm

26 **The astronomical** clock in York Minster: a memorial to fallen airmen, 1939–1945 . . . *Anon.* [York, printed by Morley, c 1960.]
  12p illus. plates 22cm

Atkins (Samuel Elliott) and Overall (William Henry)
27 Some account of the Worshipful Company of Clockmakers of the City of London. [London,] privately printed, 1881.
  xxx 346p 10 plates 25cm

***Atwood (George)**
28 Investigations, founded on the theory of motion, for determining the times of vibration of watch balances [London? 1794?]
  52p illus. 28cm
From *Philosophical Transactions of the Royal Society*, 1794.

Augustus Frederick, Duke of Sussex
29 Catalogue of the . . . collection of regulators, clocks, chronometers and watches . . . sold by auction by Christie and Manson . . . 4 July 1843 . . . [London, The auctioneers, 1843.]
  13p 26cm
The same. Another copy.
Xerox reproduction of an original with names of purchasers and prices realised.

Bailey (Francis Arthur)
30 An old watchmaker's workshop. Reprinted from *Transactions of the Ancient Monuments Society*, 1953.
  8p illus. 22cm

***Bailey (Francis Arthur) and Barker (Theodore Cardwell)**
31 The seventeenth-century origins of watchmaking in south-west Lancashire. (In Harris (J. R.), Liverpool and Merseyside. 1969. pp 1–15)

Bailey (John F.)
32 Longitude and the sea-clock . . . An illustrated extract from *History Today*, vol 20, 1970, pp 410–418. On the invention of the marine chronometer by John Harrison.

Baillie (Granville Hugh)
33 Clocks and watches: an historical bibliography . . . London, N.A.G. Press, [1951].
  xiii 414p illus. facsims. 21cm
Covers the period up to 1799.

34 Clocks and watches: an historical bibliography 1800–1899 . . . being the unpublished continuation of . . . the work published in 1951. [Typewritten, 1966.]
  13, 234 l. 34cm
Photocopy.

35 The same. The original MS from which the above copy was made.

36 The development of time measurement . . . prepared by the Worshipful Company of Clockmakers in connection with their Festival [of Britain] exhibit at the Guildhall, London, 1951. [London, Clockmakers' Company, 1951.]
  32p illus. 4 plates 18cm

37 Watch and clockmakers of the world. London, Methuen, 1929.
  xiv 416p 26cm

38 Watch and clockmakers of the world. London, N.A.G. Press, 1951.
  xxxiii 388p maps 22cm
3rd edition reprinted 1969.

39 The same. Another copy, interleaved with MS additions.

***40** Watches: their history, decoration and mechanism . . . London, Methuen [1929].
  xxiii 383p 76 plates 24cm (Connoisseur's Library)

Bain (Alexander)
41 A short history of the electric clocks, with explanations of their principles . . . London, Chapman, 1852. (*See* plate I.)
  31p illus. 21cm

42 Short history of the electric clock; edited by W. D. Hackman. London, Turner & Devereux, [1973]
  xv 31p illus. 15cm

Barker (Robert)
43 A list of Sunderland clockmakers. [Typewritten, 1965.]
  32p map 33cm

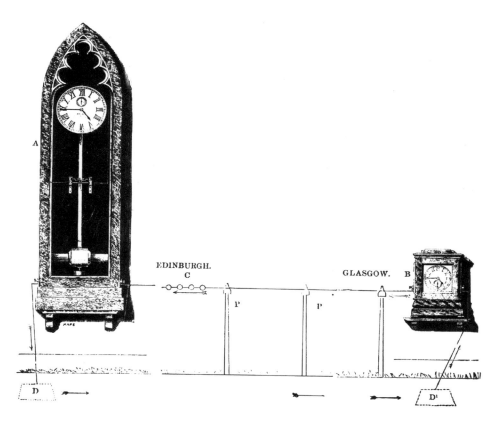

PLATE I Drawings from *A Short History of the Electric Clocks*, by Alexander Bain, 1852. Alexander Bain (1810–77) was the Scottish pioneer of electrical timekeeping. This drawing illustrates a successful demonstration of an earth-return circuit carried out by Bain in 1846. One of his electric clocks (A) in Edinburgh was connected to a second receiving or slave clock (B) in Glasgow by means of the above ground telegraph wire (P), connecting the railway stations of these cities. A 'voltaic battery' (C) supplied the current and each clock was connected to a metal plate (D) and (D¹) respectively, buried in the ground (an ample conductor), and thus the electrical circuit was completed. The two clocks worked in complete unison. (No. 38)

Barraud (Enid Mary)
44 Barraud: the story of a family. London, Research Publishing Co., [1967].
190p plates 24cm

45 The same. Another copy annotated by the author.

Barraud & Lunds
46 [Illustrated price catalogue of chronometers, watches and clocks. London, Barraud, c 1875.]
23p illus. 12cm

Barrett (C. R. B.)
47 The history of the Society of Apothecaries of London . . . London, Elliot Stock, 1905.
xxxix 310p frontis. 25cm

Bassermann-Jordan (Ernst von)
48 The book of old clocks and watches. 4th edition. Translated from the German by H. Alan Lloyd. London, Allen & Unwin, [1964].
xiii 522p illus. plates 24cm

*Baume and Co. Ltd.
49 A hundred years of time: the story of Baume and Company, watchmakers. London, [The company, 1949].
28p illus. ports. facsims. 18cm

Beckett (Edmund) *see* **Denison (Edmund Beckett)**

Bedfordshire
50 Parish registers; edited by F. G. Emmison . . . vol 13 . . . Bedford, County record office, 1936.
157p 33cm
The registers of Northill, containing records of the Tompion family.

Bedini (Silvio A.)
51 . . . The scent of time: a study of the use of fire and incense for time measurement in oriental countries . . . Philadelphia, American Philosophical Society, 1963.
50p illus. 30cm (American Philosophical Society Transactions, new series, vol 53, pt 5, 1963).

Beeson (Cyril Frederick Cherrington)
52 Clockmaking in Oxfordshire, 1400–1850. Oxford, Museum of the History of Science, 1967.
     193p illus. plates (inc. map) 24cm
Pts 1–2 first published in 1962 as monograph 2 of the Antiquarian Horological Society and as Records, vol 4, of the Banbury Historical Society.

53 English church clocks, 1280–1850: history and classification. London, Antiquarian Horological Society, [1971].
     128p illus. plates 24cm (Antiquarian Horological Society monograph 5)

Beillard (Alfred)
54 Recherches sur l'horlogerie, ses inventions et ses célébrités. Notice historique et biographique . . . Paris, E. Bernard et Cie, 1895.
     viii 209p frontis. illus. 23cm

*Bell (Arthur Ernest)
55 Christian Huygens and the development of science in the seventeenth century. London, Edward Arnold, 1950.
     220p plates (inc. ports.) 23cm

Bell (Geoffrey Howard) and Bell (Ellen Florence)
56 Old English barometers. Winchester, Warren, 1952.
     ix 42p plates (inc. ports.) 24cm

Bellchambers (Jack Kenneth)
57 Devonshire clockmakers. [Torquay,] 1962.
     41p plates 22cm

58 Somerset clockmakers. [London,] Antiquarian Horological Society, 1968.
     79p plates 25cm (Antiquarian Horological Society, Monograph 4)
Folding map inside back cover.

Bembo (Pietro), Cardinal
59 . . . Epistolae omnes quotquot extant, Latinae puritatis studiosis ad imitandum utilissimae . . . [c 1550?]
     743 11p 16cm
p 734. First recorded mention of an alarm clock in a letter to the author's son dated at Rome 1544.
Not in Baillie.

Bennett (Sir John)
60 The depression of the watch and clock manufacture with its remedy . . . London, Bean, Webley, printers, 1886.
     8p 21cm

*Bennett (Sir John) Ltd.
61 Gog and Magog: the house of Bennett 1750–1920. [London, 1920.]
     24p illus. port. 20cm

Benson (James W.)
62 Time and time-tellers . . . London, Robert Hardwicke, 1875.
     vii 190p illus. 18cm

Bertele (Hans von)
63 Clockwork globes and orreries . . . London, Antiquarian Horological Society, [1958].
     15p illus. 25cm
Reprinted from *Horological Journal* vol 100, 1958, pp 800–814.

64 Globes and spheres . . . Lausanne, Swiss Watch & Jewelry Journal [1961].
     63p illus. 26cm

Berthelé (Joseph)
65 Les 'Cloches et fondeurs de cloches' de M. Louis Régnier . . . Extrait du *Bulletin Monumentale*, Année 1896.
     pp 352–366 22cm

66 La vieille cloche de l'église de Châteauneuf (Vendée). Vannes, Imprimerie Lafolye, 1899. Extrait de la *Revue du Bas-Poitou*.
     8p 25cm

Berthoud (Ferdinand)
67 L'art de conduire et de régler les pendules et les montres: A l'usage de ceux qui n'ont aucune connoissance d'horlogerie [2nd edition] . . . A la Haye, chez Pierre Gosse Junior, 1761.
     xii 107p 4 fold. plates tables 13cm

68 De la mesure du temps, ou Supplément au Traité des horloges marines, et à l'Essai sur l'horlogerie; contenant les principes de construction, d'exécution & d'épreuves des petites horloges à longitude. Et l'application des mêmes principes de construction, &c. aux montres de poche, ainsi que plusieurs constructions d'horloges astronomiques, &c. . . . A Paris, chez J. G. Merigot le jeune, 1787.
     xvi 275p 11 fold. plates 27cm

69 De la mesure du temps par les horloges dans l'usage civil . . . Paris, Bandelot, 1797.
     16p 10cm

70 Eclaircissemens sur l'invention, la théorie, la construction, et les épreuves des nouvelles machines proposées en France, pour la détermination des longitudes en mer par la mesure du temps. Servant de suite a l'Essai sur l'horlogerie & au Traité des horloges marines, et de réponse à un écrit qui a pour titre: Précis des recherches faites en France pour la détermination des longitudes en mer par la mesure artificielle du temps . . . A Paris, chez J. B. G. Musier fils, 1773.
     viii 164p 26cm

71 The same. Another copy.

72 Essai sur l'horlogerie: dans lequel on traite de cet art, relativement à l'usage civil, à l'astronomie et à la navigation . . . 2e édition. Paris, Merigot, 1786.
     2 vols plates 26cm

73 Histoire de la mesure du temps par les horloges . . . A Paris, de l'imprimerie de la République. An X (1802 v.s.)
     2 vols Vol 1 xxviii 374p 13 fold. plates
     Vol 2 xvi 448p 13 fold. plates 28cm

74 The same. Another copy of Vol 1 only.

75 Les longitudes par la mesure du temps, ou méthode pour déterminer les longitudes en mer avec le secours des horloges marines . . . A Paris, chez J. B. G. Musier fils, 1775.
xxiv 90p fold. plates tables 26cm
Followed by an extract from *Voyage fait . . . pour éprouver en mer les horloges marines inventées par M. Ferdinand Berthoud*, by M. d'Eveux de Fleurieu. Paris, 1773. (*See* no. **327**.)
18p

76 Suite du *Traité des montres à longitude*, contenant la construction des montres verticales portatives, et celle des petites horloges horizontales pour servir dans les plus longues traversées . . . Paris, Bandelot, 1796.
viii 116p plates 26cm

77 Traité des horloges marines, contenant la théorie, la construction, la main-d'oeuvre de ces machines, et la manière de les éprouver, . . . A Paris, chez J. B. G. Musier fils, 1773.
xl 590p 27 fold. plates 26cm

78 Traité des montres à longitude, contenant la construction, la description & tous les détails de main-d'oeuvre de ces machines . . . A Paris, de l'imprimerie de Ph. D. Pierres, 1792.
xii 230 ii 20 16 23p 6 fold. plates 26cm
With three appendices.

79 Supplément au *Traité des montres à longitude*, suivi de la notice des recherches de l'Auteur depuis 1752 jusques en 1807 . . . A Paris, de l'imprimerie de J. M. Eberhart, 1807.
ii 88p 1 fold. plate 26cm

Binning (Rex Austin)
80 Group clocks tell a story.
Illustrated extracts from *Brighton Hospitals Bulletin*, Feb. 1971, pp 1, 6–7, and March 1971, p 7.
Account of clocks owned by the Brighton Hospitals Group.

Bird (John)
81 The method of constructing mural quadrants, exemplified by a description of the brass mural quadrant in the Royal Observatory at Greenwich . . . Published by order of the Commissioners of Longitude. London, 1768.
27p 3 fold. plates 26cm

82 The method of dividing astronomical instruments . . . Published by order of the Commissioners of Longitude. London, 1767.
vi 14p fold. plate 25cm

Birmingham. Museum of Science and Industry.
83 . . . [Catalogue of an] exhibition of British watches and clocks . . . [31 October 1953–28 February 1954. Birmingham, The Musuem, 1953.]
18p 1 plate 20cm

Blackburne (Richard)
84 Thomae Hobbes angli Malmesburiensis philosophi vita. *Anon.* Carolopoli [i.e. London,] apud Eleutherium Anglicum, 1682.
10, 67p port. 21cm

Blagrave (John)
85 The art of dyalling in two parts . . . London, printed by N. O. for Simon Waterson, 1609.
viii 152p illus. 19cm
See plate 2.

Blakesley (George H.)
86 The London Companies Commission: A comment on the majority report . . . London, Kegan Paul, Trench & Co, 1885.
63p 21cm

Bobinger (Maximilian)
87 Alt-Augsburger Kompassmacher: Sonnen-, mond- und Sternuhren, astronomische und mathematische Geräte, Räderuhren. Augsburg, Rösler [1966].
448p illus. port. facsims. 23cm (Abhandlungen zur Geschichter der Stadt Augsburg, Schriftenreihe des Stadtarchivs Augsburg, 16.)

88 Kunstuhrmacher in alt-Augsburg: erster Teil, Johann Reinhold, Georg Roll und ihr kreis; zweiter Teil, die Generationen der Buschmann. Augsburg, Rösler, [1969].
128p plates (inc. maps, facsims.) 23cm (Abhandlungen zur Geschichte der Stadt Augsburg: Schriftenreihe des Stadtarchivs Augsburg, 18.)

Bonniksen (B.)
89 The karrusel watch, by its inventor. *Anon.* [Sevenoaks, Gardner, 1969?]
48p illus. port. 20cm
A catalogue, reprinted from the original of 1905.

Booth (Mary Louise)
90 New and complete clock and watchmakers' manual . . . With an appendix containing a history of clock and watchmaking in America . . . New York, John Wiley & Sons, 1882.
xvii 294p 12 fold. plates 20cm

Bougainville (Louis Antoine de)
91 Voyage autour du monde, par la frégate du Roi la Boudeuse, et la flûte L'Etoile, en 1766, 1767, 1768 & 1769. Seconde édition augmentée. A Paris, chez Saillard & Nyon, 1772.
Vol I xliii 336p 6 maps
Vol II 456p 14 maps 20cm
Preface signed 'de Bougainville.'

Bowring (John)
92 Report on the commerce and manufactures of Switzerland . . . Presented to both Houses of Parliament . . . London, printed by W. Clowes & Sons, 1836.
148p 33cm

Boyd (Perceval)
93 Roll of the Drapers' Company of London . . . Croydon, J. A. Gordon at the Andress Press, 1934.
iii 207p 27cm

Boyle (Patrick Reginald), 13th Earl of Cork and Orrery
94 Catalogue of the . . . orrery made by . . . John Rowley which will be sold by auction . . . 24th June 1974 . . . [London, Sotheby, 1974.]
[12p] illus. 24cm

THE ART OF DYALLING
IN TWO PARTS.

The first shewing plainly, and in a ma-
ner mechanichally to make dyals to all
plaines, either Horizontall, Murall, declining, reclining or inclining, with the
theoricke of the Arte.

The second how to performe the selfe same , in a
more artificiall kinde, and without vse of Arithmeticke, together with concaue and conuex Dyals, and the inserting
of the 12. signes, and the howres of any other country
in any dyall, with many other things to the
same Art appertaining.

The whole differing much from all that hath beene heretofore
written of the same Art by any other, and the greater part wrought
by diuerse new conceits of the Author, neuer yet
extant , now published.

By IOHN BLAGRAVE of Reading Gentleman, and Mathemati-
cian this yeare, 1 6 09.

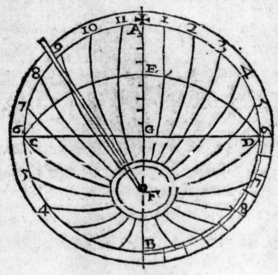

AT LONDON,
Printed by N. O. for *Simon Waterson*, and are to be sold at his shop in Paules
Church yard, at the signe of the Crowne, 1 6 0 9.

PLATE 2 Title-page of *The Art of Dyalling*, by J. Blagrave, 1609. Before clocks
and watches had been developed so as to be reasonably accurate, time was obtained
by sun dials of many different types. To compute and design an accurate dial
required a knowledge of spherical geometry as well as of astronomy; hence a
comprehension of these subjects was regarded not only as an attainment but also as
a civilized recreation. (No. 85)

Branston (A. W.)
95 Herefordshire clock and watch makers prior to 1870. [Typewritten, 1966.]
34 l. 33cm

British Clock and Watch Manufacturers Association
96 Five centuries of British timekeeping; an exhibition of modern clocks and watches . . . with historical specimens by the old master clockmakers, at Goldsmiths Hall . . . October 1955. [London, The Association, 1955.]
79p illus. 18cm

97 Pendulum to atom . . . an exhibition of modern clocks and watches . . . with historical specimens . . . [held at] Goldsmiths Hall . . . October . . . 1958 . . . [London, The Association, 1958.]
84p illus. 22cm

British Horological Institute
98 . . . British clockmakers' heritage exhibition . . . [London, The Institute, 1952.]
93 xi p 32 plates 24cm
Held at the Science Museum, South Kensington.

99 Catalogue of English books [in the library]. 1951.
28p 33cm
Typescript.

British Museum
100 Clocks in the British Museum, by Hugh Tait. London, The Museum, 1968.
55p illus. 25cm
Includes the Ilbert collection.

Britten (Frederick James)
101 Former clock and watchmakers and their work: including an account of the development of horological instruments from the earliest mechanism . . . a directory of over five thousand names . . . London, E. & F. N. Spon, 1894.
viii 397p 19cm

102 Old clocks and watches and their makers . . . London, Batsford, 1899.
viii 500p illus. 22cm

103 Old clocks and watches and their makers . . . to which is added a list of ten thousand makers . . . 2nd edition. London, Batsford, 1904.
viii 735p 22cm

104 Old clocks and watches and their makers . . . 3rd edition. London, Batsford, 1911.
viii 790p illus. ports. 22cm

105 Old clocks and their makers . . . With a list of over eleven thousand makers . . . 4th edition. London, Batsford, [1919].
x 597p 23cm
Preface dated 1919, signed A. M. Britten.

106 Old clocks and watches and their makers. Being an historical and descriptive account of the different styles of clocks and watches of the past, in England and abroad. To which is added a list of nearly 12,000 makers

. . . 5th edition, much enlarged . . . London, E. & F. N. Spon. [1922].
xii 822p frontis. 23cm
Preface dated 1922, signed Annie Britten.

107 Old clocks and watches and their makers . . . 6th edition. London, E. & F. N. Spon, [1933].
viii 891p illus. port. 22cm

108 Old clocks and watches and their makers . . . 7th edition. London, Spon, 1956.
xx 518p illus. plates 28cm
Edited by G. H. Baillie, C. Clutton, and C. A. Ilbert.

109 Old clocks and watches and their makers . . . 8th edition by Cecil Clutton, G. H. Baillie and C. A. Ilbert . . . London, Eyre Methuen, [1973.]
xxii 532p illus. plates 28cm

110 Old English clocks (the Wetherfield collection), with an introduction and notes. London, Lawrence and Jellicoe, 1907.
xi 133p illus. 38cm

111 On the springing and adjusting of watches . . . London, E. & F. N. Spon, 1898.
152p 18cm

112 The watch and clockmakers' handbook . . . 4th edition. London, W. Kent & Co., 1881.
172 iiip 20cm

113 The watch and clockmakers' handbook . . . [5th edition.] London, Kent & Co., 1884.
312p 20cm

114 The watch and clockmakers' handbook . . . 13th edition. London, E. & F. N. Spon, 1922.
504p illus. 21cm

115 The watch and clockmakers' handbook . . . 14th edition. London, E. & F. N. Spon, 1938.
vi 548p illus. 21cm

116 The watch and clockmakers' handbook . . . 15th edition. London, E. & F. N. Spon, [1955].
598 xxiip illus. 22cm

Britten (Frederick William)
117 Horological hints and helps. 2nd edition. London, Technical Press, 1934.
xi 361p 18cm

Bromley (John Frederick)
118 The armorial bearings of the guilds of London; a record of the heraldry of the surviving companies . . . with forty plates in full colour and numerous line drawings by Heather Child . . . London, Warne, [1961].
xii 282p illus. plates 23cm

Brown (Howard Miles)
119 Cornish clocks and clockmakers. [2nd edition.] Newton Abbot, David & Charles, [1970].
94p plates 18cm

Bruton (Eric)
120 Clocks and watches. [Feltham,] Hamlyn, [1968].
140p illus. 28cm

121 Clocks and watches 1400–1900. London, Barker, [1967].
208p illus. plates 24cm
Two copies.

122 From lantern to long-case. Illustrated extract from *Discovering antiques*, No. 17, pp 400–404, 1970.
Account of English clocks before 1750.

123 The longcase clock. London, Arco publications, 1964.
146p illus. plates 22cm

Buckley (Francis)
124 Old Manchester clock and watchmakers. 17th & 18th centuries. Uppermill, Moore & Edwards, 1929.
6p plates 22cm
MS additions.

125 Old watchmakers: Ellicott. Uppermill, [Moore & Edwards, printers,] 1930.
[6]p plates 27cm

126 Old watchmakers II: George Graham. Uppermill, Moore & Edwards, 1929.
6p plates 26cm

127 Old watchmakers III of London, 1600–1750. Uppermill, Moore & Edwards, 1929.
8p 22cm
MS additions.

128 Old watchmakers IV: Daniel Quare . . . Uppermill, Moore & Edwards, 1930.
6p plates 25cm

129 The watch and clockmakers of Northumberland and Durham of the 17th and 18th centuries recorded in newspapers, directories, etc. . . . Overprint from *Archaeologia Aeliana*, 4th series, vol 7. Newcastle-upon-Tyne, Northumberland Press Ltd., 1930.
pp 57–67 22cm

Buckley (Francis) and Buckley (George Bent)
130 Clock and watchmakers of the 18th century in Gloucestershire and Bristol . . . From *Transactions of the Bristol and Gloucestershire Archaeological Society*, vol. 51, 1929.
pp 305–319 22cm

*****131** Watch and clockmakers [of Worcestershire of the 18th century]. Reprinted from *Berrow's Worcester Journal*, 1930.

Burgess (Edward Martin)
132 World time sculptural clock in the banking hall of J. Henry Schroder Wagg & Co., Ltd. . . . designed by Martin Burgess . . . 1969; descriptive and pictorial manual of operation and maintenance . . . [Boreham, Burgess metallic art Ltd., 1969.]
4 vols illus. 27cm
Typewriter script.

Burkitt (E. H.)
133 A short history of the Worshipful Company of Curriers . . . [London, The Company, 1906.]
72p frontis. (arms) 2 plates 18cm

Bury St Edmunds. Corporation.
134 The John Gershom Parkington memorial collection of time measurement instruments. Compiled by S. Benson Beevers. Reprinted from *The Connoisseur Year book*, 1958.
15p illus. 31cm

135 The John Gershom Parkington memorial collection of time measurement instruments. Based on a catalogue compiled by S. Benson Beevers.
Illustrated extract from *The Connoisseur*, vol 176, no. 708, February 1971, pp 93–105.

C. (H.) *see* **A Short** chat . . .

Camus (Charles Etienne Louis)
136 A treatise on the teeth of wheels, pinions, &c., demonstrating the best forms which can be given to them for the various purposes of machinery; such as mill-work, clock-work &c. . . . translated from the French of M. Camus; with additions . . . London, printed by W. Stratford, 1806.
xvii 144p 15 plates 23cm

Caspari (E.)
137 Les chronomètres de marines . . . Paris, Gauthier-Villars, [1894].
203p 19cm

Cassini (Jean Dominique de)
138 Voyage fait par ordre du Roi en 1768, pour éprouver les montres marines inventées par M. Le Roy . . . Avec le mémoire sur la meilleure manière de mesurer le tems en mer, qui a remporté le prix double au jugement de l'Académie Royale des Sciences . . . A Paris, chez Charles Antoine Jombert, 1770.
viii 144p tables xxivp Mémoire 60p map 6 fold. plates 25cm

Cerchiari (Giacinto)
139 Trattato grafico analitico di gnomonica . . . Imola per Ignazio Galeati, 1835.
123p 8 fold. tables 14 fold. plates 28cm

*****Cescinsky (Herbert)**
140 The Old English master clockmakers . . . 1670–1820. London, Routledge, [1938].
xii 182p illus. ports. 25cm

Cescinsky (Herbert) and Webster (Malcolm R.)
141 English domestic clocks . . . London, Routledge, 1913.
353p illus. port. 31cm

Chamberlain (Paul M.)
142 Watches. The Paul M. Chamberlain collection at the Art Institute of Chicago. 1921 . . .
Not paged. 54p 2 plates 24cm
(*See* plate 3.)

143 Its about time . . . New York, Richard R. Smith, 1941.
xvi 490p illus. 26cm

No. 123—ALARM WATCH BY THOS.
MUDGE

No. 191—"H. Z. Culver, Elgin, Ill. Pat. No. 1800." Full plate, 18 size, key wind, 15 jewels, compensation balance. Made 1867. See cut 158-23. The Natn'l. Watch Co. of Chicago, Illinois was incorporated in 1864. In 1874, the name of the Company was changed to "The Elgin National Watch Co."

No. 192—"T. M. Avery, Elgin, No. 415726." "Elgin Natn'l Watch Co." Full plate, 18 size, nickel balance, 7 jewels, key wind. Made in 1876. See cut 158-24.

No. 193—"Francis Rubie. National Watch Co., Elgin. Patent Pinion. Moseley's Patent No. 50832." 10 size, three-quarter plate, compensated balance, 15 jewels, key wind. Made in 1878. See cut 158-22.

No. 194—"Dexter St., National Watch Co., Elgin, Patent Pinion, No. 201110." Three-quarter plate, 10 size, key wind, 7 jewels, compensated balance. Made in 1872. See cut 158-21.

No. 195—"Lady Elgin, Elgin, Ill., Patent, Moseley Patent. No. 76705." Three-quarter plate, 10 size, 15 jewels, compensated balance. Made in 1871.

No. 196—"Gail Borden, Elgin, Patent Pinion, Patent, 186012." Key wind, 10 size, three-quarter plate, 15 jewels, compensated balance. Made about 1872. Resembles cut 158-21.

No. 197—"Atlas Watch Co., Chicago." No number. Made by Water-

PLATE 3 Illustration from a catalogue of the Paul M. Chamberlain Collection of watches that was on exhibition at the Art Institute of Chicago in 1921. Major Chamberlain (1865–1940) formed two watch collections, one before and the other after the First World War. He was also the author of *It's About Time*, 1941 (No. 143), a work of great importance. (No. 142)

*Chancellor (Edwin Beresford)
144 The collection of watch-papers belonging to the Clockmakers' Company at Guildhall.
(In *Connoisseur*, vol 83, 1929, pp 339–344.)
See List of Prints, &c., item 1151 *post*.

Chancellor (John)
145 A treatise, in nine sections on the properties and advantages of a new invented escapement, with reference to all its parts by engraved diagrams . . . Dublin, printed for John Cumming, 1833.
22p fold. plate 22cm

Chapuis (Alfred)
146 De horologiis in arte: l'horloge et la montre à travers les âges . . . Lausanne, Editions du Journal Suisse d'horlogerie et de bijouterie, 1954.
154p illus. plates 30cm

147 Geneva watches and enamels: the H. Wilsdorf collection . . . Geneva, Rolex, 1945.
136p 23cm
Translated from French edition of 1944.

148 Histoire de la boîte à musique et de la musique mécanique . . . Lausanne, Edition Scriptar, 1955.
319p illus. plates 27cm

149 Montres et émaux de Genève, Louis XIV, Louis XV, Louis XVI et Empire. Texte de Alfred Chapuis, Dr H. C. Avant-propos de Paul Chaponnière. Geneva, Collection H. Wilsdorf, 1944.
234p 48 col. plates 28cm
(Half-title): Il a été tiré de cet ouvrage 600 exemplaires. Exemplaire hors commerce.

150 Relations de l'horlogerie suisse avec la Chine: la montre chinoise . . . Neuchâtel, Attinger Frères, [1919].
xiii 272p illus. 28cm

151 Urbain Jurgensen et ses continuateurs. A propos d'un manuscrit inédit. Neuchâtel, Imprimerie Paul Attinger, 1923.
46p frontis. (port.) plates 20cm

*Chapuis (Alfred) and Droz (Edmond)
152 Automata: a historical and technological study, translated from the French by Alec Reid. Neuchâtel, Griffon, [1958].
407p illus. plates 28cm

*153 Les automates . . . Neuchâtel, Griffon, [1950].
425p illus. 18 plates 28cm

Chapuis (Alfred) and Jacquet (Eugène)
154 The history of the self-winding watch 1770–1931. English adaptation by R. Savaré Grandvoinet . . . London, Batsford, [1956].
246p illus. 28cm

Charmasse (Anatole de)
155 L'horlogerie et une famille d'horlogers à Autun et à Genève, aux seizième et dix-septième siècles.
In *Mémoires de la Société Eduenne*. Nouvelle série. Tome 16e. Autun, Imprimerie Dejussieu Père et Fils, 1888.
pp 175–213 25cm

Chasin (Martin)
156 The Lees clock in the rare book collection . . . Reprinted from the Library Chronicle of the University of Pennsylvania, vol 34, no 1, 1968.
11p 1 plate 23cm

Chaucer (Geoffrey)
157 A treatise on the Astrolabe; addressed to his son Lowys by Geoffrey Chaucer, AD 1391. Edited from the earliest MSS by the Rev Walter W. Skeat . . . London, published for the Early English Text Society by H. Trubner & Co., 1872.
lxix 120p 7 plates 22cm

Chenakal (Valentin L.)
158 Watchmakers and clockmakers in Russia 1400 to 1850 . . . Translated by W. F. Ryan. London, Antiquarian Horological Society, 1972.
64p ports. 14cm (Antiquarian Horological Society monograph, 6.)

Christie, Manson and Woods
159 Catalogue of watches, clocks and instruments: T. B. Williams Esq and the late Laurence Bateman Esq . . . which will be sold at auction . . . 8 October 1968 . . . [London, Christie, 1968.]
35p plates 24cm

Cipolla (Carlo Maria)
160 Clocks and culture 1300–1700. London, Collins, 1967.
191p illus. plates 21cm

City and Guilds of London Institute
161 City & Guilds of London Institute for the advancement of technical education. Proposals of Executive Committee, January 1879.
4p 38 × 10cm

162 City and Guilds of London Institute for the advancement of technical education. Report to the Governors, 14 March 1881.
37p 25cm

Clapham (Sir John)
163 The Bank of England. A history . . . Cambridge, University Press, 1944.
2 vols plates 24cm

Clerke (Gilbert)
164 The spot-dial, very useful to shew the hour within the house: together with directions how to find a true meridian, the azymuth and declination . . . London, printed by J. M. for Walter Kettilby, 1687.
ii 26p 20cm

Clockmakers Company
165 [Association oath roll of members of the Company witnessing to the loyalty to William III and supporting the rightful succession, 1697.]
s.sh. 83 × 56cm
Facsimile of the original MS in the Public Record Office.

166 [Circular urging those engaged in clockmaking who are entitled to do so to take up their freedom. London, 1812.]
3p

167 [Collection of acts, regulations, oaths, standard letters and forms, etc. relating to the company, 1809–17.] Includes Livery list, 1812, and Observations on the art and trade of . . . watchmaking . . . [*Anon.*] 1812.

168 [Collection of forms, and other documents, relating to admission to the freedom, court of assistants and livery of the company, during the Clerkship of George Atkins, 1809–40.]

169 [Collection of summonses to the quarterly Court of Assistants, 1794–1879.]
3 vols

170 [Freemen 1631–1896.] Compiled alphabetically by Charles E. Atkins from a manuscript list made by . . . H. C. Overall . . . *c* 1900.
154 l.   33cm
Photostat copy.

171 Abstracts from Acts of Parliament, &c., Orders, and bye-laws of the Worshipful Company of Clockmakers, London: and regulations for the manufacture of clocks, watches and mathematical instruments. Hoxton, Richardson, printer.
14p   17cm

172 Appeal to the trade to maintain the authority of the Clockmakers' Company, so that illicit practices may be stopped. Hoxton, Richardson, printer, 1812.
3p   33cm   2 copies.

173 Catalogue of books in the Library of the Company of Clockmakers of the City of London. London, printed by B. McMillan, 1830.
iii   26p interleaved with MS additions   22cm

174 The same. Another copy.

175 A catalogue of books, manuscripts, specimens of clocks, watches and watch-work, paintings, prints, etc., in the Library and Museum of the Worshipful Company of Clockmakers of the City of London. London, printed by E. J. Francis & Co., 1875. Compiled by William Francis Overall.
vii   103p   23cm

176 The same, interleaved, 2 copies.

177 Catalogue of the library . . . 2nd edition. London, [The Company,] 1898.
205p   23cm

178 Another copy. Inlaid on large paper.

179 A catalogue . . . of the collection of clocks, watches, chronometers presented . . . by . . . H. L. Nelthropp . . . [with additions to 1897]. London, The Company, 1895–97.
2 vols in 1   illus. port.   24cm

180 A catalogue . . . of the collection of clocks, watches, chronometers . . . presented . . . by . . . H. L. Nelthropp . . . 2nd edition. London, [The Company,] 1900.
85p illus.   24cm
Bound with Catalogue of the Museum of the Worshipful Company of Clockmakers . . . 2nd edition. 1902.

181 The same. Another copy.

182 Catalogue of the Museum . . . 2nd edition. London, [The Company,] 1902.
viii   95p   24cm

183 The same. Another copy.

184 3rd edition [Compiled by G. H. Baillie.] London, Mowbray, 1949.
v   137p   22cm

185 Clocks and watches in the collection of the Worshipful Company of Clockmakers [by] Cecil Clutton and George Daniels. London, Sotheby Parke Bernet, 1975.
xx   123p   illus. plates   28cm

186 Catalogue of books in the library. 1820.
MS with names of donors and prices paid for purchases.

187 Catalogue of the library . . . 3rd edition. London, The Company, 1951.
v   79p   22cm

188 Charter and bye-laws of the Worshipful Company of Clockmakers of the City of London, incorporated 1631 . . . Printed by M. Couchman . . . by order of the Master, Wardens and Fellowship, 1825.
104p printed on one side only   frontis. (arms)   23cm

189 The Charter and bye-laws of the Company of Clockmakers of London. London, printed by R. S. Kirby, [*c* 1800].
72p   interleaved   17cm

190 A second copy has a MS note: 'Examined by George Atkins with Justin Vulliamy, 24 April 1817'.

191 Guide to the Museum of the Clockmakers' Company of London, by G. H. Baillie. [London, Butler & Tanner,] 1939.
73p   15 plates   13cm

192 A list of the names of the Master, Wardens, Assistants and livery . . . 1784, 1785, 1786–89, 1796–97, 1801–15, 1817, 1880, 1891–1946, 1949–57, 1960, 1963, 1968, 1971 [to date].

193 A memorial to the Lords of his Majesty's Treasury, on the subject of the illicit importation of foreign clocks & watches into these realms. Dated Dec 9th 1841. [London, The Company, 1842?]
12p   32cm

194 Register of apprentices . . . from its incorporation in 1631 to . . . 1931; compiled from the records . . . by Charles Edward Atkins . . . [London,] privately printed, 1931.
xvi   338p   frontis.   25cm

195 A statement of the various proceedings and transactions that have taken place between the Court of Assistants of the Clockmakers' Company of the City of London and his Majesty's Government, in relation to the importation of foreign clocks and watches into these realms, subsequent to the 5th of March, 1832. Ordered to be printed . . . the 8th of July, 1833: and the addenda . . . to be printed . . . 1841. London, printed by John Ollivier, 1841.
pp 41–59, incl. the addenda only   25cm

196 Another copy, without the addenda. London, printed by E. H. Blagden, 1833.
40p   24cm

197 Another copy. London, printed by B. McMillan, 1832.
vi 73p 24cm

Clutton (Cecil)
198 Collector's collection. [A description of the author's collection of watches and small timepieces.] London, Antiquarian Horological Society, 1974.
95p illus. 24cm

Clutton (Cecil) and Daniels (George)
199 Watches. London, Batsford, [1965.]
xvi 159p plates 30cm

Collard (F. Bernard Royer-)
200 Skeleton clocks. London, N. A. G. Press, [1969.]
154p illus. port. facsims. 28cm

Collins (John)
201 Geometrical Dyalling: or, Dyalling performed by a line of chords onely, or by the plain scale . . . London, printed by Thomas Johnson for Francis Cossinet, 1659.
iv 82p frontis. 18 plates 18cm

202 The sector on a quadrant, or a treatise containing the description and use of four several quadrants; two small ones and two great ones, each rendred many wayes . . . Also an appendix [by John Lyon] touching reflected dyalling . . . London, George Hurlock, 1659.
[386]p illus. plates 18cm
Pts 2 and 3 and appendix have separate title pages all dated 1658.

Commissioners of Longitude
203 Explanations of timekeepers constructed by Mr Thomas Earnshaw and the late Mr John Arnold. London, T. Bensley, 1806.
iii 63p 6 fold. plates 28cm

204 Minutes of the proceedings of the Commissioners appointed by Act of Parliament for the discovery of the longitude at sea, at their meetings [in May and June] 1765. With respect to carrying into execution so much of an Act . . . as relates to giving Mr John Harrison a reward, upon his making a discovery of the principles of his watch or timekeeper. Printed in the year 1765.
15p 25cm
Another copy in 976/15 post.

205 The principles of Mr Harrison's time-keeper, with plates of the same. London, W. Richardson and S. Clark, 1767.
31p 10 fold. plates 26cm
See also 976/20E post.

206 Tables for correcting the apparent distance of the moon and a star from the effects of refraction and parallax. Cambridge, The Commissioners, 1772.
xii [1066] p 34cm

Coole (Philip George)
207 Investing in clocks and watches by P. W. Cumhaill [pseudonym for Philip George Coole]. London, Barrie, [1967].
159p illus. 30cm

Coole (Philip George) and Neumann (Erwin)
208 The Orpheus clocks. London, Hutchinson, [1972].
164p illus. plates 24cm

*Cooper (Thomas Parsons)
209 The old clockmakers and watchmakers of York. Reprinted from the Associated Architectural Societies' reports and papers, vol 30, pt 1, 1909.
18p 20cm

Cork and Orrery, Earl of see **Boyle (P.R.)**

Cousins (Frank William)
210 Sundials . . . London, Baker, [1969].
247p illus. 25cm

Coventry. Public Libraries.
211 Catalogue of a collection of horological and scientific books, etc. presented to the library by the watch manufacturers of the city of Coventry. Coventry, [The Library,] 1876.
36p 20cm

Cox (James)
212 A descriptive inventory of the several exquisite and magnificent pieces of mechanism and jewellery, comprised in the schedule annexed to an Act of Parliament . . . for enabling Mr James Cox . . . to dispose of his Museum by way of lottery. London, printed by H. Hart for Mr Cox, 1773.
46p 16cm

Crespe (François)
213 Essai sur les montres à répétition . . . à l'usage des horlogers . . . A Genève, chez J. J. Paschoud, An XII–1804.
xiv 284p 19cm

Crisp (W. B.)
214 Prize essay on the compensation balance and its adjustments in chronometers and watches . . . Printed by Turner & Co, London, [1875].
30p 2 plates 22cm

Crom (Theodore R.)
215 Horological wheel cutting engines, 1700 to 1900. Gainesville, Fla., [The author,] 1970.
ix 150p illus. port. facsims. 23cm

Croucher (Joseph)
216 Analytical hints, on the patent marine time keeper, made by Joseph Croucher, no. 27 Cornhill . . . [London, The author, c 1828.]
14 l. 20cm
Photocopy of original pamphlet.
A marine chronometer by Croucher is in Clockmakers Museum, no. 619.

Cudworth (William)
217 Life and correspondence of Abraham Sharp . . . with memorials of his family . . . London, Sampson Low, 1889.
xvi 342p illus. plates 25cm

Cumhaill (P. W.), pseudonym for Philip George Coole, see **Coole (Philip George)**.

Cumming (Alexander)
218 The elements of clock and watch-work . . . London, printed for the author, 1766.
[vi] 192 [xiii] p 16 fold. plates 28cm
See plates 4, 5.

219 The same. Another copy with MS notes by Thomas Grignion, jnr.

220 The same. Another copy.
Interleaved with MS notes by the author: 'This is the most correct coppy [*sic*] if a second edition should be wanted. Apr. 1803.'

221 The same. Another copy.
With MS notes by James Short, John Rowning and the author.

Cunynghame (Henry Hardinge)
222 Royal Society of Arts. Cantor Lectures on the theory and practice of clockmaking . . . London, printed by William Trounce, 1909.
59p 25cm

223 Time and clocks: A description of ancient and modern methods of measuring time. London, Archibald Constable & Co. Ltd., 1906.
200p frontis. illus. 19cm

Cuss (Theodore Patrick Camerer)
224 The Country Life book of watches. London, Country Life Ltd., [1967].
128p illus. 25cm

225 The story of watches. London, Macgibbon, 1952.
172p illus. 22cm

*Daniell (J. A.)
226 The clockmakers of Leicestershire . . . [*c* 1949.]
9 l. 25cm

227 The making of clocks and watches in Leicestershire and Rutland . . . Leicester, Leicestershire Archaeological Society, 1952.
36p plates 25cm
Reprinted, with revision, from the Transactions of the Society, vol 27, 1951.

Daniels (George)
228 The art of Breguet. A study of the art and techniques of the great horologist. London, Sotheby Parke Bernet, 1975.
xi 394p illus. ports. plates facsims. 32cm

229 . . . The astronomical watch by George Margetts in the possession of the Royal Institution, and some other timekeepers of Margetts . . . Reprinted from Proceedings of the Royal Institution, vol 42, no 199, 1969
[20] p illus. 22cm

230 Catalogue of watches presented to the Worshipful Company of Clockmakers by Howard A. Collinson . . . [MS and photocopy.] 1968.
[40] l. 33cm

231 English and American watches. London, Abelard-Schuman, [1967].
127p illus. 22cm
pp 69–76: biographical notes.

232 The same. Another copy.

Dawson (Percy G.)
233 The design of English domestic clocks, 1660–1700 . . . London, Antiquarian Horological Society, 1956.
23p illus. 25cm

De Bougainville (Louis Antoine) *see* **Bougainville (Louis Antoine de)**

De Carle (Donald)
234 British time. London, Crosby Lockwood, [1947].
199p 46 plates fold. map 21cm

235 Clock and watch repairing (including complicated watches) . . . London, Pitman, [1959].
viii 312p illus. 22cm

236 Clocks and their value . . . with a unique chart of all known Tompion Clocks. London, N.A.G. Press, [1968].
vi 144p illus. 20cm

237 The same. 2nd edition. London, N.A.G. Press, [1971].
vi 159p illus. 20cm

238 Practical clock repairing . . . [2nd edition.] London, N.A.G. Press, [1968].
x 244p illus. 22cm

239 Practical watch repairing . . . [3rd edition.] London, N.A.G. Press, [1969].
viii 319p illus. 21cm

240 Watch and clock encyclopedia . . . [2nd edition.] London, N.A.G. Press, 1959.
307p illus. 21cm

241 The watchmaker's lathe and how to use it . . . [2nd edition.] London, Hale, [1971].
xi 164p illus. 22cm

242 With the watchmaker at the bench. A book for the practical watchmaker . . . 3rd edition. London, Sir Isaac Pitman & Sons, 1938.
xi 243p fold. plates 18cm

Defossez (L.)
243 Les savants du XVIIe siècle et la mesure du temps . . . Lausanne, Edition du Journal Suisse d'Horlogerie et de bijouterie, 1946.
341p 44 plates 24cm

Denison (Edmund Beckett) *afterwards* **Edmund Beckett and First Baron Grimthorpe**
244 A rudimentary treatise on clock and watch making: with a chapter on church clocks; and an account of the proceedings respecting the great Westminster clock. With numerous drawings . . . London, John Weale, 1850.
xii 279p frontis. 18cm

245 A rudimentary treatise on clocks, watches and bells . . . 6th edition, revised and enlarged. London, Lockwood & Co., 1874.
xi 384p fold. frontis. 18cm

246 A rudimentary treatise on clocks, watches and bells . . . 7th edition, 1883.
xiii 400p fold. frontis. 18cm
See also Gordon (G. F. C.) (no. 375 *post*).

THE
ELEMENTS
OF
CLOCK and WATCH-WORK,

Adapted to PRACTICE.

In TWO ESSAYS.

By ALEXANDER CUMMING,
Member of the Phil. Soc. Edinb.

LONDON: Printed for the AUTHOR;
And sold by him, and the following Booksellers;

A. MILLAR, and D. WILSON, in the Strand; J. DODSLEY, Pall-mall; S. BAKER, York-street, Covent-garden; Messrs. RICHARDSON and URQUHART, at the Royal Exchange; Messrs. FLETCHER and ANDERSON, St. Paul's Church-yard; T. PAYNE, at the Meuse Gate; J. ROBSON, New Bond-street: And by A. KINCAID, G. HAMILTON, and J. BALFOUR, in Edinburgh.

MDCCLXVI.

PLATE 4 Title-page of *The Elements of Clock and Watch-work* by Alexander Cumming, 1766. There are three annotated copies of this famous work by Cumming (c 1732–1814) in the Clockmakers Company library. One of these contains notes by Thomas Grignon; another has comments by James Short, John Rowning and the author himself, while in the third Cumming has noted, 'This is the most correct copy if a second Edition should be wanted. Apr. 1803.' Two of these copies also contain the comparatively rare page of *errata*; see Plate 5. (Nos 218–219)

E R R A T A.

Parag. Line.

1.	4.	*for* conftrued, *read* conftructed
47.	2.	*after* are, *infert* in theory
68.	2.	*for* only is the motive force, *read* alone is the moving power
70.	4.	*for* motive force, *read* moving power
98.	2.	*after* fixed point, *infert* within the ball
152.	6.	*for* that will corroborate, *read* to corroborate
203.	1.	*for* planes, *read* plane
226.	——	*The laft part of the firft note of this paragraph is wrong expreffed; but as the firft part comprehends the whole meaning, the Reader may draw his pen through that part which follows, i. e.*
271.	8.	*for* being, *read* been
296.	2.	*for* Pl. 7. *read* Pl. 5.
311.	13.	*for* pivots, *read* points
334.	11.	*for* upwards, *read* downward
	12.	*for* downward, *read* upwards
343.	9.	*for* rod, *read* rods
		Page 98. line 5. from the bottom; *for* dilation, *read* dilatation
365.	11.	*for* eafily, *read* eafie
380.	5.	*for* therefore, *read* but
399.	13.	*for* vibration, *read* vibrations
424.	1. & 2.	*for* is as its thicknefs, *read* increafes with its thicknefs
440.	5.	*for* in the proportion, *read* in proportion
479.	10.	*after the word* expect, *infert* that
526.	——	In the firft line of the note, *for* pl. 16. *read* pl. 15.
552.	——	*From the beginning; read* If the train be continued the fame, the number of leaves in the third-wheel pinion may be increafed, in the fame proportion as the number of teeth in the horizontal wheel, &c.
546.	4.	*for* any how leffened, *read* fenfibly leffened

In the conclufion, page 192. line 5. *for* practical theory, *read* a practical theory.

Whereas fome perfons feem either to mifunderftand the author's meaning, or are difpofed to difpute about words; it is proper here to mention, that

By MOMENTUM, is meant, *the effective power*, or force which a body exerts before its whole motion is deftroyed;

By MOVING POWER, that force which caufes motion, whether it takes effect in whole or in part;

And by the FORCE IMPRESSED is meant, fuch part of the *moving power* as really takes effect.

Thus if a wheel be moved by a ftream of water, the whole ftream is the *moving power*: but the force which it *impreffes* depends as much on the velocity of the wheel, as on the velocity or force of the ftream; for if the wheel moves with a velocity equal to that of the ftream, the latter can *imprefs no force* on the former, nor add to its velocity.

By MOTIVE FORCE, is meant, the quantity of motion generated by the *impreffed force.*

And in this fenfe the author apprehends thefe words have always been underftood.

PLATE 5 Page of *errata* from *The Elements of Clock and Watch-work*, by Alexander Cumming, 1766. This page of *errata* is only found occasionally in copies of this well known work. See also Plate 4. (Nos 218–219)

Dennison (Franklin)
247 Historic horology: being a catalogue of a collection of antique watches belonging to the Franklin Dennison collection and exhibited by the Dennison Watch case Company at the Jewellers' Exhibition, 1913. [With supplement, 1914.] London, 1913–14.
 2 vols in 1 16cm

Dent (Edward John)
248 An abstract from two lectures on the construction and management of chronometers, watches and clocks, delivered before the members of the United Service Institution, May 1841 . . . Published by the Author . . . London, 1841.
 30p 21cm

249 Dent on the errors of chronometers and explanation of a new construction of the compensation balance. [Cover title. London, 1842.]
Reprint of an appendix, pp 13–24. 21cm
Another copy from the *Nautical Magazine*, 1842, pp 760–8.

250 A description of the dipleidoscope, or double reflecting meridian and altitude instrument; with plain instructions for the method of using it in the correction of timekeepers . . . London, published by the Author, 1843.
 24p frontis. 21cm

251 New edition. [*Anon.*] London, Dent, 1875.
 28p illus. 1 plate 21cm

252 A paper on the patent azimuth and steering compass, invented by Edward J. Dent. Presented to the meeting of the British Association . . . at York. Published by the Author . . . 1844.
 10p 21cm
Includes a paper on the shape of the wheel teeth in the clock for the Royal Exchange.

Dent (G.)
253 The clock and watch makers of the old parish of Halifax, 1624 to about 1850. [Halifax, Halifax Printing Co., 1947.]
 26p plates 22cm

Department of the environment: Ancient monuments and historic buildings.
254 The astronomical clock, Hampton Court Palace; by Brian Hellyer and Heather Hellyer. London, H.M.S.O., 1973.
 28p illus. ports. 16cm

Derham (William)
255 The artificial clockmaker. A treatise of watch and clock-work . . . Also the history of clock-work, both ancient and modern . . . by W. D., MA. London, printed for James Knapton, 1696.
 xii 132p fold. plate 17cm
See plate 6.

256 The same. Another copy.

257 The artificial clockmaker . . . The second edition enlarged. To which is added a supplement, containing, 1. The anatomy of a watch and clock . . . 2. Monsieur Romer's satellite instrument . . . 3. A nice way to correct pendulum watches. 4. Mr Flamsteed's equation tables. 5. To find a meridian line, for the governing of watches . . . 6. To make a telescope to keep a watch by the fixed stars. London, printed for James Knapton, 1700.
 xii 150p 3 fold. plates 2 fold. tables 16cm

258 The same. Another copy.

259 The artificial clockmaker . . . The third edition, with large emendations and additions. By W. D., FRS. London, printed for James Knapton, 1714.
 xvi 140p 3 fold. plates 2 fold. tables 16cm

260 The artificial clockmaker . . . The fourth edition, with large emendations. 1734. Same collation.

261 The artificial clockmaker . . . The fourth edition, corrected. London, Knapton, 1759.
 xvi 160p 3 fold. plates 2 fold. tables 17cm

262 Philosophical experiments and observations of the late eminent Dr Robert Hooke . . . London, printed by W. & J. Innys, 1726.
 vi 397p 3 plates 2 fold. plates 19cm
Photostats have been substituted for all the plates.

263 Traité d'horlogerie pour les montres et les pendules . . . Traduit de l'Anglois de M. Derham . . . A Paris, chez Grégoire Dupuis, 1731.
 viii 191p 3 fold. plates fold. table 16cm
Translation of *The artificial clockmaker*.

De Rivaz (Pierre Joseph) *see* **Rivaz (Pierre Joseph de)**

Desargues (Gérard)
264 . . . Universal way of dyaling or plain and easie directions for marking . . . sun-dyals . . . [translated] by Daniel King . . . London, printed by Tho. Leach, 1659.
 [16,] 108p illus. 19cm

265 Description of the very ancient and curious Roman clock constructed and finished by the famous artist Isaac Habrecht, anno 1589. *Anon.* [London?, c 1850.]
 12p Engraving of clock on paper cover.
The clock appears to be the one in the British Museum.

266 A description of two curious clocks intended as a present from the East India Company to the Emperor of China, made by English artists. *Anon.*
 In Annual Register for 1766, pp 230–31. 21cm

267 Descrizione di una nuova chiave da orologia, inventata ed esequita dal signore Stefano Thorogood . . . presentata all' Accademia Reale li 25 Gennajo 1781 . . . *Anon.* [1782?]
 8p fold. plate 19cm

De Servière (Nicolas Grollier) *see* **Grollier de Servière (Nicolas)**

268 [**Designs** for chasing watch cases, 18–?.]
 117 plates 10 × 17cm
Spine title.
See plate 7.

Deutsche Gesellschaft für Chronometrie *see* **Freunde alter Uhren**

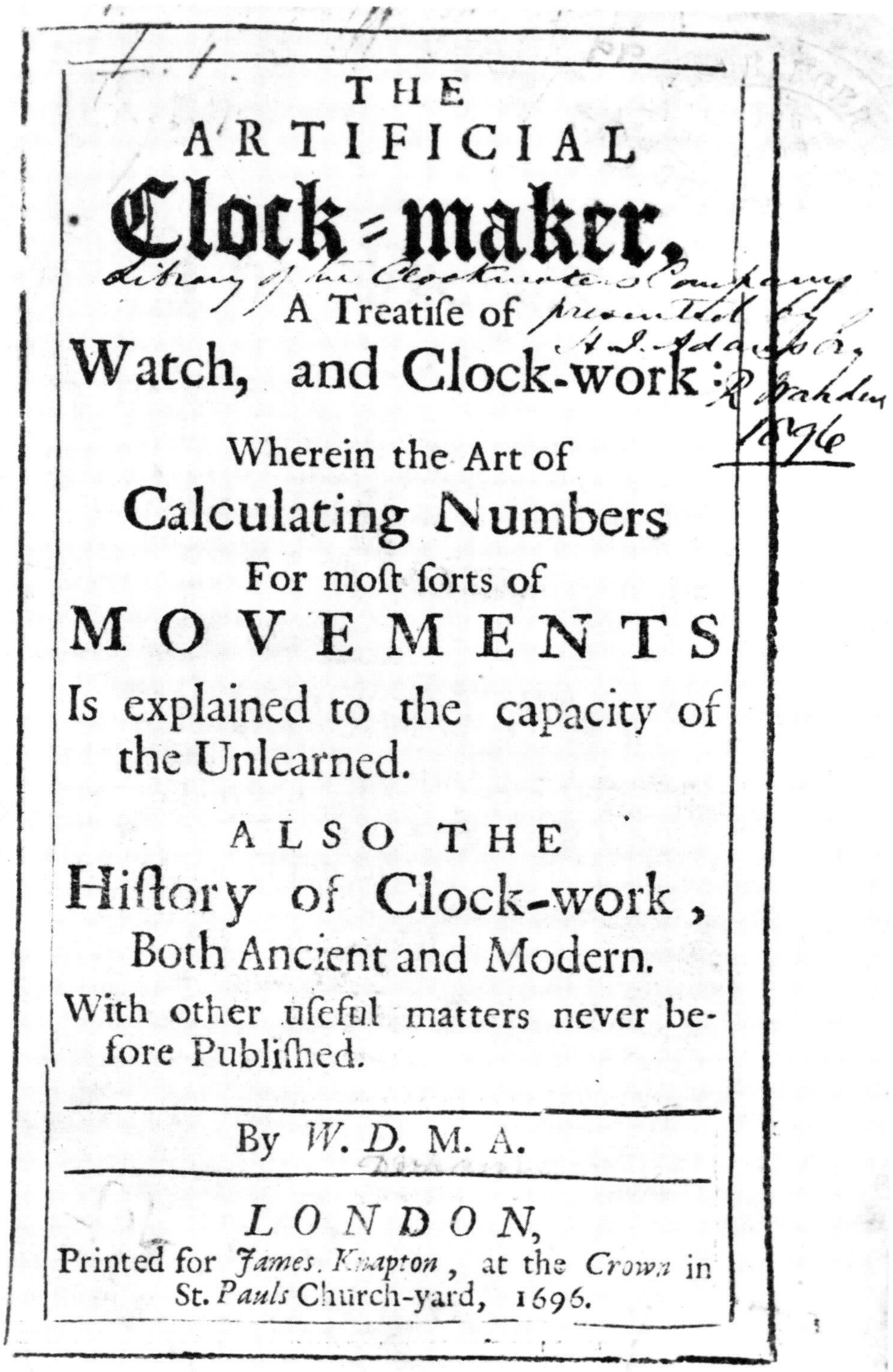

THE ARTIFICIAL Clock=maker,

A Treatise of Watch, and Clock-work:

Wherein the Art of

Calculating Numbers

For most sorts of

MOVEMENTS

Is explained to the capacity of the Unlearned.

ALSO THE

History of Clock-work,

Both Ancient and Modern.

With other useful matters never before Published.

By *W. D.* M. A.

LONDON,

Printed for *James Knapton*, at the *Crown* in St. *Pauls* Church-yard, 1696.

PLATE 6   Title-page of *The Artificial Clockmaker*, by W. Derham, 1696. The first edition of this famous early work by Dr W. Derham M.A. (1657–1735), an Essex clergyman and a Canon of Windsor. The term 'artificial', as used here, refers to clocks made by human skill as opposed to sundials or time-tellers dependent on the heavens. The work is one of the first attempts to give practical help to a working clockmaker and also to record a history of horology. There were five editions, some of which were translated into French and German. (No. 255)

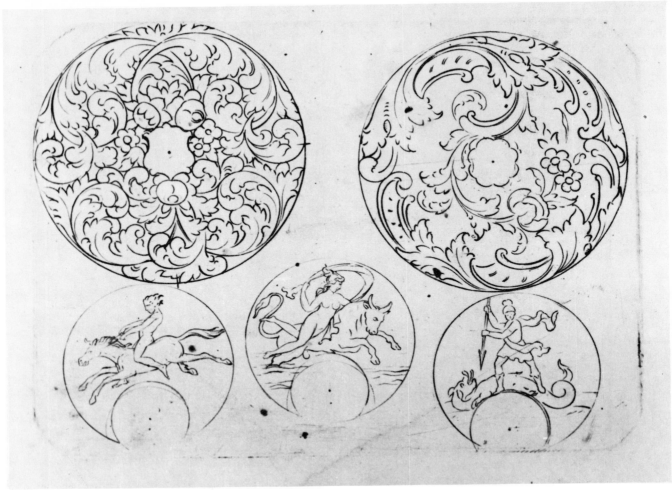

PLATE 7 Designs for chasing watch cases. This book of designs was compiled anonymously, probably during the mid-19th century. The designs are suitable not only for chasing or embossing but also for engraving, enamelling and generally ornamenting watch cases and watch dials. (No. 268)

De Vaux (Charles Grant, Viscount) *see* **Grant (Charles, Viscount de Vaux)**

Develle (Edmond)
269 Les horlogers blésois au XVIe et au XVIIe siècle. Blois, Rivière, 1913.
  150 copies printed.

270 Album d'horlogerie blésoise . . . du XVIe et du XVIIe siècle. 2e édition. Blois, Rivière, [1917].
  30 plates 28cm

The Dial: June 1920–February 1927
271 London, Dennison Watch Case Co., 1920–27.
  2 vols in 1 illus. 21cm
Published monthly. None published for April–October 1921, April 1922–October 1925.
Numbering erratic.

Dinsdale (N.V.)
272 The old clockmakers of Yorkshire . . . The

Dalesman Publishing Company, Yorkshire, 1946.
  82p 8 plates 21cm

Ditisheim (Paul)
273 The timing of chronometers and watches. A review of the history and progress of adjusting.
Extract from *English Mechanics*, March–April 1926.
On cover: Translated from *La Science Moderne*.
  14p 27cm

Drepperd (Carl W.)
274 American clocks and clockmakers . . . Garden City, N.Y., Doubleday & Company Inc., 1947.
  312p 21cm
pp 196–293: List of American makers.

Drost (William E.)
275 Clocks and watches of New Jersey. Elizabeth, N. J., Engineering Publications, [1966].
  xi 291p illus. facsims. 25cm
Arranged alphabetically under makers' names.

Drover (C. B.)

276 The Brussels miniature: an early fussee [*sic*] and a monastic alarm. Reprinted from *Antiquarian Horology*, vol III, no. 12, 1962.
[67] p illus. 25cm

277 A medieval monastic water-clock. Reprinted from *Antiquarian Horology*, December 1954.
[6] p illus. 25cm

278 Thomas Dallam's organ clock. Reprinted from *Antiquarian Horology*, vol 1, no. 10, 1956.
4p illus. 25cm

Dryander (Joannes)

279 Sonnawern allerhandt künstlich zumachen. An die Maurn und wende. Auff eyn ebne und gleichen Platz. An die Seitten eyns viereckenten und würffelechten Klotz. [Getruckt zu Marpurg durch Christianum Egenolphum,] 1543.
18p 2 plates 19cm

Dubois (Pierre)

280 Collection archéologique du Prince Pierre Soltykoff. Horlogerie: description et iconographie des instruments horaires du XVIᵉ siècle; précédée d'un abrégé historique de l'horlogerie au Moyen Age et pendant la Renaissance; suivie de la bibliographie complète de l'art de mesurer le temps depuis l'antiquité jusqu'à nos jours. Paris, Librairie Archéologique de Victor Didron, 1858.
214p 19 plates 27cm

281 The same. Another copy.

282 Histoire de l'horlogerie depuis son origine jusqu'à nos jours. Précédée de recherches sur la mesure du temps dans l'antiquité et suivi de la biographie des horlogers les plus célèbres de l'Europe . . . Paris, Administration du Moyen Age et la Renaissance, 1849.
iv 408p col. frontis. 24 plates 3 col. plates 13 fold. plates 27cm

283 La Tribune Chronométrique, scientifique et bibliographique, à l'usage des membres de la Corporation des Horlogers . . . Paris, 1852.
362p 3 fold. plates 26cm Issued in numbers. Publication stopped in 1853.

Duley (Antony J.)

284 The medieval clock of Salisbury Cathedral, its history, restoration and method of operation . . . [Salisbury, Friends of Salisbury Cathedral, 1972.]
[9] p illus. 21cm

Du Plat (Edward Austin)

285 A short history of the various methods of measuring time together with the Guide and Catalogue of the Exhibition of old and modern clocks and watches 14th May to 15th June, 1895 . . . London, Royal Aquarium & Summer & Winter Garden Society, Limited, 1895.
141p frontis. illus. 21cm

Earnshaw (Thomas)

286 Longitude 1806.
Single sheet 32 × 35cm

287 Longitude. An appeal to the public: stating Mr Thomas Earnshaw's claim to the original invention of the improvements in his timekeepers, their superior going in numerous voyages, and also as tried by the Astronomer Royal . . . and his consequent right to national reward . . . London, printed for the Author, 1808.
iv 280p Appendices & Conclusion 34p 21cm
See plate 8.

Eckhardt (George H.)

288 Pennsylvania clocks and clockmakers . . . [New York,] Bonanza Books, [1955].
xviii 229p illus. ports. 25cm

Edey (Winthrop)

289 . . . French clocks. London, Studio Vista, [1967].
83p illus. 21cm (Collector's blue books)
Covering the Renaissance to the Revolution.

Edwardes (Ernest Lawrence)

290 The grandfather clock . . . [2nd edition]. Altrincham, Sherratt, [1952].
253p plates 25cm

291 The grandfather clock . . . [3rd edition]. Altrincham, Sherratt, [1971].
xx 271p 221 plates 25cm

292 Weight-driven chamber clocks of the middle ages and Renaissance . . . Altrincham, Sherratt, [1965].
xvi 160p plates 25cm

Eiffe (John Sweetman)

293 Accounts of improvements in chronometers, made by Mr John Sweetman Eiffe; for which a reward was granted to him by the Lords Commissioners of the Admiralty. With an appendix containing Mr Robert Molyneux' specification of a patent for improvements. Published by order of the Lords Commissioners of the Admiralty. London, printed by Palmer and Clayton, 1842.
25p 5 plates 28cm

294 Elgin reminiscences . . . Assorted reprints concerning the National Watch Company, Chicago . . . (1864–74), succeeded by the Elgin National Watch Company. Bristol, Conn., K. Roberts, 1972.
32p illus. 22cm
Facsimile reprint.

Elkington (George)

295 The Coopers: Company and craft . . . London, Sampson Low, Marston & Co. Ltd., [1933].
ix 310p 11 plates 24cm

Ellicott (John)

296 An account of the influence which two pendulum clocks were observed to have upon each other. Communicated to the Royal Society . . . [London, 1744?]
9p 21cm

297 A description of two methods, by which the irregularities in the motion of a clock, arising from the influence of heat and cold upon the rod of the pendulum may be prevented . . . Read at the Royal Society, 1752.

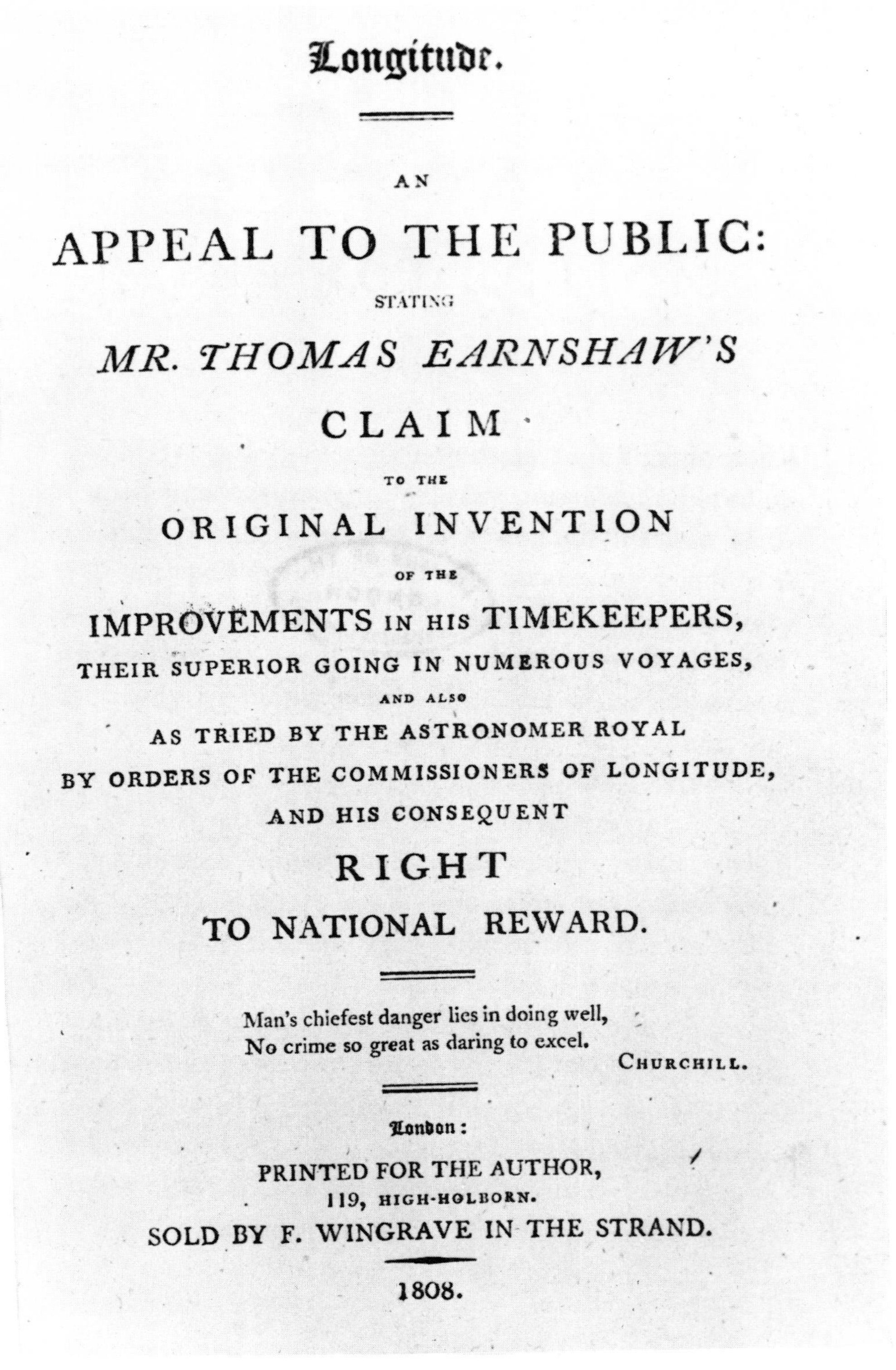

Longitude.

AN

APPEAL TO THE PUBLIC:

STATING

MR. THOMAS EARNSHAW'S

CLAIM

TO THE

ORIGINAL INVENTION

OF THE

IMPROVEMENTS IN HIS TIMEKEEPERS,

THEIR SUPERIOR GOING IN NUMEROUS VOYAGES,

AND ALSO

AS TRIED BY THE ASTRONOMER ROYAL

BY ORDERS OF THE COMMISSIONERS OF LONGITUDE,

AND HIS CONSEQUENT

RIGHT

TO NATIONAL REWARD.

Man's chiefest danger lies in doing well,
No crime so great as daring to excel.
CHURCHILL.

London:

PRINTED FOR THE AUTHOR,
119, HIGH-HOLBORN.
SOLD BY F. WINGRAVE IN THE STRAND.

1808.

PLATE 8 Title-page of *Longitude, an Appeal to the Public*, by Thomas Earnshaw, 1808. A contentious book by Thomas Earnshaw (1749–1829), the pioneer chronometer maker. From 1774 until 1828 longitude prizes of up to £10,000 were still open for award and were the source of much jealous competition amongst the leading chronometer makers of the day, including Earnshaw. In this book he extols his claim to a monetary award. (No. 287)

To which are added a collection of papers relating to the same subject . . . London, printed for R. Willock, 1753.
vii   60p   2 fold. plates   21cm

298   The same. Another copy.

Emerson (William)
299   Dialling, or the art of drawing dials, on all sorts of planes whatsoever . . . [London? 1770?].
iv   164p   18 fold. plates   20cm

300   The mathematical principles of geography . . . London, printed for J. Nourse, 1770.
viii   ii   172p   plates   20cm

301   Encyclopédie méthodique . . . Horlogerie. [By Jean Romilly. An article from La Grande Encyclopédie, c 1780.]
25p   64 plates   38cm

302   Encyclopédie méthodique . . . Horlogerie. Another version of the plates only (re-engraved).
50 plates   28cm

303   An **Explanation** of the nature of equation of time, and use of the equation table for adjusting watches and clocks to the motion of the sun; also the description of a timekeeper for astronomical and other uses. *Anon.* London, printed for F. Clay, 1731.
22p   plates   fold. equation table   24cm

*Fales (Martha Gandy)
304   Thomas Wagstaffe, London Quaker clockmaker. (In *Connoisseur*, vol 151, 1962, pp 193–201)

Fanmakers' Company
305   Worshipful Company of Fanmakers. Report of Committee . . . Competitive exhibition of fans, held at Drapers' Hall, London, July, 1878. [London, The Company, 1879.]
16p   24cm

Favarger (A.)
306   L'électricité et ses applications à la chronométrie . . . Avec 344 figures dans le texte . . . Troisième édition revue et augmentée. Neuchâtel. Editions du Journal Suisse d'horlogerie et de bijouterie, 1924.
557p   8 fold. plates   25cm
Appeared as articles in the Journal. Preface dated 1923.

Fedchenko (Feodosy Mikhailovich)
307   About the isochronous oscillation of a pendulum.
[14]l.   illus.   25cm
Photocopy.

308   Astronomical clock with an electromagnetically driven pendulum . . . [Photocopied from *Research in the field of time measurement:* proceedings of a committee of the All Union Scientific Research Institute of Physiotechnical and Radiotechnical Measurements, issue 58 (118), 1962.]
[18] l.   illus.   25cm

309   Astronomical clock Ach F-1 with isochronous pendulum. [Photocopied from *Astronomical journal of USSR*, 1957.]
[12] l.   illus.   26cm

Fedchenko (Feodosy Mikhailovich) and Fleer (A. G.)
310   Spring suspensions for a pendulum. [Photocopied from *Measurement techniques*, no. 8, August 1966.
6 l.   illus.   27cm

Fell (Robert Andrews)
311   Some notes on the balance and spring. [London, c 1946.]
[22] p.   illus.   26cm

Ferguson (James)
312   The description and use of a new machine, called the mechanical paradox; invented by James Ferguson, FRS. London, printed for the Author, 1764.
16p   fold. plate   23cm

313   An introduction to electricity . . . 2nd edition . . . London, Strahan, 1775.
140p   plates   21cm

314   The same. Another copy.

315   Lectures on electricity. A new edition, corrected, with an appendix, adapting the work to the present state of science by C. F. Partington. London, published by Sherwood & Co., 1825.
102p   2 plates   21cm

316   Lectures on select subjects in mechanics, hydrostatics, hydraulics, pneumatics, and optics . . . The fifth edition . . . London, printed for W. Strahan, 1776.
xiv   402p   23 fold. plates   21cm

317   Lectures on select subjects in mechanics, hydrostatics, hydraulics, pneumatics, optics, geography, astronomy and dialling . . . with notes . . . by David Brewster, LL.D. Third edition. In two volumes with 27 plates. Edinburgh, printed for Stirling & Slade, 1823.
2 vols in 3   plates   21cm

318   Lectures on select subjects in mechanics, hydrostatics, pneumatics, optics, and astronomy . . . A new and improved edition, adapted to the present state of science, by C. F. Partington . . . London, published by Sherwood and Co., 1825.
xlvii   452p   frontis. (port.)   10 plates   21cm

319   Select mechanical exercises: shewing how to construct different clocks, orreries and sun-dials . . . London, Strahan, 1773.
lxii   272p   9 fold. plates   21cm

320   Select mechanical exercises: shewing how to construct different clocks, orreries and sun-dials . . . 2nd edition. London, Strahan, 1778.
xliii   272p   port. 9 plates   21cm

*321   Select mechanical exercises: shewing how to construct different clocks, orreries and sun-dials . . . 3rd edition. London, Strahan, 1790.
xliii   272p   9 fold. plates   20cm

322   Tables and tracts relative to several arts and sciences . . . London, printed for A. Millar and T. Cadell, 1767.
xiv   328p   3 fold. plates   21cm

Ferriday (Peter)
323 Lord Grimthorpe, 1816–1905. London, Murray, [1957].
  xiii 230p illus. plates (inc. ports.) 22cm

Ffoulkes (Charles)
324 Some account of the Worshipful Company of Armourers and Brasiers, together with a catalogue of the arms and armour in the possession of the Company . . . Privately printed for the Company, 1927.
  iv 38p frontis. 14 plates 21cm

*__Fine (Oronce)__
325 Orontii Finei . . . protomathesis . . . Parisiis, [impensis Gerardi Morrhii & Joannis Petri,] 1532.
  [232] p illus. 38cm
Includes: De Solaribus horologiis et quadrantibus libri.

Fleet (Simon)
326 Clocks. London, Weidenfeld, [1961].
  128p illus. ports. 21cm

Fleurieu (Charles Pierre Claret d'Eveux de)
327 Voyage fait par ordre du Roi en 1768 et 1769, à différentes parties du monde, pour éprouver en mer les horloges marines inventées par M. Ferdinand Berthoud . . . A Paris, de l'imprimerie royale, 1773.
  Vol 1 lxxxix 803p Vol 2 622 xl p 4 fold. maps fold. plates 6 tables 25cm

Flint (Stamford Raffles)
328 Mudge memoirs; being a record of Zachariah Mudge and some members of his family . . . Truro, printed by Netherton & Worth, 1883.
  xx 250p 7 ports. fold. tables of ports. fold. genealogy 21cm
On verso: 100 copies printed.

329 Fonte des cloches. *Anon.* [Extract from La Grande Encyclopédie, 1765.]
  8p 8 plates 39cm

Foote (Richard)
330 . . . The pyrakodon, or fire detector . . . London, Lowe, [1841?]
  8p illus. 20cm

Fortnum & Mason Ltd.
331 Mr Fortnum and Mr Mason: the new clock. [London, 1965.]
  [2] p 18cm

Foster (Samuel)
332 Elliptical or azimuthal horologiography. Comprehending several ways of describing dials upon all kindes of superficies . . . London, printed by R. & W. Leybourn, 1654.
  iii 204p 18cm
  p 115 is a separate title-page with 333 *post.*

333 Circular Horologiography . . . London, printed for Nicholas Bourn, 1654.
  Paging is continuous.

334 Miscellanies, or mathematical lucubrations of Mr Samuel Foster . . . Published, and many of them translated into English, by John Twysden . . . London, printed by R. & W. Leybourn, 1659.
  xii 290p 6 plates 4 fold. plates 32cm
A title-page in Latin precedes the English one. Seventeen parts, each with title-page and all of the same date and imprint.
With 10p of contemporary (?) MS 'Errata additionala'.
? John Twisden's own copy.

*__335__ Posthuma Fosteri: the description of a ruler upon which is inscribed divers scales, and the uses thereof . . . in astronomie, navigation, and dialling . . . London, Bourn, 1652.
  80p 19cm

Foster (Sir William)
336 A short history of the Worshipful Company of Coopers of London . . . Cambridge, printed for the Company by the University Press, 1914.
  viii 147p frontis. 12 plates 21cm

Foulkes (Robert K.)
337 Thirty-hour Tompion clocks. 1951. An illustrated extract from *Apollo*, vol 54, pp 99–102, 106.

Fox (C. A. O.)
338 An anthology of clocks and watches . . . Swansea, [The editor, 1947].
  68p 14 plates 21cm

Franklin Institute Library, Philadelphia
339 Horological books and pamphlets in the . . . library; compiled by Emerson W. Hilker . . . 3rd edition. Philadelphia, The institute, 1974.
  185p 28cm

Freund der Künsten *see* **Selbstlehrende Uhrmacher**

Freunde alter Uhren
340 Schriften der Freunde alter Uhren in der Deutschen Gesellschaft für Chronometrie. Heft 1– Heidelberg, Impuls, 1960–.
In progress.

*__Friendly Society of Clock and Watch-makers__
341 Articles, rules . . . London, printed Jarratt, 1818.
  27p 20cm

Frodsham (William James)
342 Results of experiments on vibrations of pendulums, with different suspending springs; being the substance of a paper read . . . before the Royal Society, June 21, 1838. London, [Whiting,] 1839.
  8p 27cm

Furtwangen. Ingenieur Schule für Feinwerktechnik.
343 Festschrift zum 100 jahrigen Bestehen der Staatlichen Uhrmacherschule . . . [Furtwangen, 1950.]
  xlv 63p 28cm

Gallucci (Giovanni Paolo)
344 . . . De fabrica, et usu cuiusdam instrumenti ad omnia horarum genera describenda . . . Venetiis, apud Io. Baptistam Ciottum, 1592.
  [11,] 62p illus. 23cm
See plate 9.

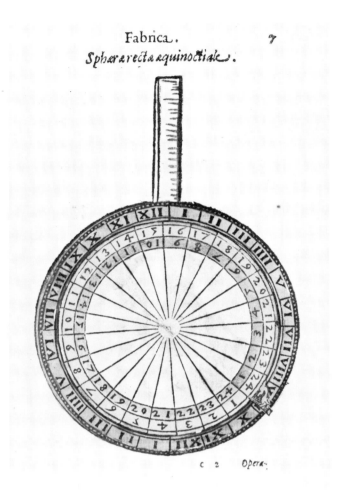

Fabrica. 7
Sphæra recta æquinoctiale.

c 2 Opera.

PLATE 9 Illustration from *De fabrica, et usu cuiusdam instrumenti ad omnia horarum genera describenda*, an early work on dialling by G. P. Gallucci, 1592. G. P. Gallucci (*fl.* 1569–93) published this work in Venice. Written in Latin, it gives illustrated instruction on how to make and use elaborate sundials. This illustration is one of a series showing components of a sundial; it is hand-coloured and, unusually, the central disc, or volvelle, can be rotated by the reader of the book. (No. 344)

Gardner (Malcolm), bookseller
345 Catalogue XVI: horology, printed books, MS, etc. on clocks, watches . . . and other allied subjects . . . offered for sale on behalf of the executors [of the late Professor D. S. Torrens]. [Sevenoaks, 1971.]
   138p   22cm

Garrard (F. J.)
346 Clock repairing and making. A practical handbook dealing with the tools, materials and methods used in cleaning and repairing all kinds of English and foreign timepieces, striking and chiming clocks, and the making of English clocks . . . With 120 original illustrations. London, Crosby Lockwood & Son, 1914.
   viii   168p   19cm

Garrett (Frank)
347 . . . English long-case & bracket clocks, being a collection made by the late Frank Garrett . . . with a foreword & . . . catalogue descriptions by Herbert Cescinsky . . . To be sold by auction . . . New York, The Anderson Galleries, 1926.
   [x]   56p   illus.   24cm

Gatty (Margaret; Mrs Alfred Gatty)
348 The book of sun-dials. New and enlarged edition, edited by H. K. F. Gatty and Eleanor Lloyd, with an appendix on the construction of dials by W. Richardson. London, George Bell and Sons, 1889.
   viii   520p   frontis.   plates   3 fold. plates   22cm

349 The book of sun-dials, originally compiled by the late Mrs Alfred Gatty, now enlarged and re-edited by H. K. F. Eden and Eleanor Lloyd. London, George Bell and Sons, 1900.
   xvii   350p   frontis.   9 plates   28cm
Previous editions are dated 1872, 1889, 1890.

Gazeley (William John)
350 Clock and watch escapements. London, Heywood, 1956.
   vii   294p   illus.   22cm

351 Watch and clock making and repairing . . . [2nd edition.] London, Heywood, 1958.
   vii   434p   illus.   22cm

Gélis (Edouard)
352 L'horlogerie ancienne: histoire, décor et technique . . . Paris, Gründ, [1950].
   xvii   254p   illus.   plates   ports.   22cm
pp 59–227: catalogue of clocks and watches in the author's collection, now in the Musée Saint-Raymond, Toulouse.

General Committee for the relief of the distressed watch and clock makers
353 The case of the distressed watch and clock makers. [London, 1798.]
   39   32cm

General Post Office
354 Technical instructions, XI. Clocks and Time distribution. Engineer-in-Chief's office, General Post Office, London. London, H.M.S.O., 1927.
   69p   3 fold. plates   33cm

Gibbs (James W.)
355 Buckeye horology; a review of Ohio clock and watch makers. Columbia, Pennsylvania, Artcrafters, [1971].
   x   128p   illus.   facsims.   28cm

Giddy (Davies), afterwards Gilbert (Davies)
356 On the vibrations of heavy bodies . . . Extracted from the *Quarterly Journal*, vol 15. Printed by W. Clowes. [London, 1827.]
   15p   fold. table   20cm

357 **Gilbert (Davies)** *see* **Giddy (Davies), afterwards Gilbert (Davies)**

Gilbert (William L.) Clock Co.
358 Illustrated catalogue of clocks manufactured by the . . . company . . . 1875. [Bristol, Conn., American Clock and Watch Museum, 1967.]
 36p illus. 19cm
Facsimile reprint of the 1875 edition.

Gillgras (Alfred)
359 The book of Big Ben: the story of the great clock of Westminster . . . London, Joseph, [1946].
 47p frontis. 16 plates 25cm

Giraud (J. B.)
360 Pierre Bergier, armurier et horloger du Roi à Grenoble (1633–1641) . . . Nouvelle édition. Lyon, 1901.
 20p 22cm
Second title-page: Notes sur l'horlogerie antérieurement au XVIIIe siècle . . . First published in Bull. archéologique du Comité des Travaux historiques du Ministère de l'instruction publique, 1900.

Glasgow (David)
361 Watch and clock making . . . London, Cassell, 1885.
 xii 341p 17cm (Manuals of Technology. Edited by Professor Ayrton and R. Wormwell.)

Goaman (Muriel)
362 English clocks. London, The Connoisseur, 1967.
 119p illus. 24cm

Good (John)
363 The art of shadows, or universal dialling . . . 2nd edition. London, J. Robinson, printer, 1711.
 vi 184p 7 plates 16cm
1st edition titled: Multum in parvo, or tables exactly calculated . . . London, 1706.

Goodison (Nicholas Proctor)
364 Balthazar Knie: an immigrant barometer-maker. An illustrated extract from *Auction*, vol 2, 1969, pp 8–11.

365 Charles Orme's place in the history of the barometer . . . Firenze, Olschki, [1966?].
 10p illus. 24cm
Reprinted from *Physis*, vol 8, fasc. 4, 1966.

366 Clocks in the collection of Lord Harris at Belmont Park, Kent. Reprinted from *The Connoisseur*, vol 168, 1968.
 2 pts illus. 31cm

367 Daniel Quare and the portable barometer. Reprinted from *Annals of Science*, December, 1967.
 [7] p 25cm

368 Daniel Quare's barometers. Reprinted from *Apollo*, vol 86, 1967.
 [6] l. illus. 30cm

369 English barometers 1680–1860 . . . London, Cassell, [1969].
 xiii 353p illus. plates facsims. 28cm

370 English barometers, 1680–1860 . . . New York, Potter, [1968].
 xiii 353p illus. plates facsims. 28cm

371 The foreign origins of domestic barometers, 1800–1860. Reprinted from *The Connoisseur*, vol 170, 1969.
 [8] l. illus. 30cm

372 Gillows' clock cases. Reprinted from *Antiquarian Horology*, vol 5, 1968.
 [14] p facsims. 25cm

373 Matthew Boulton's geographical clock: an important re-discovery. Reprinted from *The Connoisseur*, vol 166, 1967.
 [9] l. illus. facsim. 31cm

Goodrich (Ward L.)
374 The modern clock. A study of time keeping mechanism; its construction, regulation and repair . . . Chicago, Hazlitt & Walker, 1905.
 502p 19cm

Gordon (G. F. C.)
375 Clockmaking past and present. With which is incorporated the more important portions of 'Clocks, Watches, and Bells,' by the late Lord Grimthorpe, relating to turret clocks and gravity escapements . . . London, Crosby Lockwood and Son, 1925.
 vi 232p 35 plates 21cm

Gould (Rupert Thomas)
376 Early marine chronometers. An illustrated lecture delivered at the British Horological Institute, London, on 21st November, 1923. Reprinted from the *Horological Journal*.
 24p 25cm

377 John Harrison and his timekeepers. Reprinted from the *Mariner's Mirror*, vol 21, no. 2, 1935.
 pp 115–139 frontis. (port.) 6 plates 34cm

378 John Harrison and his timekeepers. Extract from *Argentor*, June 1947.
 pp 107–113 and 133–136 plates port. 25cm

379 The marine chronometer, its history and development . . . Published by J. D. Potter, London, 1923.
 xvi 287p frontis. (port.) 39 plates 24cm

380 The reconstruction of Harrison's first timekeeper. From *The Observatory*, vol 56, no. 709, 1933.
 pp 193–196 plates 22cm

381 Romance of the chronometer. 1937.
Extract from *Shipping Wonders of the World*, pt 52, pp 1641–45.

382 In memory of Lieutenant-Commander R. T. Gould . . . Letters, obituaries . . . 1948–50.
 13 items in loose-leaf folder. 35cm

Graffenriedt (Hans Rudolff von)
383 Compendium sciotericorum; dass ist, ein . . . Beschreibung, wie man . . . die vier Haupt unnd alle geschregte Sonnen Uhren . . . verzeichnen soll . . . sampt einer Beschreibung des Mond Uhrlins . . . Gedruckt zu Bern. bey Abraham Wecklin, 1617.
 vi 38p fold. plate 19cm

Grafton (Edward)
384   Horology; or, a popular sketch of the history and principles of clock and watchmaking . . . London, Edward Grafton, 1846.
36p   17cm

Graham (Robert Pickersgill Howgrave-)
385   Some clocks and jacks, with notes on the history of horology . . . Oxford, printed by John Johnson for the Society of Antiquaries of London, 1928.
Extract from *Archaeologia*, vol 77, pp 257–312.
12 plates   28cm
With 1 leaf MS by John James Hall.

386   The Wells clock . . . Wells, Friends of Wells cathedral, 1971.
24p   illus.   22cm

387   Wells clock . . . Wells, Friends of Wells cathedral. 2nd edition. 1971.
24p   illus.   22cm

Graham (William)
388   A table of equation of natural days, showing how much a clock or watch ought to be faster or slower than a sun-dial, any day of the year. London, printed for William Graham, clock and watchmaker, 1728.
1 sh.   32cm

Grant (Charles, Viscount de Vaux)
389   The means of finding the longitude at sea, gradually developed, discovered and demonstrated . . . London, printed for the Author, by D. N. Shury . . . 1808.
96, 67p   frontis. (port.)   4 fold. plates   4 fold. maps   27cm
pp 23, 24 are duplicated in the second pagination and pp 33–40 are blank.

Green (F. H.)
390   Old English clocks, being a collector's observations on some seventeenth-century clocks . . . printed and published at St Dominic's Press, Ditchling Common, 1931.
ii 90p   frontis.   50 plates   29cm
300 copies only printed.

*Greenwich. National Maritime Museum.
391   Instruments of navigation: a catalogue . . . with notes . . . by H. O. Hill and E. W. Paget-Tomlinson. London, H.M.S.O., 1958.
89p   illus.   plates   18cm

392   An inventory of the navigation and astronomy collections . . . with a list of the instruments used at the Royal Observatory, 1676–1950. London, The Museum, 1970.
In loose-leaf binder to receive additions.

393   The restoration of the Old Royal Observatory, Greenwich, with a provisional list of instruments and clocks, 1676–1835. Greenwich, The Museum, 1966.
ii 16p   illus.   plans   33cm
Typewriter script.

Gregory (John)
394   De Aeris & Epochis: shewing the several accounts of time among all nations, from the Creation to the present age. London, printed by M. Clark, for Benj. Tooke, 1683.
Paged 127–173   20cm
Extract with separate title-page from the fourth edition of the Author's works, 1684–3 [*sic*].

Gregory (Olinthus)
395   A treatise of mechanics, theoretical, practical and descriptive . . . Vol 1 containing the theory of statics, dynamics, hydrostatics . . . Vol 2 containing remarks on the nature, construction and simplification of machinery . . . London, printed for George Kearsley, 1806.
Vol 1   xx   548p
Vol 2   vii   514p
37 plates in separate volume   21cm

Grimshaw & Baxter
396   Trade price list . . . of tools and appliances for watch and clock makers, jewellers, silversmiths . . . London, [Grimshaw & Baxter,] 1900.
169p   illus.   28cm
See plate 10.

Grimthorpe (Edmund Beckett Denison, 1st Baron) *see* **Denison (Edmund Beckett)**

Grollier de Servière (Nicolas)
397   Recueil d'ouvrages curieux de mathématique et de mécanique, ou description du cabinet de Monsieur Nicolas Grollier de Servière . . . par . . . son petit fils. Seconde édition revue, corrigée et augmentée de nouvelles machines. A Paris, chez Ch. Ant. Jombert, 1751.
[22,] 152p   85 plates   25cm
3rd issue of the original edition of 1719.

Gros (Charles)
398   L'échappement à ancre de Graham . . . Paris, Desforges, [*c* 1913].
31p   24cm

Grossman (Jules and Hermann)
399   Horlogerie théorique. Cours de mécanique appliquée à la chronometrie . . . Bienne, E. Magron, éditeur. Paris, Gauthier-Villars, 1908.
Vol 1   408p   2 frontis. (ports.)   13 plates
Vol 2   427p   frontis. (port.)   7 plates   23cm

Guillaume (Charles Edouard)
400   Les aciers au nickel et leurs applications à l'horlogerie . . . Bienne, E. Magron, éditeur. Paris, Gauthier-Villars, 1912.
55p   21cm

Gunther (Robert T.)
401   The astrolabes of the world, based upon the series of instruments in the Lewis Evans collection in the Old Ashmolean Museum at Oxford, with notes on the

31, 33 & 35, Goswell Road, Clerkenwell, London, E.C.

WHEEL-CUTTING ENGINES.

Wheel-cutting Engine, 14in. divided plate, with micrometer screw dividing arrangement stop point action, for flat, bevel, or angular gears and rack cutting up to 18in. length. This machine will cut flat wheels up to 6in. diameter ... £54 0 0

Wheel-cutting Engine, 14in. divided plate, with divisions ranging from No. 19 to 720, traversing slide with lever and screw action (as illustrated) for flat, bevel, or angular gears. This machine will cut flat wheels up to 5in. diameter £38 0 0

Ditto ditto, 12⅝in. divided plate, cutting up to 4½in. diameter £28 0 0

Ditto ditto, 10⅜in. divided plate cutting up to 4in. diameter £24 0 0

Ditto ditto, 8⅜in. divided plate, cutting up to 3in. diameter £18 0 0

Wheel-cutting engine with 6¼in. divided plate, traversing slide with screw action, for flat wheels only, cutting up to 2in. diameter £6 10 0

Counting up attachment fitted to above machines, from 25/- upwards.

Larger wheel cutting machines quoted for on application.

Cutters for every description of work in stock or supplied to order. Wheel and rack cutting a speciality.

Tools of every description for factory use and all kinds of special work quoted for on application.

PLATE 10 Page from a catalogue of tools issued by Grimshaw and Baxter, 1900. This catalogue of tools for clock and watchmakers, and practitioners of allied trades, is fully illustrated. (No. 396)

astrolabes in the collections of the British Museum . . . and in other public and private collections . . . Vol 1, The Eastern astrolabes. Vol 2, The Western astrolabes. Oxford, printed at the University Press, 1932.
 xvii viii 609p 2 frontis. 153 plates 28cm
Subscription copy No. 36.

Guye (Samuel) and Michel (Henri Jules)
402 Time and space: measuring instruments from the 15th to the 19th centuries. [Translated from the French: photographs by Pierre Devinoy.] London, Pall Mall Press, [1971].
 289p illus. facsims. maps 24cm

Haggar (Arthur L.) and Miller (Leonard F.)
403 Suffolk clocks and clockmakers. [London, Antiquarian Horological Society, 1974.]
 xiii 169p plates 24cm

The Hague. Gemeentemuseum.
404 De eeuw van Shakespeare. [Catalogue of an exhibition,] 1958.
 52, [76] p illus. plates 26cm

Hall (Francis), *alias* Line
405 Explicatio horologii in horto regio Londoni, in Anglia an. 1699 erecti, in quo plurima horologiorum sciatericorum genera continentur . . . Leodii Eburonum [Liège]. Apud Guilielmum Henricum Streel, Suae Serenissimae Celsitudinis Typographum, 1673.
 75p 20cm
Bound with the above are some pages of MS, mainly sermon notes in Latin. Late 17th century?

*Hall (Francis)
406 An explication of the diall sett up in the kings garden at London an. 1669 . . . Liège, G. H. Streel, 1673.
 59p plates 21cm

Hall (John James)
407 The story of Bishop Grandison's clock in the Church of St Mary of Ottery . . . Typed, with revisions, from the *Horological Journal*, 1935.
 iii 36p 2 plates 2 photos. Part typescript, part printed. 26cm

Harlow (Samuel Boulton)
408 The clock makers' guide to practical clockwork . . . for making eight-day and thirty-hour clocks . . . Birmingham, Orton & Hawkes Smith, [1813].
 8p plates 18cm
Xerox copy.
Appears to describe the beginning of the factory manufacture of 'grandfather' clock movements.

Harris (John)
409 The description and uses of the celestial and terrestrial Globes; and of Collin's pocket quadrant . . . London, printed by E. Midwinter for D. Midwinter and T. Leigh, 1703.
 iv 62p frontis. 16cm

Harrison (John), 1693–1776
410 An account of the proceedings in order to the discovery of the longitude at sea . . . *Anon.* 2nd edition. London, printed by T. and J. W. Pasham, 1763.
 viii 98p 19cm
Written by James Short? Photocopy.

411 The case of Mr John Harrison [relative to his invention of a chronometer]. [London, 1767?]
 4p 33cm
Other copies in MS 3973/18 (no. 976 *post*) and MS 6026/M, N. (no. 979 *post*).

412 A description concerning such mechanism as will afford a nice or true mensuration of time; together with some account of the attempts for the discovery of the longitude by the Moon; as also an account of the discovery of the scale of music . . . London, printed for the Author, 1775.
 114p 21cm
pp 109–114: Photocopy of Appendix, rarely found in existing copies of this work.

413 The same. Another copy.
See plate 11.

414 A narrative of the proceedings relative to the discovery of the longitude at sea . . . *Anon.* London, 1765.
 18p 20cm
Written by James Short? Photocopy.

415 Remarks on a pamphlet lately published by the Rev N. Maskelyne under the authority of the Board of Longitude. London, W. Sandby, 1767.
 34p 23cm
A second copy is in MS 3973/14 (no. 976 *post*).

Harrison (John), Junior
416 Memoirs of a trait in the character of George III . . . by Johan Horrins [pseudonym for John Harrison]. London, Edwards, 1835.
 xlviii 256p 22cm
On the intervention of George III in the case of John Harrison, clockmaker, and the Commissioners of Longitude.
 Chaps XIII–XVI only, with 10 appendices.

Hartmann (Johann Georg)
417 Johann George Hartmanns nöthiger Unterricht von Verbesserung alle Uhren durch die Höhe des Aufzuges, waagerechten Stand, und Berechnung. Mit 50 Figuren . . . Halle, im Verlag des Wäysenhauses, 1756.
 xii 210–222p frontis. (port.) 16 fold. plates 17cm
At end of contents: Das 8 Capitel oder den 2 Theil . . . habe schon 1752, zum erstenmal herausgegeben, ist iezo aber neu aufgelegt und gehöret zu diesen Werke.

418 Johann George Hartmanns nöthiger Unterricht von Verbesserung aller Uhren durch die Höhe des Aufzuges, waagerechten Stand und Berechnung . . . Nebst einer Vorrede Hrn. D. Georg Ehrhard Hambergers. Zweyte und verbesserte Auflage. Halle, im Verlag des Wäysenhauses, 1756.
 xxiii 90, 6p fold. plates 17cm

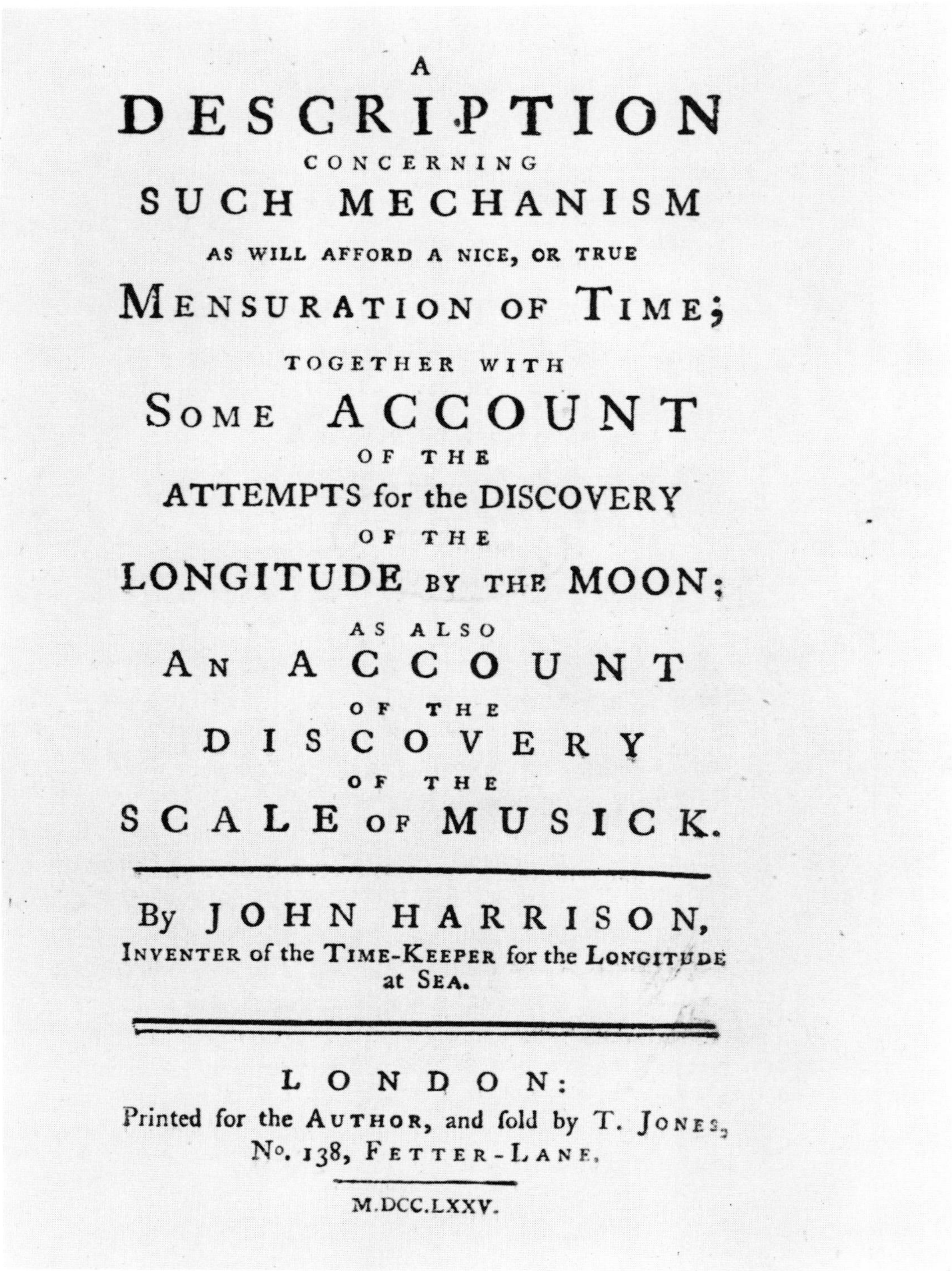

A
DESCRIPTION
CONCERNING
SUCH MECHANISM
AS WILL AFFORD A NICE, OR TRUE
MENSURATION OF TIME;
TOGETHER WITH
SOME ACCOUNT
OF THE
ATTEMPTS for the DISCOVERY
OF THE
LONGITUDE BY THE MOON;
AS ALSO
AN ACCOUNT
OF THE
DISCOVERY
OF THE
SCALE OF MUSICK.

By J O H N H A R R I S O N,
INVENTER of the TIME-KEEPER for the LONGITUDE
at SEA.

L O N D O N:
Printed for the AUTHOR, and fold by T. JONES,
No. 138, FETTER-LANE.

M.DCC.LXXV.

PLATE 11   Title-page of *A Description concerning Such Mechanism as will afford a Nice, or True Mensuration of Time*, by John Harrison, 1775. John Harrison wrote this book in 1775, the year before he died, aged eighty-two. Although not easy to follow, the book gives the only available information on his early visit to London in 1730, when he met the Astronomer Royal (Dr Halley) and George Graham. It also describes his involved theories not only on accurate timekeeping but also on music, including his proposal for a new musical scale based on π (the proportion which the radius of a circle bears to its circumference). (Nos 412–413)

Haswell (J. Eric)
419 Horology. The science of time measurement and construction of clocks, watches and chronometers . . . London, Chapman and Hall, 1928.
xvi   267p   19 plates   22cm

420 Horology. The science of time measurement and construction of clocks, watches and chronometers . . . London, Chapman and Hall. Cheaper edition with supplement 1937. Title-page otherwise the same. Same paging, but Supplement continues to p 289.

Hatton (Thomas)
421 An introduction to the mechanical part of clock and watchwork. In two parts. Containing all the arithmetic and geometry necessary, with their particular application in the said branches . . . London, printed for T. Longman, 1773.
xvi   400p   18 fold. plates   21cm

Hawkes (Arthur John)
422 The clockmakers and watchmakers of Wigan, 1650–1850 . . . Wigan, the Author, 1950.
84p   13 plates   18cm

Hayden (Arthur)
423 Chats on old clocks . . . London, T. Fisher Unwin Ltd., [1917].
302p   57 plates inc. in paging.   20cm
New edition (1951) completely rewritten by H. A. Lloyd, *q.v.*

Hayward (John Forrest)
424 Two English watches in Livrust-Kammeren [the royal armoury of Sweden] . . . Reprinted from *Livrust-kammeren*, the journal of the royal armoury [1952], vol 5, p 12, pp 233–249.
Two watches by Thomas Tompion and J. Bellette, personal relics of Charles XI and Charles XII of Sweden.

Heal (Sir Ambrose)
425 A list of clock and watch makers supplementary to that given by Britten.
An extract from *The Connoisseur*, vols 92, 93, 1943–44.

Hearn (Mrs George A.)
426 Collection of watches loaned to the Metropolitan Museum of Art of the City of New York . . . Privately printed, 1907.
35p   frontis.   9 plates   24cm

427 The same. Another copy.

Heath (John Benjamin)
428 Some account of the Worshipful Company of Grocers of the City of London . . . London, 1829. Not published.
viii   358p   frontis.   21cm   Engraved title-page.

Hellmann (C. Doris)
429 George Graham. Maker of horological and astronomical instruments . . .
Reprinted from *Vassar Journal of Undergraduate Studies*, Vol 5, May 1931, pp 221–251.

Hellmut-Kienzle-Uhrenmuseum. Schwenningen.
430 Katalog. Schwenningen, Das Museum, 1970.
19p   illus.   21cm

Henderson (Ebenezer)
431 An historical treatise on horology, shewing its rise and progress from the earliest period down to the present time . . . London, printed by S. Rothwell, 1836.
24p   23cm

432 Life of James Ferguson, FRS, in a brief autobiographical account and a further extended memoir. With numerous notes and illustrative engravings . . . A. Fullerton & Co., Edinburgh, London and Glasgow, 1867.
xiv   503p   frontis. (port.)   23cm

Henslow (T. Geoffrey W.)
433 Ye sundial booke . . . London, Edward Arnold, 1914.
iii   422p   25cm
From p 37 to p 401 there is an engraving on every page.

Herbert (Sir Alan Patrick)
434 Sundials old and new . . . London, Methuen, [1967].
198p   plates   21cm

Herbert (William)
435 The history of the twelve great Livery Companies of London, principally compiled from their grants and records. With an historical essay, and accounts of each Company, its origin, constitution, dress, customs, halls, and trust estates and charities . . . London, published by the Author, 1837.
Vol I   xvi   498p   fold. tables
Vol II (date on title-page 1836)   684p   24cm

Hildeyard (Thomas)
436 Chronometrum mirabile Leodiense; being a most curious clock lately invented by Thomas Hildeyard, Professor of mathematicks in the English college of Liège. London, printed by N. Blandford, 1727.
12p   4 fold. plates   27cm
Baillie (*Bibliography*, p 165) says 'no definite evidence that the clock was ever made'. But *see* Junquera (P.), Relojeria Palatina, 1956, plates II and IIa–d (item 496 *post*).
See plate 12.

Hobbs (James Leslie)
437 Former clock and watch makers of North Lonsdale. Reprinted from the Cumberland and Westmorland Antiquarian and Archaeological Society's Transactions, vol LVII, new series, 1958, pp 100–124.
125p   22cm

438 Former clock and watch makers of Somerset to *c* 1850. Minehead, [The author,] 1968.
90 l.   25cm
Typewritten.

Holford (Christopher)
439 A chat about the Broderers' Company. By an old boy and past master. London, George Allen & Sons, 1910.
xi   314p   frontis.(port.)   19 plates   24cm

THE CLOCKMAKERS' LIBRARY

PLATE 12 Illustration from *Chrono-metrum mirabile Leodiense*, by Thomas Hildeyard, *c* 1727. A very rare work which describes an elaborate astrono-mised clock with dials on all four sides of its bronze case as well as further tidal indicators in the finials. It was made *c* 1727 by Thomas Hildeyard, an English-man who was Professor of Philosophy and Mathematics at a school in Liège. The clock has recently been identified with the anonymous clock now in the Spanish Royal Collection. Madrid; see No. 496. (No. 436)

Holmes (Thomas Henry)
440 A brief history of the National College of Horology and Instrument Technology . . . [1946–60]. London, The College, 1960.
32p 22cm
Situated during the fourteen years of its existence at the Northampton College, Clerkenwell.

Hood (Peter)
441 How time is measured. London, Oxford University Press, 1955.
64p illus. 23cm

442 How time is measured. 2nd edition. London, Oxford University Press, 1969.
62p illus. map 28cm

Hope-Jones (F.) *see* **Jones (F. Hope-)**

Hooke (Robert)
443 A description of helioscopes and some other instruments, made by Robert Hooke . . . London, printed by T. R. for John Martyn, 1676.
37p fold. plate 21cm
Two MS lists of Hooke's inventions, 7 pp, bound in at end.

444 Lampas; or, descriptions of some mechanical improvements of lamps and water-poises; together with some other physical and mechanical discoveries made by Robert Hooke . . . London, printed for John Martyn, 1677.
54p 3 plates 21cm

445 Lectures and collections made by Robert Hooke . . . Cometa . . . Microscopium . . . London, printed for John Martyn, 1678.
vi 112p 5 fold. plates 21cm

446 Lectures de potentia restitutiva, or of spring, explaining the power of springing bodies . . . London, printed for John Martyn, 1678.
56p 2 plates fold. plate 21cm

447 The posthumous works . . . containing his Cutlerian lectures, and other discourses read at the meetings of the . . . Royal Society, to [which] . . . is prefixt the author's life . . . by Richard Waller. London, Waller, 1705.
xxviii 572, 10p plates 32cm

Horblitt (Harrison D.)
448 The celebrated library of Harrison D. Horblitt Esq removed from Ridgefield, Connecticut . . . early science, navigation and travel . . . which will be sold by auction . . . by Sotheby & Co . . . [London, 1974– .]
2 vols illus. maps facsims. 28cm
In progress.

Horne (Ethelbert)
449 Primitive sun dials or scratch dials . . . including a list of those in Somerset . . . Taunton, Barnicott, 1917.
xii 90p plates 21cm

Horological Journal
450 English clocks and watches and their makers. *Anon.* [London, printed by Silk, 1923?]
64p illus. 22cm

451 The special organ of the British Horological Institute. London, printed for the British Horological Institute and published by Kent & Co., [1859 to date].
Vols 1–60, starting 1859, 23cm
Vols 60–76, from 1917–18 to 1933–34, 25cm
Vols 77 to date, 27cm
From Vol 60 the title is: *The Horological Journal. For chronometer, watch & clock makers, jewellers, gold & silversmiths, and opticians. London, published by the British Horological Institute, Ltd. . . .*
From Vol 82, 1940, the title is: *Horological Journal. Incorporating the Watch & Clockmaker. Official organ of the British Horological Institute & of the British Clock Manufacturers' Association. Founded 1858.* Editor, Arthur Tremayne.

452 Established for promoting the science and practice of horology. No. 1, September, 1858. Price 4*d*.
14p 23cm
First issue, as published, of the *Horological Journal.*

Horrins (Johan) *see* **Harrison (John), Junior**

Horstmann (G. Henry)
453 Taschenuhren frühere Jahrhunderte aus der Sammlung Marfels . . . Berlin, Verlag Deutsche Uhrmacher-Zeitung, 1897.
15p 24 plates 24cm

Howard (E.) Watch and Clock Co.
454 Catalogue of hall striking clocks . . . 1888. [Bristol, Conn., American Clock and Watch Museum, 1963.]
27p illus. 24cm
Facsimile reprint of 1888 edition.

455 Illustrated catalogue of clocks manufactured by the . . . company [Boston, U.S.A., Batchelder, 1874.]
[63p] illus. 21cm
A reprint, 1974.

Howgrave-Graham (Robert Pickersgill-) *see* **Graham (Robert Pickersgill-Howgrave)**

Howse (Derek) and Hutchinson (Beresford)
456 The clocks and watches of Captain James Cook, 1769–1969. [Reprinted from *Antiquarian Horology*, 1969.]
[65] p illus. ports. facsims. 25cm

***Hughes (Thomas Cann)**
457 Notes on some Westmorland clock-makers. (In Cumberland and Westmorland Antiquarian & Archaeological Society, Transactions, new series, vol 35, p 42; vol 37, p 147; vol 39, p 171, 1935–39.)

Huguenin (Pierre)
458 The inside story of the Swiss watch. La Chaux-de-Fonds, Swiss Watch Chamber of Commerce, [1949].
31p illus. plates 23cm

Humane industry . . . *(Anon., 1661) see* **Powell (Thomas)**

Huygens (Christiaan)
459 Christiani Hugenii à Zulichem, const. F. Horologium. Hagae comitum, ex officina Adriani Vlacq, 1658.
15p 1 plate 19cm
Photostat copy.

CHRISTIANI
HVGENII
ZVLICHEMII, CONST· F·
HOROLOGIVM
OSCILLATORIVM·
SIVE
DE MOTV PENDVLORVM
AD HOROLOGIA APTATO
DEMONSTRATIONES
GEOMETRICÆ.

PARISIIS,
Apud F. Muguet, Regis & Illuſtriſſimi Archiepiſcopi Typographum,
viâ Cithara, ad inſigne trium Regum.
MDCLXXIII.
CVM PRIVILEGIO REGIS.

PLATE 13   Title-page of *Horologium oscillatorium*, by Christiaan Huygens, 1673.
This work, which was completed by Huygens in 1673, has been described by
G. H. Baillie as possibly 'the most important item of a horological bibliography'.
(No. 460)

460 Christiani Hugenii Zulichemii, Const. F. Horologium oscillatorium sive de motu pendulorum ad horologia aptato demonstrationes geometricae. Parisiis, Apud F. Muguet, Regis & Illustrissimi Archiepiscopi Typographum, 1673.
xiv 162p illus. diagrams 31cm
See plate 13.

Ilbert (Courtenay Adrian)
461 . . . Catalogue of the . . . English and continental clocks also . . . of Japanese clocks . . . which will be sold at auction by Christie, Manson & Woods . . . [London, The auctioneers, 1958.]
96p plates 25cm
Bought for the British Museum before the sale.

Ingraham (E.) Co.
462 . . . Illustrated catalogue and price list of clocks . . . 1880. [Bristol, Conn., American Clock and Watch Museum, 1965.]
44p illus. 18cm
Facsimile reprint of the 1880 edition.

International Congress for Chronometry
463 . . . Antique clocks; a selection of . . . clocks and watches exhibited . . . on occasion of the . . . congress . . . at Munich [1959]. Ulm, Neuen Uhrmacher-Zeitung, 1960.
168p illus. 21cm
Text in German, English and French.

Ireland. National Museum, Dublin.
464 . . . A list of Irish watch and clock makers by Geraldine Fennell . . . Dublin, Stationery Office, 1963.
vi 42p 21cm

Istanbul. Topkapi Sarayi Museum.
465 Catalogue of clocks and watches in the . . . Museum; by Wolfgang Meyer . . . [Istanbul, The Museum, 1970?]
[118] p illus. 27cm

Jackson (John Early)
466 The amateur scientist: how two distinguished amateurs set about refining the accuracy of a pendulum clock. [Photocopied from *Scientific American*, July–August 1960.]
14 l. illus. 27cm

Jackson (William)
467 The trial of William Jackson (a watch-case maker) at the Old Bailey, April 9th, 1816, on an indictment for feloniously transposing and removing the marks of the Goldsmiths' Company from one watch-case to another. London, printed by J. Diggens, 1816.
71p 20cm

Jagger (Cedric)
468 Paul Philip Barraud: a study of a fine chronometer maker, and of his relatives, associates and successors in the family business, 1750–1929 . . . London, Antiquarian Horological Society, 1968.
viii 177p illus. plates 30cm
Includes check lists of the firm's timepieces.

469 English watch cocks. [Extract from *Antique Finder*, vol 12, no. 11, November 1973, pp 34–37. illus.]

470 Watches and their chains.
Illustrated extract from *Discovering Antiques*, no. 52, 1971, pp 1244–48.

471 Clocks. London, Orbis, [1973].
64p illus. 30cm

James (Arthur E.)
472 Chester County [USA] clocks and their makers. Published under the auspices of the Chester County Historical Society, 1947.
205p illus. plates 23cm

James (Emile)
473 Bibliothèque horlogère. Les sonneries de montres, pendules et horloges, pratique et théorie . . . avec 60 figures dans le texte. 2e édition, revue et augmentée. Bienne, E. Magron, 1927.
94p 19cm

James (Walter Henry)
474 House of Commons. 1876. Mr W. H. James' Motion on the City Companies (Transcript of shorthand notes). [W. J. Adams, printer.]
45p inc. debate. 20cm

Janvier (Antide)
475 Des revolutions des corps célestes par le mécanisme des rouages . . . Paris, Imprimerie de P. Didot l'aîné, 1812.
xii 128p frontis. 8 fold. plates 28cm

476 Essai sur les horloges publiques, pour les Communes de la campagne. Dedié aux habitans du Jura . . . A Paris, de l'imprimerie de Doublet, 1811.
iii 56p 3 fold. plates 20cm

477 Étrennes chronométriques, pour l'an 1811, ou précis de ce qui concerne le tems, ses divisions, ses mesures, leurs usages, etc. Publié par Antide Janvier, au Palais des Arts, 1810.
xviii 288p frontis. 1 plate 14cm

478 Manuel chronométrique, ou précis de ce qui concerne le temps, ses divisions, ses mesures, leurs usages, etc. . . . A Paris, de l'imprimerie de Firmin Didot, 1821.
277p frontis. 5 fold. plates 17cm
The contents are similar to those of *Etrennes chronométriques* (see 477).

479 Recueil de machines composées et executées par Antide Janvier. Paris, Imprimerie de Jules Didot aîné, 1828.
vi 61p 12 plates 25cm

Jaquet (Eugène) and Chapuis (Alfred)
480 Technique and history of the Swiss watch . . . [Translated from the French by D. S. Torrens and C. Jenkins. 2nd edition.] London, Spring books, [1970.]
272p illus. plates (inc. ports., facsims.) 31cm
Text of the first English edition, 1953, with a new chapter by Samuel Guye.

Jaquet (Eugène) and others
481 Histoire et technique de la montre suisse . . . Bâle, Editions Urs Graf, 1945.
270p   288 plates   31cm

*Jefferies (Henry Beddowe)
482 The Danesfield clock. [Radnage, the Author, 1966.]
10p   plates   25cm

Jenkins (Henry)
483 A description of several astronomical and geographical clocks; with an account of their motions and uses . . . The second edition, with additions . . . London, printed for and sold by the Author, 1778.
130p   fold. frontis.   20cm

Jerome (Chauncey)
484 History of the American clock business for the past sixty years, and life of Chauncey Jerome, written by himself. Barnum's connection with the Yankee clock business. New Haven, published by F. C. Dayton Jnr, 1860.
144p   frontis. (port.)   18cm

Jerome & Co.
485 [Catalogue of clocks manufactured by the company. Philadelphia, Young & Duross, 1852.]
24p   illus.   11cm
Facsimile reprint, 1964, of the 1852 edition by the American Clock and Watch Museum.

Jerome Manufacturing Co.
486 Chauncey Jerome, manufacturer of brass clocks, a trade catalogue . . . [New Haven, Conn., printed by J. H. Benham, 1853?]
32p   illus. facsims.   20cm
Reprint, 1971, by the American Clock and Watch Museum.

*487 Jewellers' and watchmakers' pocket book. Advisory editor A. Selwyn . . . London, Heywood, [1951].
503p   11cm

Jodin (Jean)
488 Les échappemens à repos comparés aux échappemens à recul; avec un mémoire sur une montre de nouvelle construction . . . Suivi de quelques réflexions sur . . . la police des Maîtres Horlogers de Paris . . . A Paris, chez Ch.Ant. Jombert, 1766.
260p   3 plates   17cm

Jones (F. Hope-)
489 Electric clocks. With a foreword by Sir Frank Dyson . . . London, N.A.G. Press, [1931].
xv   261p   21cm

490 Electrical timekeeping; with a foreword by H. Spencer Jones. London, N.A.G. Press [1940].
xix   275p   22cm

Jones (Sir Harold Spencer)
491 The history of the marine chronometer. Reprinted from *Endeavour*, vol XIV, no. 56, pp 212–219, October 1955.
[4] p   illus. port.   28cm

492 The rotation of the earth . . . Reprinted from *Encyclopedia of Physics*, vol 47, [1955?]
23p   illus.   25cm

Jones (John)
493 A sketch of the history and principles of watch work. [London, c 1840].
16p   illus. plates   22cm

Jones (William)
494 Methods of finding a true meridian line, useful in placing horizontal sun-dials, setting clocks and watches, &c. . . . London, printed for W. & S. Jones, 1795.
8p   fold. equation table   20cm

Jordan (Ernst von Bassermann-) *see* **Basserman-Jordan (Ernst von)**

Joy (Edward Thomas)
495 The *Country Life* book of clocks. London, Country Life, [1967].
96p   illus.   25cm

Junquera (Paulina)
496 . . . Relojeria Palatina: antología dela Colección Real Espanõla. Madrid, R. C. Blasco, 1956.
x   116p   40 plates   17cm
Clock and watchwork in the Palacio Real, Madrid. *See* note to 436 *ante*.

Jupp (Edward Basil)
497 A historical account of the Worshipful Company of Carpenters of the City of London. London, William Pickering, 1848.
xix   338p   frontis.   3 plates   22cm

Jürgensen (Urbain)
498 Mémoires sur l'horlogerie exacte, contenant:
1. Remarques sur l'horlogerie exacte . . .
2. Description de l'échappement libre à double roue.
3. De l'isochronisme des vibrations du pendule . . .
4. Description d'un pendule compensateur . . .
5. De l'influence de l'air sur le régulateur des pendules astronomiques . . .
Publiés et en partie traduit du Danois par le fils aîné de l'Auteur, Louis Urbain Jürgensen. Paris, Bachelier, 1832.
63p   5 fold.plates   28cm

499 Principes generaux de l'exacte mesure du temps par les horloges; ouvrage contenant les principes élémentaires de l'art de la mesure du temps par les horloges, la description de plusieurs échappements et de deux nouveaux proposés aux artistes par l'Auteur, les meilleurs moyens de compensation des effets de la temperature, trois plans ou calibres de différentes montres, la description d'une pendule astronomique et d'une montre marine projetées par l'Auteur . . . Copenhague, Chez N. Moller et Fils, 1805.
xxxii   255p   19 fold. plates   26cm
Plates in separate volume.

Kater (Henry)
500 An account of experiments for determining the variation in the length of the pendulum vibrating seconds, at the principal stations of the trigonometrical

survey of Great Britain. From the Philosophical Transactions. London, Printed by William Bulmer & Co., 1819.
ii 170p 27cm

501 An account of the comparison of various British standards of linear measure. From the Philosophical Transactions. London, printed by W. Bulmer, 1821.
22p 27cm

502 On the error in standards of linear measure. From the Philosophical Transactions. London, printed by Richard Taylor, 1830.
pp 359–381 27cm

Kater (Henry) and Lardner (Dionysius)
503 A treatise on mechanics . . . London, printed for Longman, Rees, Orme, Brown & Green, 1830. Second title-page, The Cabinet Cyclopaedia, conducted by the Rev Dionysius Lardner . . . Natural Philosophy, Mechanics.
ix 342p 21 plates 16cm

504 Kelly's directory of the watch, clock and jewellery trades throughout England, Scotland and Wales. 3rd–16th editions. London, Kelly, 1880–1937.
14 vols 26cm
Published at irregular intervals.
1880, 1887, 1892, 1897, 1901, 1905, 1909, 1913, 1917, 1921, 1924, 1927, 1932, 1937 – no more published.

Kemlo (F.)
505 Watch-repairer's handbook; being a complete guide to the young beginner in taking apart, putting together, and thoroughly cleaning the English lever and other foreign watches, and all American watches . . . Philadelphia, Henry Carey, Baird & Co., 1882.
93p 19cm

Kendal (James Francis)
506 A history of watches and other timekeepers . . . With numerous illustrations. London, Crosby Lockwood and Sons, 1892.
ii 252p frontis. 18cm

Kennedy (Richard Hartley)
507 Memorandum of the life and public charities of Sir Jamsetjee Jeejeebhoy. *Anon.* Printed for private circulation, 1855.
32p 19cm

*Knaster (Roland)
508 Watch papers: a neglected conceit.
(In *Alphabet and image*, 7 May 1948, pp 26–32.)

Kuhlicke (Frederick William)
509 . . . Thomas Tompion . . . 1948.
An illustrated extract from the *Bedfordshire Magazine*, vol 1, pp 249–255.

La Chaux-de-Fonds. Musée d'horlogerie.
510 [A collection of illustrations of exhibits. 196–?]
99p illus. 25cm

511 . . . Montres émaillées des XVIIᵉ et XVIIIᵉ siècles; collections du Louvre et des musées parisiens . . . [La Chaux-de-Fonds, Le musée, 1970.]
48 plates 24cm

Exhibition catalogue published in collaboration with the Union des Banques Suisses on the occasion of their fortieth anniversary.

Lacroix (Paul)
512 The arts in the Middle Ages and the Renaissance . . . English edition, revised and re-arranged by W. Armstrong, and illustrated with twelve chromolithographic prints by F. Kellerhoven, and upwards of 400 engravings on wood. London, J. S. Virtue & Co., [1886].
xvi 464p col. frontis. 11 col. plates 26cm
Horology is on pp 138–152.

Lancashire Watch Co.
513 The Lancashire Watch Company, Prescot, Lancashire, England, 1889–1910 . . . Fitzwilliam, N. H., USA, Ken Roberts Publishing Co., [1973].
88p illus. 28cm

Landrock (Horst)
514 . . . Alte Uhren, aus einer Zittauer Sammlung Einführung und Erläuterungen . . . [Leipzig,] Im Prisma-Verlag, [1971].
xii 39p plates 20cm
Mainly plates.

Langman (H. R.) and Ball (A.)
515 Electrical horology. A practical manual on the application of . . . electricity to horological instruments . . . with an account of the earliest electrically driven clock mechanism . . . With 68 illustrations. London, Crosby Lockwood and Son, 1923.
xi 164p 19cm

516 Electrical Horology . . . 3rd edition, revised and enlarged by H. R. Langman. London, The Technical Press Ltd., 1946.
xii 200p 18cm

Lanz (Philippe-Louis) and Bétancourt (Augustin de)
517 Essai sur la composition des machines . . . Seconde édition, revue, corrigée et considerablement augmentée. Paris, Bachelier, 1819.
i 184p 13 fold. plates 25cm
References to equation clocks, pp 119–121, and to escapements, pp 123–136.

Le Corbeiller (Mrs Clare)
518 James Cox, a biographical review.
An illustrated extract from the *Burlington Magazine*, vol 112, no. 807, June 1970, pp 348, 351–8.
Cox, the London jeweller and toymaker and proprietor of a museum of automata.

Lecoultre (François)
519 A guide to complicated watches . . . Bienne, Rohr, 1952.
220p illus. 21cm

Lee (Ronald Alfred)
520 The first twelve years of the English pendulum clock; or the Fromanteel family and their contemporaries, 1655–1670: a loan exhibition at the . . . galleries of Ronald A. Lee . . . London, The author, 1969.
[80]p illus. 31cm
Mainly illustrations of the exhibits.

521 The Knibb family . . . [Byfleet, Manor House Press, 1964.]
  187p   illus.   30cm

Leeds. Temple Newsam House.
522 Exhibition of English clocks 1600–1850. 1949.
  27p   4 plates   24cm

Leiden. National Museum of the History of Science.
523 Descriptive catalogue of the Huygens collection . . . by C. A. Crommelin. [Leiden, The Museum, 1949.]
  31p   4 plates   19cm

Le Lionnais (François)
524 Prentice-Hall book of time. London, Prentice-Hall, [1962].
  110p   illus.   18 × 21cm   (Symbol series)

Le Locle. Musée d'horlogerie.
525 . . . Premières horloges mécaniques à poids: horloges gothiques. Le Locle, Le musée, [1969].
  70p   illus.   21cm
Catalogue of an exhibition 7 June to 17 August 1969, with an introduction by W. Hertig, from whose collection the exhibits came.

Le Locle, Musée d'horlogerie, and La Chaux-de-Fonds, Musée d'horlogerie.
526 . . . Montres du XVIe au XIXe siècle: exposition de 120 montres et automates provent des musées . . . [Le Locle, Le musée, 1970.]
  51p   illus.   24cm
Catalogue of the exhibition held at the Swiss Institute, Rome, 28 October – 7 November 1970.

527 Le pays de l'horlogerie. [Le Locle,] Association de developpement du Locle, [1970?].
  s. sh. folded   illus.   maps   42 × 30cm
Leaflet advertising the two museums.

Le Monnier (Pierre Charles)
528 Observations de la lune, du soleil, et des étoiles fixes . . . A Paris, de l'imprimerie royale, 1751–73.
  4 vols in 1   39cm

Leopold (John H.)
529 The Almanus manuscript, Staats-und Stadtbibliothek Augsburg codex in 2° No. 209, Rome c 1475 – c 1485. London, Hutchinson, [1971].
  306p   illus. facsims.   30cm

Lepaute (Jean André)
530 Copie d'une lettre écrite à Monseigneur le Duc de ***, par le Sieur Lepaute, Horloger du Roi . . . servant à la justification dudit Sieur Lepaute contre différentes imputations du Sieur Le Roi, fils aîné du Sieur Jullien le Roi, . . . [Paris,] 1752.
  9p   22cm

531 Traité d'horlogierie, contenant tout ce qui est nécessaire pour bien connoître et pour régler les pendules et les montres, la description des pièces d'horlogerie les plus utiles, des répétitions, des équations, des pendules à une roue, &c. . . . A Paris, chez Jaques Chardon, Père, 1760.
  xxviii   308   xxxvip   17 fold. plates   25cm

Le Roy (Pierre)
532 Expose succint des travaux de MM. Harrison et Le Roy, dans la recherche des longitudes en mer, & des épreuves faites de leurs ouvrages . . . A Paris, chez Nyon, 1768.
  xvi   51p   25cm
See Plate 14.
Also published in English with footnotes, some of them initialled W.H., *i.e.* (?) William Harrison the only son of John Harrison; a copy is in the British Horological Institute.

533 A memoir on the best method of measuring time at sea, which obtained the double prize adjudged by the Royal Academy of Sciences; containing the description of the longitude watch presented to His Majesty (Louis XV, King of France) . . . 1766. Translated from the French by Mr T. S. Evans . . .
In the *Philosophical Magazine*, Vol 26, 1806.
  pp 40–204   3 fold. plates   23cm

534 Mémoire sur l'horlogerie, contenant diverses remarques sur les ouvrages et les prétentions de M. R. Par M. *** Paris, 1750.
  40p   2 plates   26cm
'M. R.' is Monsieur de Rivaz. (i.e. Pierre Joseph de Rivaz).

535 The same. Another copy.

Leurechon (Jean)
536 Mathematical recreations . . . lately compiled in French by Henry van Etten, gent. [pseudonym for Jean Leurechon] and now delivered in the English tongue . . . London, printed by T. Cotes, 1633.
  xxvi   289p   illus.   16cm

Liberty (Gene)
537 The how and why wonder book of time . . . London, Transworld [1968].
  48p   illus.   27cm

Lincoln. Usher Art Gallery *see* Usher Art Gallery.

Little (John Egram) and Nettell (D. F.)
538 . . . Uffington church clock . . . 1969.
  10p   plate   22cm   (Berkshire Tracts 2.)

Liverpool. Corporation Museums.
539 Watches in the city of Liverpool museums [a handlist]. [Liverpool, The Corporation, 1971?]
  20 l.   33cm
Typewriter script.

Lloyd (Herbert Alan)
540 Chats on old clocks. [3rd edition.] London, Benn, [1951].
  186p   illus.   75 plates   20cm
A new edition of Arthur Hayden's earlier work of the same title.

541 The clocks of Sir Isaac Newton and John Flamsteed.
From the *Horological Journal*, December 1948, pp 750–768.
  28cm

EXPOSÉ SUCCINT

DES TRAVAUX

DE MM.

HARRISON ET LE ROY,

DANS LA RECHERCHE

DES LONGITUDES EN MER,

& des épreuves faites de leurs Ouvrages.

Par M. LE ROY, Horloger du Roi.

A PARIS,

Chez {
NYON, Quai des Augustins, à l'Occasion.
JOMBERT, rue Dauphine, à l'Image Notre-Dame.
PRAULT père, Quai de Gêvres, au Paradis.
}

M. DCC. LXVIII.

PLATE 14   Title-page of *Exposé succint des travaux des Mm. Harrison et Le Roy*, by Pierre Le Roy, 1768. In his book Pierre Le Roy (1717–1785) compares his marine timekeepers with the prize-winning watch, H.4., of John Harrison (1693–1776). P. Le Roy was a French chronometer maker of great inventive genius who constructed two marine timekeepers that were proved to be effective at sea two years after Harrison had competed successfully for the £20,000 longitude prize. Le Roy must have had this prize firmly in mind, as he ends his book with a plea to the French government that he, too, should be recompensed now that the 'venerable old man' has been 'worthily rewarded'. (No. 532)

542 The collector's dictionary of clocks. London, Country Life, [1964].
   214p   illus.   31cm

543 The English domestic clock, its evolution and history; a brief guide to the essential details for dating a clock . . . [London, privately printed for the author, 1938.]
   28p   illus.   24cm

544 Giovanni de Dondi's horological masterpiece, 1364. [London? 1955.]
   22p   facsims.   30cm
With 16 photographs by H. A. Lloyd of a model of the clock, 1961?

545 John Harrison . . . [1954?]
   17p   illus. port.   28cm
Reprinted from *La suisse horlogère*.

546 Old clocks. 3rd edition. London, Benn, [1964.]
   176p   plates   22cm

547 Old clocks. 4th edition. London, Benn, [1970.]
   216p   plates   22cm

548 The one and only Edward East. Reprinted from *Horological Journal*, May and June, 1950.
   7p   illus. port.   28cm

549 . . . Some outstanding clocks over seven hundred years, 1250–1950. London, Hill, 1958.
   xx   160p   illus. plates   27cm

550 . . . Tides and time. [London, reprinted from *Horological Journal*, December 1950.]
   14p   illus.   28cm

Lloyd (Herbert Alan) and Drover (Charles B.)
551 Nicholas Vallin (*c* 1565–1603). 1954.
   7 l.   illus.   31cm
Reprinted from *Connoisseur Year Book*.

London and Middlesex Archaeological Society
552 A catalogue of the antiquities and works of art, exhibited at Ironmongers' Hall, London . . . 1861. London, Harrison & Sons, 1869. Editor George Russell French.
   2 vols   19 plates   2 col. plates   2 fold. plates   37cm

London. Clock and Watch Manufacturers
553 The memorial of the undersigned Clock and watch manufacturers, and of the workmen employed in the various branches connected therewith, resident in the Metropolis, to the . . . Lords Commissioners of Her Majesty's Treasury. [1841.]
   3p   33cm

London. Corporation.
554 Extract from an Act of Common Council [15 October 1765] of the City of London, for regulating the Master, Wardens, and Fellowship of the art or mystery of clock-making. [London, Clockmakers' Co., n.d.]
   s. sh.   39 × 24cm

London County Council, afterwards Greater London Council
555 . . . Form of tender for clock winding, cleaning and repairing . . . [London, The council, 1937.]
   48p   33cm

Includes list of buildings covered by the tender. Name of tenderer: A. A. Osborne & Son.

556 London wholesale, manufacturing and retail goldsmiths, silversmiths, watchmakers, opticians and cutlers directory . . . also . . . wholesale houses . . . at Birmingham, Liverpool and Manchester . . . London, Collinson, 1861.
   320p   24cm

Loomes (Brian)
557 Yorkshire clockmakers. [Clapham, Yorks.,] Dalesman, 1972.
   192p   illus.   21cm

558 The white dial clock. Newton Abbot, David & Charles, 1974.
   172p   illus.   21cm

559 Westmorland clocks and clockmakers. Newton Abbot, David & Charles, [1974].
   120p   illus. facsims.   18cm

Lübke (Anton)
560 Die uhr von der sonnenuhr zur atomuhr . . . Düsseldorf, VDI Verlag, 1958.
   ix   441p   illus.   27cm

Mackay (Andrew)
561 The theory and practice of finding the longitude at sea or land . . . London, printed for J. Sewell, 1793.
   2 vols in 1   22cm

Mandey (Venterus) and Moxon (James)
562 Mechanick-Powers . . . Together with . . . the making of clock-work, and other engines . . . London, printed for the Authors, 1696.
   x   320p   17 fold. plates   20cm
Horology is on pp 189–242.
Earliest mention of the stackfreed regulating device.

Margetts (George)
563 Margetts' horary tables for showing, by inspection, the apparent diurnal motion of the sun, moon, and stars, the latitude of a ship, and the azimuth, time, or altitude, corresponding with any celestial object. London, printed for the Author, 1790.
xviii p containing instructions for the use of the tables, which are lacking in the Clockmakers' copy, but a copy of the Tables is in Guildhall Library collections.
   27cm

Marperger (Paul Jacob)
564 Paul Jacob Marpergers . . . Horologiographia, oder Beschreibung der Eintheilung und Abmessung der Zeit . . . durch die Sonnen-Zeiger . . . auch durch künstliche Machinas, Uhrwerke und Glocken . . . Dresden und Leipzig, 1723.
   xii   288p   frontis.   17cm

Martin (Benjamin)
565 The description and use of a table-clock upon a new construction . . . [London, 1770.]
   10p   plate   26cm

Martin (John)
566 Mechanicus and Flaven: or the watch spiritualized. London, printed for G. Keith, 1763.
xii 59p 18cm

Maskelyne (Nevil)
567 An account of the going of Mr John Harrison's watch, at the Royal Observatory, from May 6th 1766 to March 4th 1767. Together with the original observations and calculations of the same. Published by order of the Commissioners of Longitude. London, W. Richardson and S. Clark, 1767.
28 lvip 30cm

568 An answer to a pamphlet entitled 'A Narrative of Facts', lately published by Mr Thomas Mudge, Junior, relating to some timekeepers constructed by his father, Mr Thomas Mudge . . . and the resolutions of the Board of Longitude, respecting them are vindicated from Mr Mudge's misrepresentations. London, printed for F. Wingrave, 1792.
128p Appendices 40p 26cm

Mason (Bernard)
569 Clock and watchmaking in Colchester . . . fifteenth to the nineteenth centuries . . . [London,] Country Life, 1969.
436p illus. port. maps, plans, facsims. 25cm

Masters (John Neve)
570 Amusing reminiscences of Victorian times and of today (Illustrated) . . . Rye, 1921.
201p 22cm
pp 83–89, Life in a country watchmaker's shop. Pp 121–128, Sun-dials and clocks. Ancient and modern time-keepers.

Mathematical Society, London
571 A catalogue of books belonging to the Mathematical Society, London. Printed by James Whiting, 1804.
xvi 47p 20cm

Mears and Stainbank
572 A plain statement of facts relative to the Royal Exchange chimes. [London, 1850?]
4p 40cm
Answer to an attack on the firm in the Court of Common Council.

573 [Catalogue of] . . . church, clock, hemispherical and . . . other . . . bells. [London, 1911].
61p illus. 20cm

Mellor (E.)
574 Bridlington clockmakers. [1964.]
16 l. 25cm
Typewriter script. Photostat copy.

575 Memoirs of the life and mechanical labours of the late Mr Thomas Mudge . . .
An extract from the Universal Magazine, vol 97, July 1795, pp 41–47.

576 **Memorandum** of the life and public charities of Sir Jamsetjee Jeejeebhoy. *Anon.*
[London,] printed for private circulation, 1855.
32p port. 19cm

577 The same. Another copy.
Lacks portrait.

Mercer (Raymond Vaudrey)
578 John Arnold & Son, chronometer makers, 1762–1843 . . . London, Antiquarian Horological Society, 1972.
xii 302p illus. plates (inc. maps) 25cm

Meyrick (William)
579 A short account of the remarkable clock made by James Cox, in the year 1766, by order of the Hon the East India Company for the Emperor of China: Illustrated. Also a few remarks on James Cox, and some other of his works. [London,] 1868.
16p frontis. 27cm

Micheli (Pietro Adamo)
580 Della dichiaratione de l'horologio di Mantova, seconda & nuoua editione, illustrata & abbellita in cio che prima era meno bella & oscura. [Nearly full-page woodcut.] In Mantova del XLVII [1547].
Paged on every second page 1–8, IX–XIX. 15cm
The name Pier Adamo is mentioned on p 3, but Riccardi gives the Author's name as above, from evidence in Volta's *Compendio della storia di Mantova. See* plate 15.

Milan. Museo Poldi Pezzoli.
581 Gli orologi a cura di Giuseppe Brusa; le schede degli strumenti scientifici sono di Tullio Tomba. Milan, The Museum, 1974.
84p illus. 27cm
Catalogue of the Bruno Falck collection of clocks, watches and scientific instruments.

Milbourn (Thomas)
582 The Vintners' Company, their muniments, plate, and eminent members, with some account of the Ward of Vintry . . . Printed for the Vintners' Company, for private circulation, 1888.
i 136p frontis. 4 plates 25cm

Milham (Willis I.)
583 Time and timekeepers, including the history, construction, care, and accuracy of clocks and watches . . . New York, The Macmillan Company, 1923.
xix 609p frontis. 22cm

584 **Modern** watch repairing and adjusting. By a Swiss expert . . . London, N.A.G. Press, [1933?].
xiii 118p illus. plates 21cm

Mody (N. H. N.)
585 A collection of Japanese clocks . . . This is one of 200 copies, no. 43. London, Kegan Paul, Trench, Trubner & Co. Ltd., 1932.
xiv 27p 135 plates 29p of Japanese text 26cm

Moenck (Gustavus)
586 Patent detached escapement. [1847.]
s. fold. sh. with illus. 33cm
Moenck's specification of his invention patented December 1847.

PLATE 15   Title-page of *Description of the Clock at Mantua*, by Pietro Adamo Micheli, 1547. Probably the first printed book about a clock. The woodcut shows the clock at Mantua. The dial has XII and XXIIII at left and right respectively; this was usual in early times, when the Italian day commenced at sunset (that is, at XXIIII). (No. 580)

Moinet (M. L.)
587 Nouveau traité général, astronomique et civil d'horlogerie, theorique et pratique . . . Contenant une nouvelle méthode pratique et universelle de l'engrenage . . . les échappements anciens et modernes, et les échap. libres actuels, cadratures, main-d'oeuvre, tables, etc. . . . Paris, chez l'Auteur-éditeur, 1848.
Vol 1 iv 432p frontis. 18 fold. plates 9p tables
Vol 2 544p fold. plates 19–51 25cm

Moore (N. Hudson; Mrs Hannah Moore)
588 The old clock book . . . London, Heinemann, 1912.
xi 339p plates (inc. ports.) 21cm
Contains lists of English and American makers.

Morgan (Charles Octavius Swinnerton)
589 Continuation of the history and of the art of watchmaking . . . London, printed by Nichols, 1850.
17p 27cm
Reprinted from *Archaeologia*, vol 33.

590 List of members of the Clockmakers' Company of London, from the period of their incorporation in 1631 to the year 1732.
MS note: From the *Archaeological Journal*, Vol 40, No. 158, pp 193–214, 1883.
22cm
The sheets are pasted on leaves of a folio volume.

591 Observations on the history and progress of the art of watchmaking, from the earliest period to modern times . . . London, printed by J. B. Nichols & Son, 1849.
19p 29cm
From *Archaeologia*, vol 33, pp 84–100.

592 Observations on the classification and arrangement of a collection of watches . . . [London, 1875.]
17p 22cm

*Morgan (John Pierpont)
593 Catalogue of the collection of watches . . . by G. C. Williamson . . . London, Chiswick Press, 1912.
lxii 244p illus. plates 37cm
The Morgan collections were presented in 1917 to the Metropolitan Museum of Art, New York.

Morpurgo (Enrico)
594 Dizionario degli orologiai Italiani (1300–1880). [Roma,] Edizioni La Clessidra, 1950.
239p 21cm

595 Gli orologi. [Milano], Fabbri, [1966].
157p illus. 19cm
Mainly illustrations.

596 Nederlanse klokken-en horlogemakers vanaf 1300. Amsterdam, Scheltema & Holkema, 1970.
vii 152p plates 15cm

597 Precious watches from the 16th to the 19th century, with a historical survey of Italian watchmaking. [Milan? Omega publications, 1966?]
112p illus. 24cm

Mortensen (D.)
598 Jens Olsen's clock . . . Copenhagen, Technological Institute, 1957.
156p illus. port. 29cm

Mudge (Thomas), 1717–94
599 A register of the going of Mr Mudge's first time-keeper from April . . . 1780 to May . . . 1781 . . . [London? c 1781.]
16p 26cm

Mudge (Thomas), 1760–1843
600 A description with plates, of the time-keeper invented by the late Mr Thomas Mudge. To which is prefixed a narrative, by Thomas Mudge, his son, of measures taken to give effect to the invention since the reward bestowed upon it by the House of Commons in the year 1793; a republication of a tract by the late Mr Mudge on the improvement of time-keepers; and a series of letters written by him to . . . Count Bruhl, between the years 1773 and 1787 . . . London, printed for the Author, 1799.
clxi 176p 9 fold. plates frontis. (port.) 27cm
The description of the plates is by Robert Pennington.

601 A narrative of facts relating to some timekeepers, constructed by Mr Thomas Mudge, for the discovery of the longitude at sea; together with observations upon the conduct of the Astronomer Royal respecting them. London, printed for Thomas Payne, 1792.
xii 94p 19cm

602 A reply to the answer of the Rev Dr Maskelyne, Astronomer Royal, to A narrative of facts relating to some time-keepers, constructed by Mr Thomas Mudge, for the discovery of the longitude at sea, &c. . . . To which is added, a short explanation of the most proper methods of calculating a mean daily rate . . . by . . . Count de Bruhl. London, printed for Thomas Payne, 1792.
187p 23cm

Munckerus (Philippus)
603 De intercalatione variarum gentium, et praesertim Romanorum libri quatuor . . . Lugduni Batavorum, Apud Jacobum Hackium, 1680.
[xxx] 410, [16]p 18cm

Munster (Sebastian)
604 Horologiographia . . . Basiliae, Henricus Petrus, [1533].
[54,] 334p illus. 20cm
Preface and dedication with marginal notes in a late 16th-century hand.

605 Rudimenta mathematica . . . posterior vero omnigenum horologiorum docet delineationes . . . Basileae, 1551.
viii 244p fold. plate 31cm
See plate 16.

Mussey (June Barrows) and Canedy (Ruth Mary)
606 . . . Terry clock chronology; compiled for Charles Terry Treadway . . . [Bristol, Conn., Treadway, 1948.]
30 l. map 28cm
Reprint (196–?) by the American Clock and Watch Museum of the 1948 edition. Typewriter script.

Napier (Robert)
607 Catalogue of the works of art forming the

PLATE 16 Title-page of *Rudimenta mathematica*, by Sebastian Munster, 1551.
This work on mathematics by Sebastian Munster (1489–1552) was published in
Basle. The last part of the book gives instruction on making sundials and other
contemporary timekeepers. Munster, a celebrated German hebraist and cosmo-
grapher, was one of the earliest writers on the general art of dialling (gnomonics), as
opposed to the description of specific instruments. (No. 605)

collection of Robert Napier . . . Compiled by J. C. Robinson . . . London, privately printed, 1865.
x 326p 24cm
Known as the Shandon collection.

608 First – fourth portion. Catalogue of the celebrated assemblage of works of art and vertu, known as the Shandon collection, formed by . . . Robert Napier Esq. deceased . . . sold by auction . . . on April 11, 1877 and 8 following days . . . [London, Christie, 1877.]
4 pts in 1 vol 24cm

National Company
609 The National Company for the manufacture of watches. Capital £250,000, in 10,000 shares of £25 each. [London, c 1850.]
4p 30cm

Needham (Noel Joseph Terence Montgomery) and others.
610 Heavenly clockwork: the great astronomical clocks of medieval China . . . Cambridge, University Press, 1960.
xv 253p illus. plates 25cm

Needlemakers' Company
611 The Worshipful Company of Needlemakers of London; with a list of the Court of Assistants and Livery. [London, The Company,] 1876.
112p 22 × 19cm

Nelthropp (Henry Leonard)
612 A treatise on watchwork, past and present . . . London, E. & F. N. Spon, 1873.
x 310p 18cm

613 The same. Another copy.

***New Southgate. Clock and Watch makers asylum.**
614 [Rules, and list of subscribers for 1885 and 1889.] London, 1885–89.
2 vols 18cm

New York. Metropolitan Museum of Art.
615 Collection of watches loaned to the . . . museum . . . by Mrs George A. Hearn. [New York?] privately printed, 1907.
34p plates 24cm

616 The same. Another copy.

Nicholl (John)
617 Some account of the Worshipful Company of Ironmongers . . . Second edition. London, privately printed, 1866.
xiii 657p Appendix 48p 27cm

Nicholson (John)
618 The Operative Mechanic, and British Machinist; second edition. London, printed for Knight and Lacey, 1825.
xvi 796p fold. frontis. 93 plates 1 fold. plate 21cm
Horology on pp 486–528, 7 plates.

Niebling (Warren H.)
619 History of the American watch case. Philadelphia, Whitmore, [1971].
xi 192p illus. facsims. 28cm

Nixseaman (Alfred Jonathan)
620 A church clock with one hand recalling memories of Nelson and Pitt. Reprinted from *The Salisbury Times*, 28 October 1955.
5p illus. 21cm
Church clock of Stratford-sub-Castle, Wilts.

621 First production: Tompion's great clock [in Northill parish church] . . . Biggleswade, Elphick, 1953.
64p illus. port. 22cm

622 A Sussex clock. Reprinted from *Antiquarian Horology*, vol 1, no. 10, 1956.
[3]p illus. 25cm
Turret clock of Cuckfield church.

Northampton. Central Museum and Art Gallery.
623 . . . Exhibition of early clocks and watches . . . Sept. 3rd to 24th, 1966. [Catalogue] . . . [Northampton, The museum, 1966.]
16p illus. 25cm
Lists watch and clock makers of Northamptonshire.

624 The same. Another copy.

Norwich. Museums.
625 Horological exhibits . . . [Typewriter script, n.d.]
10p 25 × 30cm
Photostat copy.

Notes and Queries
626 A venerable church clock [the ancient clock of Stroud, Glos., parish church. An extract from *Notes & Queries*, 5 series, 7 September 1878, p 184].

627 **Objections** to the repeal of so much of the statute of 5th Elizabeth, cap. 4, as subjects to penalties persons who carry on or follow any trades without having served an apprenticeship thereto of seven years. *Anon.* [London, c 1815?]
3p 33cm

628 **Observations** on the art and trade of clock and watchmaking . . . showing the necessity . . . for further regulations to protect and relieve from their present state of extreme distress the persons lawfully engaged in the said art. *Anon.* Printed by J. Richardson, Hoxton, 1812.
23p 22cm

629 The same. Another copy.

Omega, Louis Brandt & frère S.A.
630 The secret of Switzerland. [Geneva, Omega, 1950.]
59p 27cm
A short study of Swiss economic history, with especial reference to the watchmaking industry.

631 **On the system** of prize chronometers at Greenwich, by Caleb Mainspring, [pseudonym]. From the *Philosophical Magazine and Annals* for December 1829. London, R. Taylor.
[5]p 23cm

Osborne (Clive Alfred)
632 Clockmakers and watchmakers of Derby and Derbyshire . . . [Typewritten, 1964.]
11 l.   25cm

Osborne (Clive Alfred) and Christmas (Leonard Edward)
633 Watchmaking in Chigwell: some notes on the Prest family. Reprinted from Vol 4 of *Antiquarian Horology* [nos. 1–2, 1962–63].
[3]p   illus.   25cm

Otte (Heinrich)
634 Glockenkunde . . . Zweite verbesserte und vermehrte Auflage. Leipzig. T. O. Weigel, 1884.
vi   220p   fold. plate   24cm

Oxford. University. Museum of the history of science.
635 Catalogue 2: Watches [by] F. R. Maddison and A. J. Turner. Oxford, The University, 1973.
vi   91p   illus.   24cm

Ozanam (Jacques)
636 Recréations mathématiques et physiques . . . avec un traité nouveau des horloges élémentaires . . . Paris, Jombert, 1696.
[12,]   583, [23]p   illus.   plates   19cm

637 Recréations mathématiques et physiques . . . 3e edition. Amsterdam, George Callet, 1698.
2 vols   plates   20cm

Padovani (Giovanni)
638 Joannis Paduanii Veronensis de compositione, et usu multiformium horologiorum solarium ad omnes totiùs orbis regiones . . . Venetijs, apud Franciscum Franciscium Senensem, 1582.
[10,]   267, [12]p   illus.   21cm
With MS notes and additions.

Palmer (Brooks)
639 The book of American clocks . . . New York, Macmillan, 1950.
viii   318p   illus.   26cm
pp 135–318, list of American clock and watch makers.

640 A treasury of American clocks. New York, Macmillan, [1967].
xi   371p   illus.   facsims.   26cm

Paris. Communauté des maîtres horlogers.
641 Mémoire signifié pour la communauté des maîtres horlogers . . . opposants à l'enrigistrement de lettres-patentes du 24 Mai, 1750. Contre Pierre de Rivaz, demandeur en enrigistrement. Paris, [De l'imprimerie de J. Lamesle, 1751].
32p   22cm

Paris. Conservatoire national des arts et métiers.
642 Catalogue . . . Horlogerie . . . [Paris, Le conservatoire,] 1949.
330p   illus.   22cm

643 Chef-d'oeuvre de l'horlogerie . . . Paris, [Les presses artistiques, 1949].
72p   16 plates   21cm

Paris. Musée Galliéra.
644 Centenaire de A. L. Breguet 1747–1823. Exposition de son oeuvre . . . [Paris, Musée Galliéra,] 1923.
37p   plate   22cm

Paris. Musée national du Louvre.
645 Catalogue de la collection [des horloges et des montres]. Paul Garnier. Publié d'après les notes du donateur. Par Gaston Migeon . . . Paris, Hachette, 1917.
112p   plates   18cm

Parker-Rhodes (Charles Elmes) *see* **Rhodes (Charles Elmes Parker-)**

Parkinson (William) and Frodsham (William James)
646 A brief account of the chronometer, with remarks on those furnished by Parkinson and Frodsham to the expeditions of Captains Ross, Parry, Sabine, King, Lyon, Foster . . . with the rate of others tried at the Royal Observatory, Greenwich, in the years 1828–29–30–31. London, printed by M. A. Pittman, 1832.
24p   21cm

647 Change of rate in chronometers, as stated to arise from their removal from one place to another on land, or by their removal from land to shipboard.
Reprinted from the *Nautical Magazine*, 1833.
8p   20cm

Parliament
648 City of London Livery Companies' Commission. Report and appendix. Vol 1, containing (1) The reports and memoranda of the Commissioners and (2) The oral enquiry. Presented to both Houses of Parliament . . . London, printed by Eyre & Spottiswoode, 1884.
5 vols   32cm

649 Copies of three letters addressed by Mr Dent to the Commissioners of Her Majesty's Woods and Forests on the 3rd of May . . . 1847 . . . Ordered to be printed 1847.
2p   32cm

650 Experiments [of Henry Kater] relating to the pendulum vibrating seconds of time in the latitude of London. Ordered by the House of Commons to be printed. London, 1818.
41p   2 fold. plates   33cm

651 A portion of the papers relating to the great clock for the new Palace of Westminster. London, printed by William Clowes & Sons, 1848.
56p   25cm

652 Report from the Committee [of the House of Commons] on the petitions of watchmakers of Coventry, &c. with the minutes of the evidence . . . Ordered to be printed, 1817.
116p   32cm

653 The same. Another copy.

654 Report from the Select Committee [of the House of Commons] appointed to consider of the laws relating to watchmakers. Ordered to be printed 1818.
24p   32cm

655 The same. Another copy.

656 Report from the select committee . . . to whom it was referred to consider of the report . . . from the committee to whom the petition of Thomas Mudge . . . was referred . . . [London,] 1793.
160p   21cm

657 Report from the Select Committee [of the House of Commons] on Hall Marking (gold and silver); together with the proceedings of the Committee . . . Ordered to be printed 1879.
xx 83p 32cm

658 Report [of the Committee of the House of Commons] on clock and watchmakers' petitions. Ordered to be printed 1798.
27p 33cm

659 Return to an order of the Hon. House of Commons, date 13 July, 1847, for copies 'of all the papers and correspondence relating to the great clock . . . for the new Palace at Westminster' . . . 1847.
62p 34cm

660 The same, with further correspondence to 1848. Reprinted London 1852.
72p 34cm

661 Return to an Order of the Hon. House of Commons, dated 4 July 1853: for copies 'of all correspondence and papers relative to improvements in chronometers received by the Board of Admiralty, the Hydrographer, and the Astronomer Royal, since the 25th day of July 1849 . . .'
32p col. plate 34cm

662 A return in obedience to an order of the House of Lords, dated 31st May, 1847, for a list of the papers relative to the great clock for the new Palace of Westminster. Ordered to be printed 1847.
58p 33cm
There are references to drawings which are absent.

663 A return to an order of the House of Lords, dated 1st July 1847, for a return of all specifications and estimates sent by Mr Dent and by Mr Whitehurst to the Office of Woods, &c., relating to the great clock. Ordered to be printed 1847.
20p 32cm

Bills
664 A Bill for granting to William III certain duties on clocks and watches, 1697.

665 A Bill for more effectually discovering the longitude at sea, [1818].

666 A Bill for the more effectual prevention of frauds and abuses . . . and for the relief of distressed workmen . . . 1818.

667 A Bill to regulate the manufacture of clocks and watches. 1819.

Statutes
668 9/10 William III, 1698. [A reprint, 1818?]

669 13 Anne. Cap. 14. 1714. 'Ch. 15, 12 Anne Stat. 2 in the Common Printed Edition' (*Rec. Comm. Statutes of the Realm*, Vol 9) (Also in MS 3973/21 no. 976 *post*); *see* plate 17.

670 27 George II. 1754.

671 2 George III. Cap. 18. 1762. (Also in MS 3973/23 no. 976 *post*.)

672 3 George III. Cap 14. 1763.

673 5 George III. Cap. 20. 1765. (Also in MS 3973/24 no. 976 *post*.)

674 14 George III. Cap. 66. 1774. (Also in MS 3973/25 no. 976 *post*.)

675 9 George IV. Cap. 76. 1828.

Parmenter (John)
676 Helio-tropes or new posies for sundials written in an old book partly in English and partly in Latin and expounded in English . . . 1625. Edited by Perceval Landon. London, Methuen & Co., 1904.
36p printed on recto only. 22cm

Parr (William)
677 A treatise on pocket watches; pointing out the defects so generally complained of in their construction . . . London, printed for the Author, 1804.
x 44p 21cm

Partington (Charles Frederick)
678 The century of inventions of the Marquis of Worcester. From the original MS with historical and explanatory notes, and a biographical memoir . . . London, John Murray, 1825.
lxxxiv 138p 16cm

679 The Mechanics Library, or Book of Trades. The clock and watch-makers' complete guide . . . theoretical and practical. London, printed for Sherwood, Gilbert and Piper, [1826].
96p 2 plates 21cm

680 The Scientific Gazette; or, Library of mechanical philosophy, chemistry and discovery . . . 1825. London, printed by James Robins & Co., 1826.
390, 32p illus. 25cm
Containing:
On compensating pendulums. By James Wilson, pp 162–164.
Portable night clock (Griebel, Paris), p 219.
Curious horological machine, pp 222–223.
History of the invention of pendulum clocks by Christian Huygens. By J. H. Van Swinden, pp 8, 9.

Patent Office
681 Abridgments of the specifications relating to watches, clocks and other timekeepers . . . [1661–1876]. London, Eyre & Spottiswoode, 1858–83.
3 vols 18cm

682 Abridgments of specifications. Class 139: watches, clocks and other timekeepers . . . 1855 [to 1908]. London, H.M.S.O., 1905–12.
9 vols in 2 illus. 27cm

683 AD 1812 No. 3620. Escapements for watches. [Samuel Smith's specification.]
2p 28cm
Photocopy of original. See exhibits nos 528, 533, 534 in Clockmakers Museum, Guildhall.

(355)

Anno Duodecimo
Annæ Reginæ.

An Act for Providing a Publick Reward for such Perſon or Perſons as ſhall Diſcover the Longitude at Sea.

Whereas it is well known by all that are acquainted with the Art of Navigation, That nothing is ſo much wanted and deſired at Sea, as the Diſcovery of the Longitude, for the Safety and Quickneſs of Voyages, the Preſervation of Ships and the Lives of Men: And whereas in the Judgment of Able Mathematicians and Navigators, ſeveral Methods have already been Diſcovered, true in Theory, though very Difficult in Practice, ſome of which (there is reaſon to expect) may be capable of Improvement, ſome already Diſcovered may be propoſed to the Publick, and others may be Invented hereafter: And whereas ſuch a Diſcovery would be of particular Advantage to the Trade of Great Britain, and very much for the Honour of this Kingdom; But beſides the great Difficulty of the thing it ſelf, partly for the want of ſome Publick Reward to be Settled as an Encouragement for ſo Uſeful and Beneficial a Work, and partly for want of Money for Trials and Experiments neceſſary thereunto, no ſuch Inventions or Propoſals, hitherto made, have been brought to Perfection; Be it therefore Enacted by the Queens moſt Excellent Majeſty, by and with the Advice and Conſent of the Lords Spiritual and Temporal, and Commons in Parliament Aſſembled, and by Authority of the ſame, That the Lord High Admiral of Great Britain, or the Firſt Commiſſioner of the Admiralty, the Speaker of the Honourable Houſe of Commons, the Firſt Commiſſioner of the Navy, the Firſt Commiſſioner of Trade, the Admirals of the Red, White, and Blue Squadrons, the Maſter of the Trinity-Houſe, the Preſident of the

4   Aaaa 2   Royal

PLATE 17   First page of the text of the Act (1714) which offered rewards of up to £20,000 to anyone who could devise a practicable method of calculating the longitude of a ship at sea. John Harrison (1693–1776) competed successfully for this great prize, which at today's values would probably represent £250,000. (No. 669)

684 No. 13, 794, AD 1888 . . . Provisional specification: improvements in escapements for lever watches and other timekeepers. [Patentee: Richard Whittaker, watchmaker.]
8p illus. 28cm
Photocopy of original. See exhibit 501 in Clockmakers' Museum, Guildhall, incorporating Whittaker's resilient lever.

685 Subject list of works on horology . . . in the Library of the Patent Office. London, printed for H.M.S.O. 1912.
56p 17cm

686 William Congreve and his clock; a reprint of the patent granted to Congreve in 1808, with an introductory note . . . [London,] Turner & Devereux, [1972].
21p illus. port. 24cm

*Peabody Museum, Salem, Mass.
687 The Peabody Museum collection of navigating instruments with notes on their makers, by M. V. Brewington. Salem, Peabody Museum, 1963.
154p 25 plates 25cm

Pearce (Arthur)
688 The history of the Butchers' Company . . . London, The Meat Trades Journal Co. Ltd. 1929.
xii 280p frontis. 24cm

Pearson (William), 1767–1847
689 . . . On the transit clock. An illustrated extract from the author's *Introduction to practical astronomy,* vol 2, 1829, pp 304–315.
Photocopy.

Peate (Iorwerth Cyfeiliog)
690 . . . Clock and watch makers in Wales. [2nd edition.] Cardiff, National Museum of Wales, 1960.
vi 107p illus. plates 21cm

Peking. Palace Museum.
691 A catalogue of various clocks, watches, automata . . . of European workmanship dating from the XVIIIth and the early XIXth centuries in the Palace Museum and the Wu Ying Tien, Peiping. By Simon Harcourt Smith. Peiping, Palace Museum, 1933.
32p [41] plates 26cm

Pellaton (James C.)
692 Watch escapements . . . [Translated from the French by S. Paris and edited by Donald de Carle.] 3rd edition. [London, N.A.G. Press, 1949.]
126p illus. 24cm

Penfold (John Blake)
693 Cumberland's first horologist: [horological records from the household books of Lord William Howard]. Reprinted from *Antiquarian Horology*, Vol 2, no. 7, June 1958.
[3]p port. facsims. 25cm

694 The life of William Clement . . . Reprinted from *Antiquarian Horology*, vol 3, no. 12, 1962.
3p illus. 25cm

Peplow (W. H.) & Son, Ltd.
695 A chronicle of time; five generations of a family of jewellers. Stourbridge Mark & Moody, 1962.
26p illus. ports. 24cm
The Peplow centenary in Stourbridge.

Perregaux (Charles) and Perrot (F. Louis)
696 Les Jacquet-Droz et Leschot. Préface de Philippe Godet. Neuchâtel, Attinger Frères, 1916.
x 270p 6 plates (2 col.) 29cm

Perron (Charles-François-Alexandre)
697 Histoire de l'horlogerie en Franche-Comté. Besançon, 1860.
iv 140p 22cm

Philadelphia. Franklin Institute *see* **Franklin Institute.**

Philippe (Adrien)
698 Les montres sans clef ou se montant et se mettant à l'heure sans clef. Origine de ces montres; avantages et inconvénients comparés; descriptions des différents systèmes; principes de construction. Les répétitions; montres à secondes indépendantes . . . A Gènève, De Châteauvieux, Libraire. A Paris, 1863.
308p 3 fold. plates 23cm

Phillips (Philip Alexander Solomon)
699 History & Genealogical chart of the family of Debaufre . . . For the Worshipful Company of Clockmakers from the compiler . . . 1933.
10 l. 32cm
Photostat copy.
One of 3 copies issued.

Philpott (Stuart F.)
700 Modern electric clocks. Principles, construction, installation and maintenance. Second edition. London, Pitman, 1935.
214p 18cm

Phipps (Constantine John), 2nd Baron Mulgrave
701 A voyage towards the North Pole undertaken by His Majesty's command 1773 . . . London, printed by W. Bowyer & J. Nichols, 1774.
viii 253p frontis. 14 fold. plates 27cm
Kendall's K.2 chronometer was tested.

Piaget (H. F.)
702 The watch; its construction, its merits and defects, how to choose it, and how to use it . . . New York, printed by C. Vinten, 1860.
iv 59p illus. 15cm

Picard (Henri) & Frere Ltd.
703 Catalogue of tools and materials for watchmakers, jewellers and the electronics industry. London, Picard, [1973].
[vi] 207p illus. 30cm
Includes price list.

Pipe (Robert William)
704 The automatic watch . . . London, Heywood, 1952.
viii 156p illus. 19cm

Plana (Jean)
705 Mémoire sur le mouvement d'un pendule dans un milieu resistant. Turin, de l'imprimerie royale, 1835.
167p   27cm

Planchon (Mathieu)
706 L'évolution du mécanisme de l'horlogerie depuis son origine. Bourges, Imprimerie Vve. Tardy-Pigelet et Fils, 1918.
46p   23cm

707 L'horloge, son histoire rétrospective, pittoresque et artistique. Cent sept illustrations. Paris, Henri Laurens, [1898].
ii   264p   21cm

Player (Joseph William)
708 Watch repairing. [2nd edition.] London, Crosby Lockwood, [1952].
vi   157p   illus.   plates   18cm

Pleasure (Myrom)
709 . . . Precision pendulum clocks. [Illustrated extracts from *Horological Journal*, vol 113, 1970, August pp 7–11, September pp 12–13, October pp 6–10.]

Poppe (Johann Heinrich Moritz)
710 Ausführliche Geschichte der theoretisch-praktischen Uhrmacherkunst, seit der ältesten Art den Tag einzutheilen, bis an das Ende des achtzehnten Jahrhunderts. Leipzig, bey Koch und Cie, 1801.
x   566p   21cm

711 Versuch einer Geschichte der Entstehung und Fortschritte der theoretisch-praktischen Uhrmacherkunst. Göttingen, Vandenhock und Ruprecht, 1797.
x   90p   18cm

Powell (John)
712 A letter addressed to Edward Ellice Esq. MP on the general influence of large establishments of apprentices, in producing unfair competition . . . London, printed by Richard & Arthur Taylor, 1819.
32p   20cm

713 A letter to Peter Moore Esq. MP Chairman of the Committee appointed to enquire into the state of the watch trade, on the distressed state of those employed in that profession . . . London, printed by Geo. Pigott, 1817.
22p   16cm

Powell (Thomas)
714 Humane industry: or, a history of most manual arts . . . *Anon.* London, printed for Henry Herringman, 1661.
xiv   188p   16cm
pp 1–13: On the invention of dyals, clocks, watches etc.

Preud 'homme (Louis Baptiste)
715 Considérations pratiques sur les engrenages de roues et pignons en horlogerie; accompagnées de la description & des usages d'un compas de proportion de nouvelle invention. Genève, 1780.
95p   fold. plate   table   16cm

Price (Derek J. de Solla)
716 Clockwork before the clock . . . Reprinted from the *Horological Journal*, vol 97, 1955.
9p   illus.   25cm

Priestley (John Boynton)
717 Man and time. London, Aldus Books 1964.
319p   illus.   27cm

Quill (Raymond Humphrey)
718 James Harrison long case clock, Guildhall Museum Exhibit no. 553. [A report. Typewritten. 1954.]
5 l.   illus.   33cm

719 John Harrison: the man who found longitude. London, Baker, [1966].
xiv   255p   plates (inc. port.)   22cm

Raingo
720 Description d'une pendule à sphère mouvante, inventée par M. Raingo . . . (Extrait des *Annales de l'industrie nationale et étrangère*, tome 10, p 152.) Paris, chez l'Auteur, 1823.
24p   fold. plate   20cm

Ramsden (Jesse)
721 Description of an engine for dividing mathematical instruments . . . Published by order of the Commissioners of Longitude. London, printed by William Richardson, 1777.
ii   14p   4 fold. plates   26cm

Rawlings (A. L.)
722 The science of clocks and watches . . . Second edition. London, Pitman, 1948.
xi   303p   23cm

Rees (Abraham)
723 Rees's clocks, watches and chronometers (1819–20): a selection from *The cyclopaedia; or, universal dictionary of arts, sciences and literature.* [Newton Abbot, David & Charles, 1970.]
viii   295p   illus.   28cm
A facsimile reprint of selected articles from the 1819–20 edition of Rees's *Cyclopaedia*.

Reid (C. Leo)
724 North Country clockmakers of the 17th, 18th, and 19th centuries . . . Reprinted from *Archaeologia Aeliana*. Newcastle-upon-Tyne, Andrew Reid & Co. Ltd., 1925.
140p   6 plates   22cm

Reid (Thomas)
725 Horology. [The article contributed to Brewster's *Edinburgh Cyclopaedia*, with plates 300–8, interleaved and with MS notes by the Author. Edinburgh, 1819.]
pp 114–176   27cm
The cover is inscribed: To the Worshipful Company of Clockmakers . . . with the greatest respect . . . Thomas Reid, 1819.

726 Treatise on clock and watch making, theoretical and practical. Edinburgh, printed for John Fairburn, etc. 1826.
xii   476p   20 fold. plates   23cm
See also 992 post.

727 The same. Another copy.

Rhodes (Charles Elmes Parker-)
728 Universal reading of time, Os., midnight to 24 hours, midnight . . . London, [Free International Institute for Commerce, 1885].
15p 18cm

Rigg (Edward)
729 On the compensation of clocks, watches, and chronometers, a paper read before the Society of Arts, March, 1879.
59p 25cm

730 Society for the encouragement of arts, manufactures and commerce. Cantor lectures. Watchmaking . . . Delivered before the Society of Arts, February 1881. London, printed by William Trounce, 1881.
39p 25cm

Rivaz (Pierre Joseph de)
731 Mémoire pour Pierre de Rivaz, demandeur aux fins de l'enregistrement des lettres-patentes à lui accordées par le Roi . . . pour les horloges de son invention. Contre la Communauté des Maîtres Horlogers de la Ville & Faubourgs de Paris, opposans à l'enregistrement . . . De l'Imprimerie de J. Chardon, [1750?]
45p 22cm

732 Réponse du Sieur de Rivaz, à un mémoire publié contre ses découvertes en horlogerie. Paris, chez J. Ch Chardon Fils, 1751.
ii 96p 22cm
See also 534 ante.

Robert (Henri)
733 Considérations pratiques sur l'huile employée en horlogerie. Fragment d'un ouvrage intitulé Etudes sur diverses questions d'horlogerie. Paris, chez l'Auteur, 1851.
80p 21cm

734 Etudes sur diverses questions d'horlogerie. Paris, [Imprimerie de Pillet fils aîné,] 1852.
viii 5–276p 4 plates 23cm

Roberts (Kenneth D.)
735 The contributions of Joseph Ives to Connecticut clock technology, 1810–62. Bristol, Conn., American Clock and Watch Museum, 1970.
xiv 338p illus. ports. facsims. 28cm

Robertson (John Drummond)
736 The evolution of clockwork, with a special section on the clocks of Japan . . . together with a comprehensive bibliography of horology . . . London, Cassell, [1931].
xvi 358p illus. 22cm

Robertson (William Bell) and Walker (Frederick)
737 The royal clocks in Windsor Castle, Buckingham Palace, St James's Palace, and Hampton Court . . . London, Walker, [1904].
x 42p illus. 24cm

*Robinson (Frank)
738 Dickens, the schoolmaster and the clock. [Washington, Co. Durham, Northern Notes, 1971.]
12p 21cm
Thomas Humphreys, clockmaker of Barnard Castle, the inspiration of *Master Humphrey's clock.*

Robinson (T. R.)
739 Modern clocks. Their repair and maintenance. London, N.A.G. Press, 1934.
xiv 110p 4 plates 21cm

Robison (John)
740 A system of mechanical philosophy . . . With notes by David Brewster . . . In four volumes and a volume of plates. Vol 4. Edinburgh, printed for John Murray, 1822.
684p 10 fold. plates 22cm
Watchwork is on pp 538–609, plates 8 and 9.

Roche (J. C.)
741 The history, development and organization of the Birmingham Jewellery and allied trades . . . Birmingham, published by Dennison Watch Case Company, [1927].
116p 22cm

Rodanet (Auguste Horaire)
742 1886–87. L'horlogerie astronomique et civile; ses usages, ses progrès, son enseignement à Paris . . . Paris, Vve Ch. Dunod, éditeur, [1887].
xi 208p illus. port. 24cm

Rogers (Inkerman)
743 The progress of horology. [With a list of Devon clockmakers, with notes on ancient clocks at Barnstaple. A lecture delivered before the British Watch and Clock Makers Guild, 13 October, 1921.]
24p illus. 19cm

744 Some ancient clocks in North Devon . . . Reprint from Devon & Cornwall Notes & Queries. Exeter, James G. Commin, 1923.
8p 3 plates 21cm

Rohde (R. T.)
745 A practicable decimal system for Great Britain and her Colonies . . . London, printed by William Brown & Co., [1884 or 1885].
17p 21cm

Rolex Watch Company
746 The Rolex Story. [London? The company, 1973.]
11p illus. port. 20cm

Rosedale (Honyel Gough)
747 A short history of the Worshipful Company of Horners . . . London, Blades, East & Blades, 1912.
46p 2 plates 22cm

Rosenberg (Charles)
748 American pocket watches . . . Traders Publishing Co., [1965?].
[58]p illus. 21cm

Ross (Sir John)
749 Observations on chronometers from the appendix to Capt. Sir John Ross's narrative of his second expedition to the Arctic Regions, from 1829 to 1833. [London, C. Whiting, 1834.]
8p 27cm

Royal Observatory
750 [An account of the rate of chronometers on trial, February 1822 to October 1832.] [London, 1822–32.]
[407]p 26cm
Monthly returns, with a MS list of latitude and longitude of many places in London.

Royer-Collard (F. Bernard) *see* **Collard (F. Bernard Royer-)**

Sabine (Sir Edward)
751 An account of experiments to determine the figure of the earth, by means of the pendulum vibrating seconds in different latitudes . . . London, John Murray, 1825.
xv 509p 3 maps 27cm

Salomons (Sir David Lionel Goldsmid-Stern-)
752 Breguet (1747–1823). Illustrated with over 150 photographic reproductions and other plates. London, printed for the Author, 1921.
233p inc. 118 paged plates, frontis. (port.) 23cm

753 Supplement. Breguet (1747–1823). Illustrated with over 40 photographic reproductions. London, printed for the Author, 1921.
35p inc. 20 paged plates, frontis. (port.) 23cm

754 Breguet (1747–1823) . . . Edition revue, corrigée et augmentée . . . Traduit de l'anglais par Louis Desoutter. Londres, imprimé pour l'Auteur, 1923.
330p inc. 170 paged plates 3 frontis. plates 24cm

Saunders (Harold Nicholas)
755 The astrolabe; a brief account of its history and construction . . . Bude, The author [1971].
35p illus. 18cm

Saunier (Claudius)
756 Guide-Manuel de l'horloger, traitant des notions de calcul et de dessin . . . de la main-d'oeuvre . . . de l'outillage . . . très nombreux procédés et indications pratiques utiles à l'artiste et à l'ouvrier . . . 2e. édition. Paris, Bureau de la Revue Chronométrique, 1873.
vi 262p 8 fold. plates 18cm

757 Recueil des procédés pratiques usités en horlogerie, formant la deuxième partie du Guide-Manuel de l'horloger . . . Paris, Bureau de la Revue Chronométrique, 1874.
pp 267–514 fold. plates 9–14 18cm

758 Traité des échappements et des engrenages . . . Paris, Dufour, Mulet et Boulanger, 1855.
400p 10 fold. plates 23cm

759 Traité d'horlogerie moderne, théorique et pratique . . . Deuxième édition . . . Paris, Bureau de la Revue chronométrique, 1875.
viii 832p 21 col. plates 26cm

760 Treatise on modern horology in theory and practice. Translated from the French of Claudius Saunier . . . by Julien Tripplin . . . and Edward Rigg . . . London, published by J. Tripplin and at New York, [1881].
xvi 844p 21 plates in oblong folio 25cm

761 The watchmakers' handbook . . . Intended as a workshop companion for those who are engaged in watchmaking and the allied mechanical arts. English edition, translated, revised and considerably augmented by Julien Tripplin . . . and Edward Rigg . . . London, published by J. Tripplin and at New York, 1881.
xiv 482p 14 double plates 18cm

762 The same. An edition dated 1882, without change.

*Savory (Thomas Cox)
763 Thomas Cox Savory . . . maker of superior watches . . . [London, printed by Clowes, 183–?]
24p illus. 20cm
A priced catalogue.

Savoye (Ch.)
764 Exposition collective du Doubs 1878. 1793–1878. Notice sur l'origine de la fabrique d'horlogerie de Besançon, son état present, chiffres officiels à l'appui. [Paris, Imp. Paul Dupont, 1878.]
20p 23cm

765 [English translation of 764 *ante*, same imprint.]
20p 23cm

Schadaeus (Oseas)
766 Summum Argentoratensium templum: das ist, ausführliche und eigentliche Beschreibung dess viel künstlichen, sehr kostbaren und in aller Welt berühmten Münsters zu Strassburg . . . Strassburg, in Verlegung Lazari Zetzners Seligen Erben, 1617.
x 112 ivp 6 fold.plates 18cm
Plate 4 is of the clock.

Schmidt (Julius)
767 Zur Errinnerung von Heinrich Otte . . . Zur Glockenkunde. Herausgegeben von der Historischen Kommission der Provinz Sachsen . . . Halle a.d.S.Otto Hendel, 1891.
50p 25cm

Schott (Gaspar)
768 P. Gasparis Schotti Regiocuriani e Societate Jesu . . . Technica curiosa, sive mirabilia artis, libris XII, comprehensa; quibus varia experimenta, varique technasmata, pneumatica, hydraulica hydrotechnica . . . chronometrica . . . proponunter . . . Sumptibus Wolfgangi Mauritii Endteri. Excudebat Jobus Hertz Typographus Herbipol., 1687.
xxxvi 1044 xiip frontis. (port.) 19 fold. plates 20cm
Preceded by engraved title-page.
2nd edition.
See plate 18.

Schwenningen. Hellmut-Kienzle-Uhrenmuseum *see* **Hellmut-Kienzle-Uhrenmuseum.**

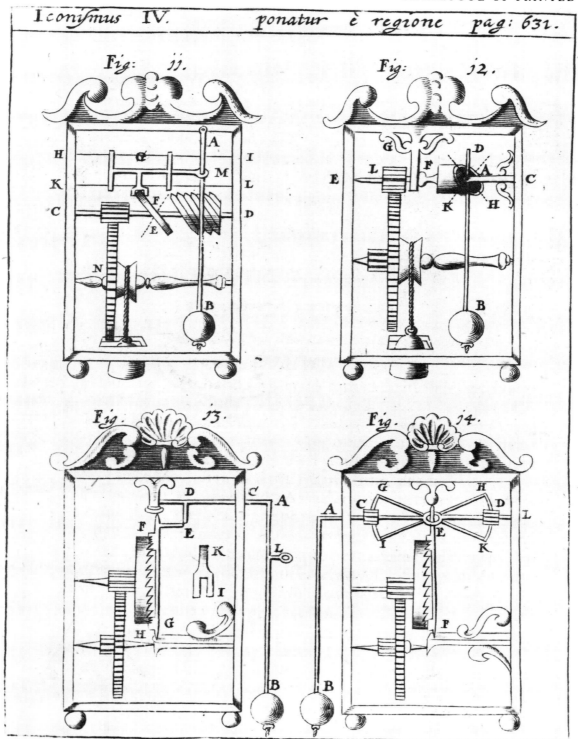

PLATE 18 Illustrations from *Technica curiosa*, by Gaspar Schott, 1687. The second edition of an early book on a wide range of technical curiosities, including clock escapements, by Gaspar Schott (1606–1666), a professor of mathematics at Wurzburg. The two upper illustrations show clocks with swash-plate or wobbling escapements. Figs 13 and 14 (below) are two forms of verge escapement, one employing a forked crank and the other dual racks. Clear explanations of these curiosities are given by P. Chamberlain in his *It's About Time* (No. 143) and by G. H. Baillie in his *Clocks and Watches, An Historical Bibliography* (No. 33). (No. 768)

Science Museum. South Kensington.
769 . . . Clocks and watches . . . by F. A. B. Ward . . . London, H.M.S.O. 1972–.
Pt 1   illus.   5cm   (Science Museum illustrated booklets)

*770 Descriptive catalogue of the collection illustrating time measurement. By F. A. B. Ward . . . London, H.M.S.O. 1966.
vii   150p   plates   22cm

771 Tercentenary of Christiaan Huygens' pendulum clock, December 1656– December 1956: exhibition arranged by the Science Museum and the Antiquarian Horological Society . . . [London, 1956.]
28p   illus.   25cm

772 Timekeepers. London, H.M.S.O. 1963.
48p   illus.   15cm   (Science Museum illustrated booklets)

773 Der **Selbstlehrende** Uhrmacher oder genugthuende Anweisung alle Geh-, Schlag-, und Repetiruhren und Sonnenuhren richtig zu berechnen . . . Von einem Freund der Künsten . . . Frankfurt am Mayn, in der Kesslerischen Buchhandlung, 1786.
xvi   208p   10 fold. plates   14cm

Sellink (J.L.)
774 Dutch antique domestic clocks c 1670–1870. Leiden, Stenfert Kroese, 1973.
vii   367p   illus.   26cm

Shadwell (Charles F. A.)
775 Notes on the management of chronometers and the measurement of meridian distances . . . London, J. D. Potter, 1855.
xii   158p   23cm

Sharp (Isaac)
776 Daniel Quare [Extract from the *Friends Quarterly Examiner*, no. 133, January 1900, pp 31–45].
15p   20cm
With MS notes and printed items inserted to illustrate Quare clocks and barometers formerly owned by C. F. Bell.

Shears (Philip James)
777 Huguenot connections with the clockmaking trade in England. Presidential address delivered at the annual meeting of the Huguenot Society of London, 11 May 1960. Reprinted from the Proceedings, vol XX, [1965].
21p   22cm

Sherwell (John W.)
778 A descriptive and historical account of the Guild of Saddlers of the City of London . . . For private circulation, 1889.
xxiv   240p   5 fold. plates   4 double plates   6 plates   21cm

779 The same. Another edition. [London, 1937.]

780 A **Short** Chat on the long-case clock. From the Architect & Contract Reporter, 18 October, 1918.
pp 215–216   2 plates and illus.   32cm
Illustrated from clocks in the collection of D. A. F. Wetherfield.
Signed H. C.

Shpolyansky (V. A.) and Chernyagin (B. M.)
781 Fedchenko's electronic-mechanical pendulum astronomical clock. [Photocopied from the authors' *Elektricheskie pribory vremeni*, Moscow, 1964.]
[3] l.   illus.   27cm

*Smethurst (W.)
782 The old clock makers of Ashbourne. [Ashbourne, printed by Henstock, 1940?]
15p   18cm
Reprinted from the *Ashbourne Telegraph*, January 1940.

Smith (Alan)
783 The Exeter Lovelace clock. An illustrated extract from *Liverpool Bulletin*, Museums number, vol 12, 1963–64, pp 4–12.

784 . . . Clocks and watches . . . London, Connoisseur, [1975].
222p   illus.   plates   21cm   (Connoisseur illustrated guides)

Smith (Mrs B. N. D.)
785 Watches, clocks and their parts. [A guide to sources of information on manufacturers for the Birmingham area 1860–1914. Birmingham, Typewritten, 1965.]
8 l.   33cm

Smith (Eric P.)
786 Repairing antique clocks; a guide for amateurs. Newton Abbot, David & Charles, 1973.
231p   illus.   21cm

Smith (Mrs Grace Howard) and Smith (Eugene Randolph)
787 Watch keys as jewelry: collecting experiences of a husband and wife. Syracuse, N.Y., University Press, [1967].
135p   illus.   24cm
Mainly illustrations. The text is a sentimental journey in quest of watch keys.

Smith (John), c 1650– c 1725
788 Horological dialogues. In three parts shewing the nature, use, and right managing of clocks and watches: with an appendix containing Mr Oughtred's method for calculating of numbers . . . By J. S., Clockmaker. London, printed for Jonathan Edwin, 1675.
xii   120p   15cm
See plate 19.

789 The same. Another copy.

790 The same. Another copy.

791 Horological disquisitions concerning the nature of time, and the reasons why all days, from noon to noon, are not alike 24 hours long. In which appears the impossibility of a clock's being always kept exactly true to the sun. With tables of equation . . . London, printed for Richard Cumberland, 1694.
ii   92p   fold. table   17cm

792 Another copy, bound with a MS of 11 pages: An explanation of what is meant by a 24 hour day . . . and of the difference from a civill day . . . and a further MS

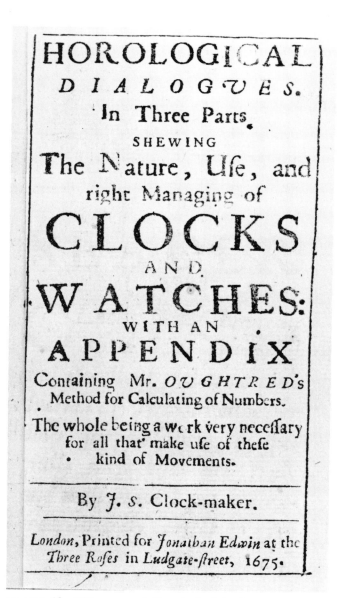

PLATE 19 Title-page of *Horological Dialogues*, by 'J. S. Clock-maker' (John Smith), 1675. The earliest book dealing with clocks and watches to be published in England. (No. 788)

entitled 'Some account of John Smith, clockmaker' taken from Robert Wallace's *Antitrinitarian biography*, London, 1850.
See plate 20.

Smith (John), messenger, Royal Bank of Scotland
793 A handbook and directory of old Scottish clockmakers from 1540 to 1850 AD. Edinburgh, published by William J. Hay, [1903].
xiv 97p printed on recto only frontis. 11 plates 18cm

794 Old Scottish clockmakers. From 1453 to 1850. Compiled from original sources with notes . . . Second edition, revised and enlarged . . . London, Edinburgh, Oliver & Boyd, 1921.
xv 436p frontis. 24 plates 23cm

Smith (Simon Harcourt) *see* **Peking Palace Museum**

Smith (S.) and Son Ltd.
795 Guide to the purchase of a watch . . . [London, *c* 1900.]
56p illus. 28cm
The firm is now known as Smith's Industries. *See* plate 21.

796 The same. Photocopy of edition *c* 1928.

Smyth (William Henry)
797 Description of an astrological clock belonging to the Society of Antiquaries communicated to the Society . . . London, printed by J. B. Nichols & Son, 1848.
30p frontis. 27cm
On the facing page: From *Archaeologia*, vol 33, pp 8–35. Earliest clock with a fusee.

Snell (Willebrord)
798 De re nummaria liber singularis. Amsterdam, Apud Henricum Laurentii, 1635.
[vi] 72p 18cm

Snoxell (William)
799 Catalogue of the . . . collections of the late William Snoxell . . . comprising his wonderful collection of mechanical automata . . . sold by auction . . . June 9 [1879]. London, Puttick & Simpson, [1879].
4 pts in 1 vol 24cm

Société Jersiaise
800 Jersey names on grandfather clocks. [St Helier, The Society, 1965?]
[4]p 22cm

801 Some **Particulars** Relative to the Discovery of the Longitude; mentioning several foreign premiums, and exactly narrating the particulars of the British Acts of Parliament, respecting that affair. With a list of the present Commissioners, etc. *Anon*. London, printed for George Burnett, 1765.
39p 21cm

Spencer-Jones (Sir Harold) *see* **Jones (Sir Harold Spencer-)**

Statter (Dover)
802 The decimal system, as a whole, in its relation to time, weight, capacity, and money, in unison with each other . . . London, Groombridge & Sons, Liverpool, 1856.
38p 22cm
There is a decimal watch by the Author in the Clockmakers Museum (item no. 493).

Statutes *see* **Parliament**

Stirrup (Thomas)
803 Horometria, or the compleat diallist . . . Whereunto is added an appendix shewing how the parallels of declination; the Jewish, Babylonish and Italian houres; the azimuths, almicanters etc. may be easily inscribed on any dial . . . by W. L. [*i.e.* William Leybourn.] London, printed by R. & W. Leybourn, 1652.
viii 203p illus. 17cm

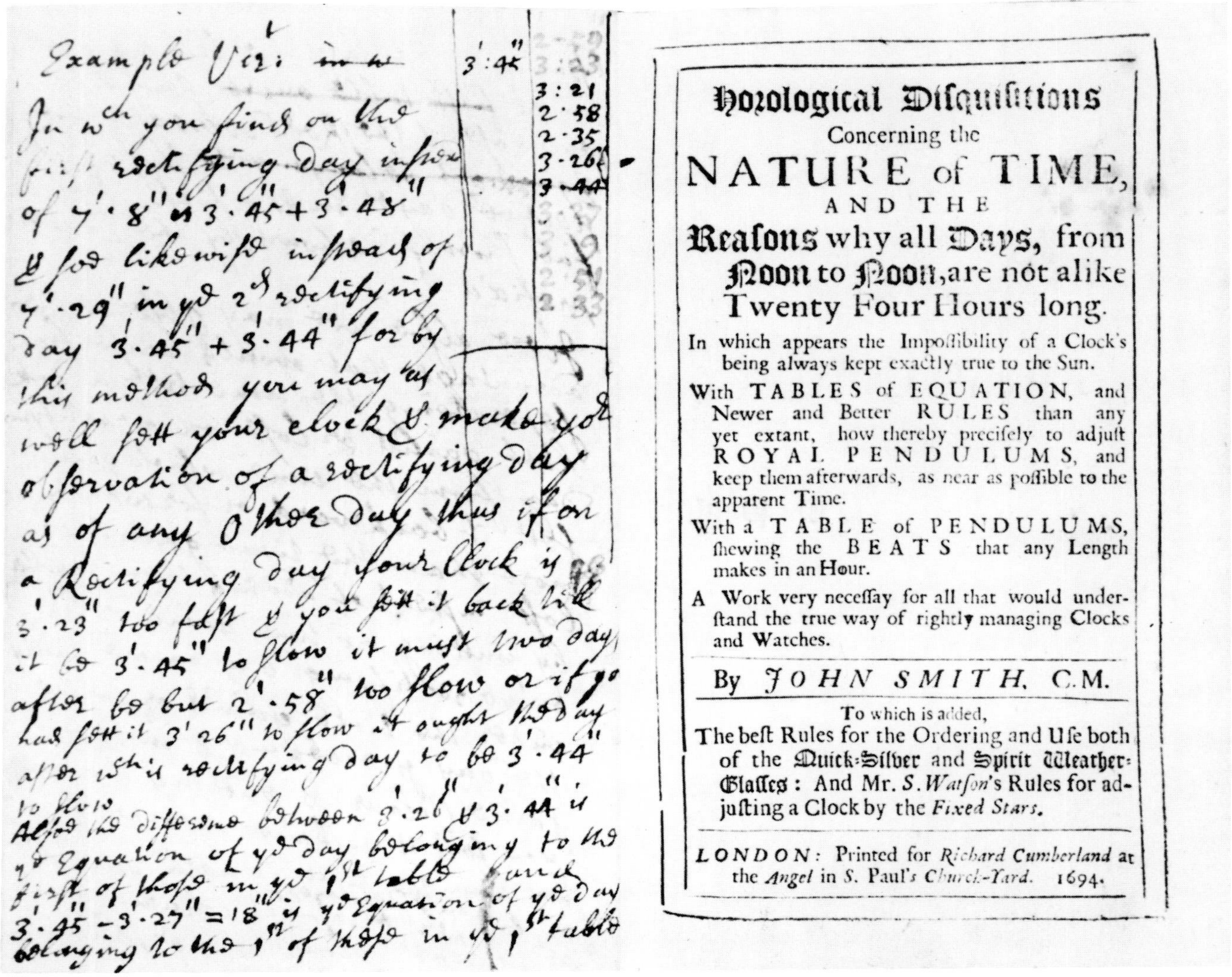

PLATE 20 Title-page of *Horological Disquisitions*, by John Smith, 1694, with a page of manuscript notes. The first edition of Smith's second work on clocks and watches. The eleven pages of manuscript notes are in an unknown hand. (No. 792)

Stone (Arthur Carlyon Stanley-)
804 The Worshipful Company of Turners of London . . . London, Lindley-Jones, 1925.
  vii 337p plates 22cm

*Stone (John)
805 [Collection of trade cards and watch papers to serve as an engraver's pattern book. *c* 1770.]

Streeter (Edwin William), late Hancock
806 Catalogue with designs and prices of diamond ornaments and machine-made jewellery . . . also of English machine-made watches and clocks . . . 13th edition. London, [The author, *c* 1873.]
  84p illus. plates 19cm

*Strode (Thomas)
807 A new and easie method to the art of dyalling . . . London, J. Taylor, 1688.
  66p illus. 19cm

Stuckey (Norman)
808 The watch and clock collection of the Worshipful Company of Clockmakers at Guildhall, London. Illustrated extract from the *Horological Journal*, vol 109, September 1966, pp 12–17.

809 A Succinct Account of the proceedings relative to the discovery of the longitude at sea, by means of artificial timekeepers particularly Mr Harrison's . . . In the *Annual Register* for the year 1765, pp 113–133.
  22cm
Another copy in MS 3973/16 (no. 976 *post*).

S. SMITH & SON, 9 STRAND, LONDON.

The Finest Specimen of Horological Work that can Possibly be Made.

ENGLISH SPLIT-SECONDS MINUTE REPEATER.
No. 148.

Minute Repeater, Perpetual Calendar, Minute and Seconds Chronograph, Split-Seconds and Phases of the Moon, with Class "A" Certificate from Kew.

This Watch was **Five** Years in course of construction. When it is considered that for Each Distinct Action Separate Mechanism has to be Constructed and so Fitted In as not to Increase the Size, it must be apparent that a Vast Amount of Time and Skill is required. Each Complication performs its work without interfering with the operations of the others; nothing is sacrificed in order to preserve the Size.

The first of the Five Combinations is the **Perpetual Calendar**: this shows the Year, the Month, Day of the Month, Day of the Week, and Phases of the Moon, and the Hour, Minute and Seconds of the Day. From its name, Perpetual Calendar, it is quite Automatic, requiring no setting whether the Month has 31, 30, or 28 days, as in Leap Year, the changes are always correct.

The Second Combination is the **Minute Repeater**, made upon the Slide System. By pushing a Slide in the Band of the Case the Watch will repeat Hours, Quarters and Minutes on Pure-toned Gongs.

The Third Combination is the **Minute and Seconds Chronograph**. In this Watch the Most Perfect Adjustment has been used; the Jewellings are of the Finest Description, all Pivots of the Most Carefully Tempered Steel.

The Fourth Combination is the **Split-Seconds**. This is described fully on page 72; and upon this action, the Best Workmanship and the Experience of Many Years has been bestowed, and produced that which only Money can obtain, viz., Perfection.

The Fifth Combination is the **Phases of the Moon**. This is as Unfailing in its Accuracy as the others; from Month to Month and Year after Year the Moon waxes and wanes; and beyond this the Watch gained **First Honors at Kew Observatory for Accurate Timekeeping**. Case about 5 ozs.

£375 0 0

N.B.—The Only One Manufactured.

"HECLA WORKS,
SHEFFIELD,
Messrs. S. SMITH & SON,   1st Dec., 1896.
9 Strand,
London, W.C.

DEAR SIRS,
I have much pleasure in stating that the Gold Perpetual Calendar Minute Repeater Watch that you supplied me with some time ago has given entire satisfaction. As the Watch is often subject to large variations in temperature, I think its excellent performance under these conditions should be specially satisfactory to you. As proving the excellence of the calendar portion of the Watch, I may say that during leap year the perpetual calendar acted quite correctly, and I think such correctness is a remarkable example of the perfection to which you have carried the construction of your Watches.

Yours truly,
R. A. HADFIELD."

Second Quality of above, £185 0 0.
This Watch All English, £450. The Most Expensive Watch Made.

CLOCK WATCH.
No. 149.

Perpetual Calendar, Repeater, Minute and Seconds Chronograph and Split-Seconds and Phases of the Moon. Part Swiss Made, but **Finished** and **Adjusted** by **English** Workmen in **London**.

This Remarkable Watch is the **Rarest of all Combinations**. In addition to the Complications detailed in the description of No. 148, it is a Clock Watch; that is, a Watch which strikes on Gongs the Hours and Quarters as they pass, exactly as a Striking Clock does. To combine this with the other actions within the compass of a Watch requires the Best Mechanical Skill.

Two Main Springs are required to give the necessary Motive Power; they are, however, both wound at the same time, and by the same action; there are also provided Two Small Levers that can be moved by a Slight Pressure of the finger: one causes the Clockwork to become Silent, the other to put it on Half Strike, viz., Quarters only; Every Part is Jewelled in the Most Complete Manner; Cased in Heavy 18-Ct. Gold Full-Hunting Cases. Case about 4 ozs.

£250 0 0

With Class "A" Kew Observatory Certificate, £275.

Clock Watch Only, Without Chronograph, Calendar or Changes of the Moon, £75.

Arms, Crest, Monogram and Inscription Emblazoned on these Watches, Engraved and Enamelled Free of Charge.

74

PLATE 21   *Guide to the Purchase of a Watch.* Page from a catalogue issued *c* 1900 by S. Smith and Son, 9 The Strand, London, describing their wide range of watches, chronometers and kindred articles. This firm is now named Smiths Industries Ltd. (No. 795)

810 A **Succinct** Account of the proceedings relative to the discovery of the longitude from the year 1714 to the present time.
In the *Monthly Review*, July 1765, pp 63–73.   32cm
Other copies in MS 3973 (976/19, 19A, 20D *post*).

811 La **Suisse** Horlogère. International edition in English . . . April 1955 to date. La Chaux-de-Fonds, [Société du Journal 'La Suisse horlogère,' 1955–].
In progress.
Published quarterly.

Sully (Henry)
812 Description abrégée d'une horloge d'une nouvelle invention, pour la juste mesure du temps sur mer. Avec le Jugement de l'Académie Royale des Sciences sur cette invention. Et une dissertation sur la nature des tentatives pour la découverte des longitudes dans la navigation, & sur l'usage des horloges, pour la mesure du temps en mer. A Paris, chez Briasson, 1726.
Suite de la description abrégée d'une horloge . . . A Bordeaux, chez Raymond la Bottière . . . A Paris . . . A Amsterdam, 1726.
  The first part has vi 48p 2 fold. plates
  The second part, with title-page and preface, continues the page numbering from 49 to 290.
  Each part, 26cm
The clock described is in the Clockmakers Museum (item no. 597). *See also* no. 990/13 *post*.
See plate 22.

813 Règle artificielle du temps. Traité de la division naturelle et artificielle du temps des horloges et des montres de différentes constructions . . . Nouvelle édition corrigée et augmentée de quelques mémoires sur l'horlogerie par M Julien Le Roy . . . Paris, Gregoire Dupuis, 1737.
  [xxii] 433p 5 fold. plates 17cm

Sussex, Duke of *see* **Augustus Frederick, Duke of Sussex**

Sutermeister (Moriz)
814 Die Glocken von Zürich. Die Glockengiesser, Glocken und Giess-statten im alten und neuen Zürich. Zürich, Verlag von M. Sutermeister, 1898.
  71p 21cm

Swinburne (Sir James)
815 The mechanism of the watch . . . London, N.A.G. Press, 1950.
  88p illus. 21cm

Symonds (Robert Wemyss)
816 A book of English clocks. [2nd edition.] London, Penguin Books, [1950].
  79p 64 plates 18cm (King Penguin Books, 28)

817 Furniture making in seventeenth- and eighteenth-century England . . . London, Connoisseur, 1955.
  xiv 238p illus. plates 35cm
With a chapter on the restoration of clock movements and cases.

*818 Masterpieces of English furniture and clocks . . . of the 17th and 18th centuries. London, Batsford, [1940].
  xii 172p illus. 33cm

819 Thomas Tompion, his life and work . . . London, Batsford, [1951].
  xvi 320p illus. plates (inc. facsims.) 29cm

Tait (Hugh) *see* **British Museum**

Tardy, publisher
820 Bibliographie générale de la mesure du temps . . . Paris, Tardy, [1947].
  352p 23cm

821 Dictionnaire des horlogers français. Paris, Tardy, [1972].
  2 vols illus. ports. 24cm

822 La pendule française . . . Paris, [1950].
  5 vols in 1 illus. 32cm
The parts are entitled:
(1) Gothique, Renaissance, Louis XIII, Louis XIV. 42p
(2) Régence, Louis XV. 34p
(3) Louis XVI, Directoire. 42p
(4) De l'Empire à nos jours. 56p
(5) Art régional, styles étrangers. 54p

823 La pendule française des origines à nos jours; [new edition.] Paris, Tardy, [1969–74].
  3 vols illus. 31cm

*Taylor (Edward Wilfrid) and others**
824 At the sign of the orrery: the origins of Cooke, Troughton & Simms, Ltd. . . . [York? Cooke, Troughton & Simms, 1967?]
  7p illus. ports. map 23cm

Tennant (Winifred Coombe)
825 The clock in the Curfew Tower.
In *Report of the Society of the Friends of St George's . . .* to 31st December 1945, pp 15–18.
  plate 21cm

Thiout (Antoine)
826 Traité de l'horlogerie, méchanique et pratique . . . A Paris, chez Charles Moette, etc., 1741.
  2 vols in 1 41 fold. plates 25cm
Plates bound separately.

Thompson (Edward John)
827 A description of some of the watches, movements, etc., belonging to the Museum of the Company of Clockmakers preserved in the Guildhall Library and Museum. [London, Napier, printer.]
  14 and 28p 16cm
Two parts, each preceded by a letter addressed to the members of the Court of the Clockmakers' Company, dated 1889 and 1890.

828 The same. Another copy.

Thomson (Adam)
829 Time and timekeepers . . . London, T. & W. Boone, 1842.
  xii 195p illus. 17cm

Thomson (Richard)
830 Antique American clocks and watches. Line drawings by Gordon Converse jnr. Princeton, Van Nostrand, [1968],
  192p illus. plates 23cm

DESCRIPTION ABREGÉE
D'UNE
HORLOGE
D'UNE NOUVELLE INVENTION.

Pour la juste mesure du Temps sur Mer.

AVEC

Le Jugement de l'Academie Royale des Sciences
sur cette Invention.

ET

UNE DISSERTATION
SUR LA NATURE DES TENTATIVES

pour la Découverte des Longitudes dans la Navigation, &
sur l'usage des Horloges, pour la mesure du Tems en Mer.

Par HENRY SULLY, *Horloger de* S. A. S.
Monseigneur LE DUC D'ORLEANS.

A PARIS,

Chez BRIASSON, ruë Saint Jacques, à la Science.

M. DCCXXVI.

Avec Approbation & Privilège du Roy.

PLATE 22 Title-page of *Description abrégée d'une horloge*, by Henry Sully, 1726. One of the earliest books on a longitude timekeeper. Henry Sully (1680–1728) was an Englishman who worked in France where, *c* 1724, he constructed a marine timekeeper which is now in the Clockmakers Museum (exhibit no. 597). This timekeeper is described and illustrated in Sully's book. (No. 812)

Thwaites & Reed Ltd.
831   The Congreve clock. [London, Thwaites & Reed, 1971.]
[7]p illus.   27cm
Catalogue and cuttings about new copies of the clock made by Thwaites & Reed; a prospectus for purchasers.

832   The Dwerrihouse clock. [London, Thwaites & Reed, 1972.]
8p illus. facsims.   27cm
Prospectus inviting subscriptions for reproductions of the clock.

833   The 18th-century rack clock. [London, Thwaites & Reed,] 1973.
Prospectus inviting subscriptions for reproductions of the clock.

Tobler (A.)
834   L'horlogerie électrique . . . Edition française revue et augmentée par L. de Belfort de la Roque . . . Avec 65 figures dans le texte. Paris, Bernard Tignol, [1891].
152p   18cm

Townsend (George E.)
835   Almost everything you want to know about American watches . . . [Vienna, Virginia, the Author, 1971.]
v 87p illus.   24cm

Tripplin (Julien)
836   Rapport sur l'état de l'horlogerie Anglaise en 1900 fait á la requête de la Commission Royale Anglaise pour le Gouvernement Française. London, printed by Wyman & Sons Ltd. 1900.
7p   21cm

837   Royal Commission, Paris Exhibition 1900. Report on the exhibits in class 96: clocks, watches and timepieces . . . Reprinted from the general Report of the Royal Commission. London, printed by William Clowes and Sons Ltd., 1901.
6p   21cm

838   Watch and clock making in 1889; being an account and comparison of the exhibits in the Horological Section of the French International Exhibition . . . London, Crosby Lockwood and Son, 1890.
viii 142p frontis.   21cm

Troughton (Edward)
839   Graduation. [1830?]
Illustrated excerpt from Edinburgh Encyclopedia, vol 10, pp 348–84.

Turner (G. L'E.)
840   The auction sale of Larcum Kendall's workshop, 1790.
(In Antiquarian Horology, vol 5, September 1967, pp 269–75.)

Tyler (Eric John)
841   The craft of the clockmaker. London, Ward Lock, [1973].
96p illus.   25cm

842   The clock of St George's church, Esher. [Reprinted from Antiquarian Horology, vol 5, no. 5, December 1966.]
[10]p illus.   24cm

843   Clocks and watches. London, Sampson Low, 1975.
80p illus. facsims.   29cm (Sampson Low Collectors' Library)

844   European clocks. London, Ward Lock, [1968].
258p illus. plates   19cm

845   The same. Another copy.

846   The evolution of the pendulum.
An illustrated extract from Discovering Antiques, no. 18, 1971, pp 423–27.

847   Die **Uhrteile** in fremder Sprache. [Deutsch, Englisch, Französisch.] Ulm, Neue Uhrmacher-Zeitung, [1957].
52p illus.   21cm

Ullyett (Kenneth)
848   British clocks and clockmakers . . . With 8 plates in colour and 24 illustrations in black and white. London, Collins, 1947.
48p 8 col. plates   22cm

849   . . . Clocks and watches . . . London, Hamlyn, [1971].
159p illus. facsims.   18cm

850   In quest of clocks. London, Rockliff, [1950].
xv 264p illus. 45 plates (inc. ports.)   22cm

Ungerer (Alfred)
851   Les horloges astronomiques et monumentales les plus remarquables de l'antiquité jusqu'à nos jours par Alfred Ungerer . . . En appendice: Table chronologique, table onomastique, table bibliographique. Strasbourg, chez l'Auteur, 1931.
514p frontis.   27cm

852   Les horloges d'édifice. Leur construction, leur montage, leur entretien. Guide pratique à l'usage des personnes qui s'interessent aux horloges monumentales, suivi d'une nomenclature des horloges monumentales les plus remarquables . . . Paris, Gauthier-Villars & Cie., [1926].
xi 334p illus.   25cm

United Kingdom Electric Telegraph Company
853   Proceedings of the banquet and testimonial to the Chairman Mr A. Angus Croll . . . at Willis's rooms on Wednesday, March 22nd 1871.
31p plates   22cm

Usher Art Gallery, Lincoln
854   Watches in the Usher collection. [Lincoln, The gallery, 1972?]
12p illus.   8cm

Usher & Cole Ltd.
855   A watchmaking centenary . . . 1861–1961. [London, The Company, 1961.]
[20]p illus.   25cm

Van Etten (Henry) *see* **Leurechon (Jean)**

Victoria and Albert Museum
856 English watches, by J. F. Hayward. [2nd edition.] London, H.M.S.O. 1969.
14p 59 plates 21cm

Vienna. Österreichisches Museum für angewandte Kunst.
857 Theatrum orbis terrarum: die Erfassung des Weltbildes zur Zeit der Renaissance und des Barocks; herausgegeben von Gerhart Egger. Wien, Das Museum, 1970.
104p 72 plates 24cm
Catalogue of an exhibition of items relating to cartography, horology and the sciences commemorating the 400th anniversary of the publication of Ortelius's *Theatrum Orbis*.

Vigniaux (P.)
858 Horlogerie pratique, à l'usage des apprentis et des amateurs. A Toulouse, chez l'Auteur, 1788.
viii 342p 12 fold. plates 20cm
See plate 23.

Vulliamy (Benjamin Lewis)
859 On the construction and theory of the dead escapement for clocks . . . London, John Olliver, 1846.
36p 5 fold. plates 22cm

860 Some considerations on the subject of public clocks, particularly church clocks; with hints for their improvement . . . London, printed by B. McMillan, 1828. For private circulation only.
15p 25cm

861 A supplement to the paper entitled 'Some considerations on the subject of public clocks . . . 1828': consisting of a correspondence with the Committee for building the new church at Bermondsey, on the subject of a clock for that church . . . London, printed by B. McMillan, 1830. For private circulation only.
33p 25cm

862 Watch.
17p plates 28cm
Extract from Rees' Cyclopaedia, vol 37, 1819.

863 The same. Another copy. London, 1818.
18p plates 29cm
Contains a description of Stogden's repeating mechanism.

Wadsworth (J. H. Francis)
864 A history of repeating watches. Reprinted from *Antiquarian Horology*, [vol 5, nos 1–3, 1965–66].
[14]p illus. 25cm

Walcott (J. P.)
865 The problem of longitude . . . 1967.
23p 28cm
Photocopy of typescript.

Wales (William)
866 The method of finding the longitude at sea by timekeepers: to which are added tables of equations to equal altitudes . . . London, printed by C. Buckton, 1794.
xvi 116p fold. plate 20cm

867 The method of finding the longitude at sea by time-keepers . . . [2nd edition.] London, Wingrave, 1810.
xvi 104p plates 20cm

Walford (Cornelius)
868 Gilds: their origin, constitution, objects, and later history . . . (Reprinted from Vol V of *Insurance Cyclopaedia*.) Printed for private circulation, 1879.
57p 25cm

Waltham Precision Instrument Co. USA.
869 Catalogue . . . of English and Continental watches formed by Franklin Dennison . . . which will be sold by Christie, Manson & Woods . . . [London, Christie,] 1961.
48p plates 24cm

870 Watch and Clock maker . . . vols 1–10, March 1928 – February 1938. [London, 1928–38.]
10 vols illus. 27cm
Published monthly.
Prior to August 1930 called: Practical watch and clock maker.
From May 1939 incorporated with the *Horological Journal, q.v.*

No. 46, Vol 4, 15 December, 1931.
Contains various articles in connection with the Tercentenary of the Company of Clockmakers, pp 309–24. Also a list of makers working at the date of incorporation, by G. H. Baillie.

*Watch and Clockmaker Benevolent Institution
871 [Report and rules for 1888.] London, [The institution,] 1889.
16p 18cm

872 Watch and clockmakers. Objections to 'A bill for forming and regulating a company to be called the British Watch and Clock making Company'. London, printed by Gilbert and Rivington, 1842.
2p 25cm

873 Watch and clock Yearbook 1958–1965. London, N.A.G. Press, [1958–65.]
8 vols illus. 22cm
No more published.

874 Watchmaker, jeweller and silversmith annual directory of trade names and punch-marks, 1954 [to date]. London, Heywood, 1953–.
In progress.

*Waters (Ivor)
875 A note on Chepstow clock and watch makers. Chepstow, [privately printed,] 1952.
7p 20cm

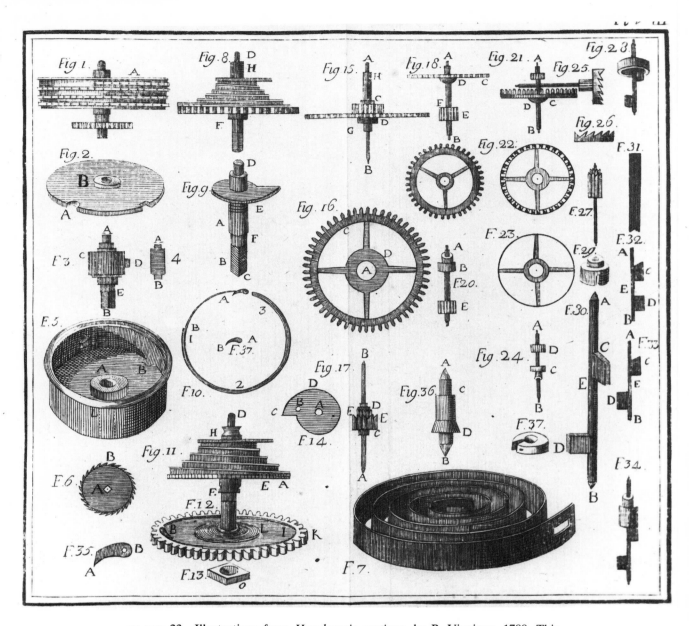

PLATE 23   Illustrations from *Horologerie pratique*, by P. Vigniaux, 1788. This French book of horological instruction includes an exceptionally full description of how to make a verge for a watch. Figs 30–34 help to illustrate the technique. (No. 858)

Watkins (Henry George)
876 Affectionate advice to apprentices; and other young persons engaged in trades or professions . . . The tenth edition stereotyped. London, published by Seeleys, 1852.
ii 56p 17cm

Watney (John)
877 Some account of the Hospital of St Thomas of Acon, in the Cheap, London, and of the plate of the Mercers' Company . . . Privately printed by Blades, East & Blades, 1892.
xi 308p 6 plates 28cm

Webster (Percy)
878 The Percy Webster collection: catalogue of the important collection of early clocks and watches . . . sold by auction by . . . Sotheby & Co. . . . [London, Sotheby, 1954.]
2 pts plates 25cm
With list of prices and buyers' names.

Welch (Charles)
879 Coat-armour of the London Livery Companies. An enquiry based upon original research by Charles Welch, FSA . . . With a biographical list of authorities and a reproduction in collotype of Richard Wallis' 'London Armory' published in 1677. London, printed for private subscription, 1914.
vii 79p 105 plates 29 cm
880 History of the Worshipful Company of Pewterers of the City of London, based upon their own records . . . London, Blades, East & Blades, 1902.
2 vols illus. plates facsims. 24cm

Welch (Kenneth)
881 Time measurement; an introductory history. Newton Abbot, David & Charles, [1972].
120p illus. 22cm

Wenham (Edward)
882 Old clocks for modern use . . . London, Bell, 1951.
xvii 174p illus. plates 22cm
883 Old clocks for modern use . . . [2nd edition.] London, Spring Books, [1964].
xv 174p illus. plates 22cm

Western Clock Manufacturing Co.
884 [Catalogue of clocks manufactured by the company. La Salle, The Company, 1902.]
28p illus. 23cm
Facsimile reprint, 1966, by the American Clock and Watch Museum, of the 1902 edition, taken from a copy with MS annotations.

Wetherfield (David Arthur Fasham)
885 The Wetherfield collection of 222 clocks. Sold by W. E. Hurcomb on 1st May, 1928 . . . [London, Hurcomb, 1929.]
95p illus. 28cm
886 The same. [2nd edition.] [London, Hurcomb, 1929.]
95p illus. 28cm

Wheeler (Maurice)
887 Account of the inclined plane clock, 1684 . . . edited . . . by A. J. Turner. London, Turner & Devereux, [1972].
24p plates 25cm
Facsimile reprint of original edition.

Wheeler (Willard H.)
888 Catalogue of the Willard H. Wheeler collection of watches, the property of Timex Watches [sold by auction by Sotheby & Co.] October 16th 1961. [London, Sotheby,] 1961.
30p plates 25cm

White (Allen)
889 The chain makers: a history of the watch fusee chain industry. Christchurch, Hants. The Author, 1967.
38p illus. port. facsims. 22cm

White (William Douglas)
890 Derbyshire clockmakers before 1850: the Whitehurst family. Issued as a supplement to *Derbyshire Miscellany*, the bulletin of the local history section of the Derbyshire Archaeological and Natural History Society. [1958.]
12p port. 26cm
Typewriter script.

Whitehurst (John)
891 Tracts, philosophical and mechanical . . . London, printed for W. Bent, 1812.
34p 3 fold. plates 27cm

Whitrow (Gerald James)
892 What is time? London, Thames & Hudson, [1972].
191p 21cm

Wilding (J.)
893 How to make a skeleton clock. Ashford, Brand Wright Associates, [1974].
83p illus. port. plans 25cm
Folding plan in pocket.

Wilkes (John), of Milland House, Sussex
894 Horology.
An illustrated extract from *Encyclopaedia Londinensis*, vol 10, 1811, pp 287–369.

Willet Holthuysen Museum, Amsterdam
895 . . . Hoe laat was het? Het Nederlandse uurwerk. [Amsterdam, Gemeente Musea, 1956.]
[24]p 20 plates 26cm
Catalogue of an exhibition of clocks and watches, 15 March – 1 May 1956, to which items were lent by the Clockmakers' Company.

Wise (S. J)
896 Electric clocks . . . [2nd edition.] London, Heywood, [1951].
168p illus. 22cm

Wollaston (Francis)
897   Directions for making an universal dial capable of being set to any latitude, which shall give the mean solar time at noon by inspection . . . London, printed for G. & T. Wilkie, 1793.
   7p   fold. plate   fold. table   27cm

Wood (Edward J.)
898   Curiosities of clocks and watches from the earliest times. London, Richard Bentley, 1866.
   x   443p   frontis.   20cm

*Wright (Lawrence)
899   Clockwork man. London, Elek, [1968].
   260p   illus.   plates   facsims.   24cm
A history of time-keeping devices.

Wyke and Green
900   [Catalogue of watchmakers' tools. Liverpool, Wyke & Green, *c* 1770–75.]
   62 plates   26cm
A photocopy.
Plates 30, 37, 39, 42, 44, 46, 49, 50 are missing.

Young (Thomas)
901   A course of lectures on natural philosophy and the mechanical arts. In two volumes. London, printed for Joseph Johnson, 1807.
   2 vols   plate   27cm
Contains: On timekeepers (Vol 1, pp 188–202, plate 16). Catalogue of articles in journals on clocks, watches and pendulums (Vol 2, pp 191–96).

INDEX TO THE CATALOGUE
OF PRINTED BOOKS

Note: This is a subject index together with references to names *additional to* those in the alphabetical sequence of the catalogue.

CATALOGUE OF MANUSCRIPTS

NOTE
Appended to each entry is the Guildhall Library
MS call number, which, together with the volume
number or numbers where relevant, is sufficient when
requesting any particular manuscript.

CLOCKMAKERS' COMPANY: RECORDS

902 Court minute books, 1632–1933. Engrossed copy.   14 vols.   MS 2710

Vol 1. 1632–80	Vol 8. 1828–45
2. 1680/81–99	9. 1845–64
3. 1699–1729	10. 1864–78
4. 1729–78	11. 1878–88
5. 1778–1804	12. 1888–1900
6. 1804–15	13. 1900–15
7. 1815–28	14. 1915–33

(For subject index to c 1815 *see* MS 3975 (no. 984 *post*). *See* plate 24.

903   Rough Court minutes books, 1637–56, 1673–1812. 12 vols.   MS 2711

Vol 1. 1637–56	Vol 7. 1740–55
2. 1673–84/5	8. 1755–71
3. 1684/5–97	9. 1772–81
4. 1698–1706	10. 1781–92
1708–09	11. 1792–1804
5. 1719–31	12. 1804–12
6. 1731–40	

904   Master's Court agenda book, 1846–49, 1857–97. 9 vols.   MS 2712

Vol 1. 1846–49	Vol 6. 1878–81
2. 1857–63	7. 1881–84
3. 1863–69	8. 1884–88
4. 1869–72	9. 1888–97
5. 1873–78	

905   Junior assistant's Court agenda book, 1813–16, 1846–49, 1858–89.   8 vols.   MS 2713

Vol 1. 1813–16	Vol 5. 1869–72
2. 1846–49	6. 1873–78
3. 1858–63	7. 1878–81
4. 1863–69	8. 1881–89

906   Clerk's Court agenda book, 1811–12, 1846–49, 1858–81, 1884–91, 1899–1906.   9 vols.   MS 2714

Vol 1. 1811–12	Vol 6. 1873–77
2. 1846–49	7. 1878–81
3. 1858–63	8. 1884–91
4. 1863–69	9. 1899–1906
5. 1869–73	

907   Receipts at Courts, searches, meetings, audits, and other concerns of the Company, 1671–76, 1688–93, 1709–16, 1732–1907.   9 vols.   MS 2715

Vol 1. July 1671–March 1676	
2. Oct. 1688–Oct. 1693	
3. Oct. 1709–Oct. 1716	
4. Oct. 1732–Oct. 1741 (Also contains analysis of the accounts 1742–59.)	
5. Oct. 1742–Oct. 1775	
6. Jan. 1776–Oct. 1811	
7. Oct. 1811–Dec. 1851	
8. Jan. 1852–Dec. 1883	
9. Jan. 1884–Dec. 1907	

908   Renter Wardens' accounts, 1836, 1843–51, 1861–77.   27 vols.   MS 2716

Vol 1. 1836	Vol 10. 1851	Vol 19. 1869
2. 1843	11. 1861	20. 1870
3. 1844	12. 1862	21. 1871
4. 1845	13. 1863	22. 1872
5. 1846	14. 1864	23. 1873
6. 1847	15. 1865	24. 1874
7. 1848	16. 1866	25. 1875
8. 1849	17. 1867	26. 1876
9. 1850	18. 1868	27. 1877

909   Freemen's Admission book, 1712–1916. (Stamped for inland revenue.)   4 vols.   MS 2717

Vol 1. Nov. 1712–Oct. 1723	
2. Sept. 1720–Sept. 1757	
3. Nov. 1757–Mar. 1786	
4. Apr. 1786–Sept. 1811	

910   Freemen's enrolment or conformity book, 1728–1911.   5 vols.   MS 2718

Vol 1. Jan. 1728/9–Apr. 1736	
2. July 1736–Dec. 1777	
3. Jan. 1778–Dec. 1809	
4. Jan. 1808–Dec. 1811	
5. Oct. 1811–Apr. 1911 (redemption)	
6. Oct. 1811–Oct. 1934 (patrimony and servitude)	

911   Alphabetical register, showing date of admission to livery, profession, residence and offices filled, 1766–1809.   MS 2719

912   Chronological register of liverymen, 1766–1912, with addresses, occupations and offices held. Compiled c 1829 and continued thereafter. Indexed.   MS 2719A

913   Alphabetical register of freedom admissions with offices held, 1767–1878.   MS 2719B

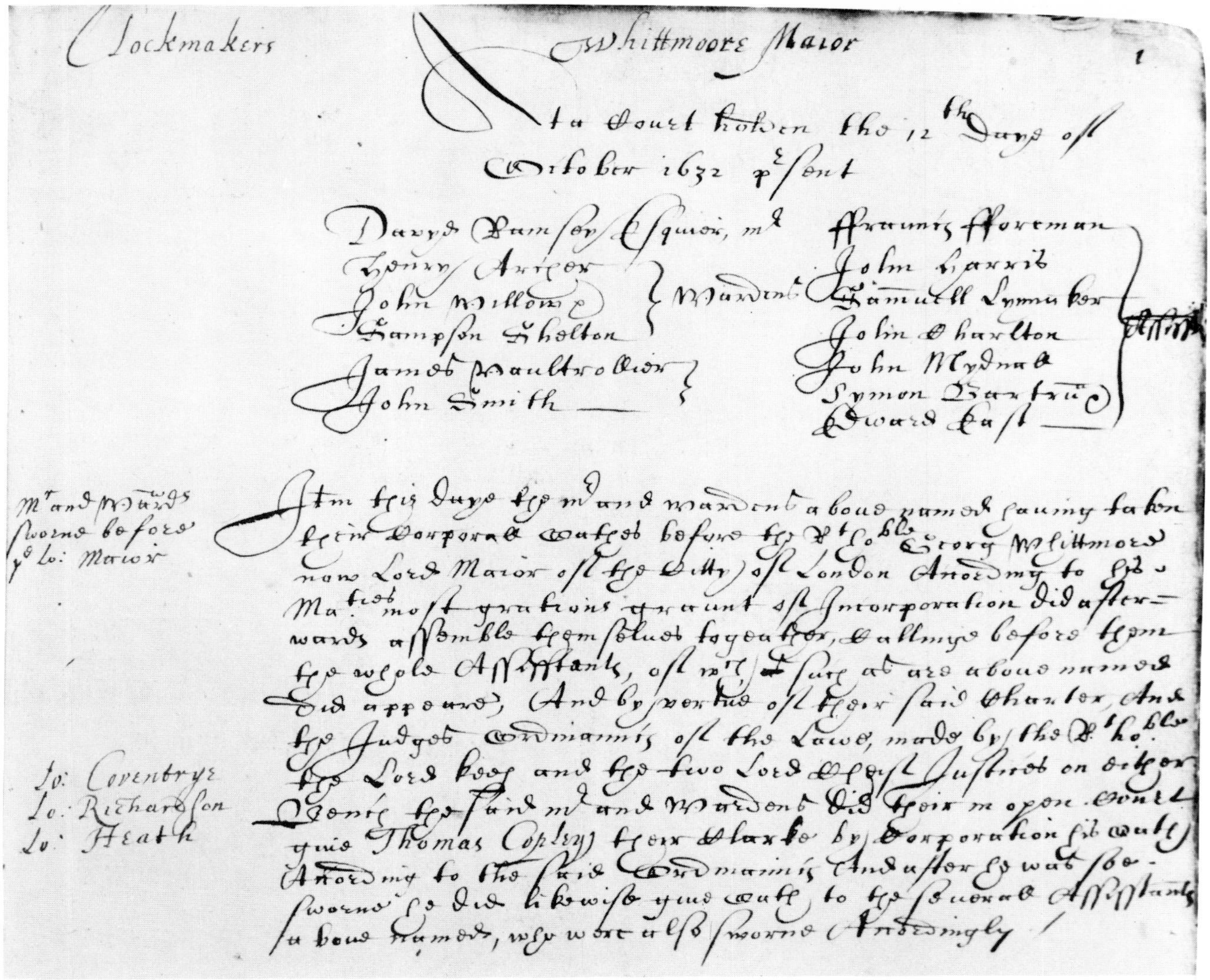
Clockmakers — Whittmoore Maior — Ata Court holden the 12th Daye of October 1632 present

Davyd Ramsey Esquier, Mr; Henry Archer, John Willowe, Sampson Shelton (Wardens); James Vaultrollier, John Smith; Francis Foreman, John Harris, Samuell Lynnaker, John Charlton, John Mydnall, Symon Bartram, Edward East (Assistants)

Mr and Wardens sworne before ye Lo: Maior

Item this daye the Mr and Wardens above named having taken their Corporall oathes before the Rt Hoble George Whittmore now Lord Maior of the Citty of London According to his Maties most gracious graunt of Incorporation did afterwards assemble themselves togeather, Callinge before them the whole Assistants, of which such as are above named did appeare, And by vertue of their said Charter, And the Judges Ordinaunces of the Lawe, made by the Rt Ho: the Lord Keeper and the two Lord Chiefe Justices on either Benche the said Mr and Wardens did their in open Court give Thomas Copley their Clarke his Corporation oath According to the said Ordinaunces And after he was sworne he did likewise give oath to the severall Assistants above named, who were also sworne Accordingly.

Lo: Coventrye
Lo: Richardson
Lo: Heath

PLATE 24 Heading to the page recording the first meeting of the Court of the Clockmakers Company.

Clockmakers		Whittmoore Maior [Lord Mayor]	
		Ata Court holden the 12th Day of October 1632 present	
Davyd Ramsey Esquier, M[r] [Master]		Francis Foreman	Assistants
Henry Archer	Wardens	John Harris	
John Willowe		Samuell Lynnaker	
Sampson Shelton		John Charlton	
James Vaultrollier		John Mydnall	
John Smith		Symon Bartram	
		Edward East	

(No. 902)

914 List of apprentices, chronologically arranged, with index, 1760–1890. 2 vols. MS 2720
    Vol 1. 1760–1811   Vol 2. 1811–90

915 Register of apprentices, with duty paid to the Chamberlain for the relief of city orphans, 1694–1861. 2 vols. MS 2721
    Vol 1. 1694–1781   Vol 2. 1781–1861

916 Register of turnover of apprentices, 1771–1808, preceded by copies of summonses to attend the various meetings of the Company, 1770. MS 2722

917 Quarterage book, 1698–1705, 1745–51, 1771–1808, 1819–50. 7 vols. MS 2723
    Vol 1. 1698–1705   Vol 4. 1789–98
        2. 1745–51   5. 1799–1808
        3. 1771–78   6. 1819–28
                     7. 1829–50
Each volume arranged alphabetically.

918 Collecting books for the payment of quarterage, arranged in topographical walks, 1774–83, 1785–86. 12 vols. MS 2724
    Vol 1. 1774   Vol 5. 1778   Vol 9. 1782
        2. 1775   6. 1779   10. 1783
        3. 1776   7. 1780   11. 1785
        4. 1777   8. 1781   12. 1786

919 Printed list of members liable to quarterage, showing the amount due on 31 Dec. 1822, with manuscript lists of those excused the payment of April 1822, and related papers 1822. MS 6436

920 Schedule of the various walks, arranged for the purpose of search and collection of quarterage from members of the craft, giving their names and particular occupations. 3 vols. 1800. MS 2725
    Vol 1. City, Whitechapel, Greenwich, Vauxhall
        2. Islington, St Luke's, Hoxton
        3. Strand, Westminster, Oxford Street, Holborn, Clerkenwell

921 Certificates issued to clock and watch makers qualified to practice, 1813–23, with list of masters and wardens, 1632–1812. MS 2726

922 Minutes of proceedings of the Committee for correspondence and laws, and for the more effectual suppression of malpractices in the trade, 1808–15. 2 vols. MS 2727
    Vol 1. 24 Oct. 1808–22 Nov. 1813
        2. 14 Dec. 1813–29 Dec. 1815

923 Minute book of the Committee appointed relative to the illicit introduction of foreign clocks and watches, 1814–19. MS 2728

924 Minutes of proceedings of the Committee appointed 2 Sept. 1816, for the affairs of freemen and apprentices, relating to the admission to the freedom of Richard Brettel Bate, mathematical instrument maker, 1816–17. MS 2729

925 Extracts from the minutes, 1701–24, of the Quarterly Court relating to the administration of the gift of Charles Gretton, with a copy of the indenture establishing the trust, 1701, and the accounts, 1702–1847. MS 2730

926 Declaration from 'professors of the art and mystery of clock and watch making' asking for the countenance and support of the Company against the evils arising from the importation of foreign watches, Nov. 1780. MS 2731

927 A list of all the clockmakers, both free men and farreners, alians, and outliers, 26 June 1662. (Inserted in a volume of extracts from the Court Minute books, 1632–1787, made by Edward Tutet.) MS 2732

928 List of the invitations to the livery to dine with the Court of Assistants at the annual quarter Court at Michaelmas, 1837–45. MS 2733

929 Persons invited to the Stewards' feast, 1732–56, 1759; and lists of the Master, Wardens, and Court of Assistants, 1759, 1761, 1764–73. MS 2734

930 Lists of freemen, 1700–71. MS 2735

931 Declaration of freemen and liverymen, 1882–1926. MS 3334

932 A folio volume containing lists of:
  1. Apprentices, 1632–96, and freemen, 1632–94. Alphabetical. Compiled *c* 1700.
  2. Stewards, 1639–96. Compiled *c* 1700.
  3. Masters, 1717–84. Compiled *c* 1784.
  4. Apprentices who had not taken the freedom, *c* 1700.
  5. Members paying quarterage, with trades and residences, *c* 1742.
  6. 246 clock and watchmakers in or near the City of London, 1782. Alphabetical. MS 3939

933 A folio volume of papers relating to patents, hallmarks and foreign importations, 1687–1842. 161 items. MS 3940

Contents
  1. Order of the King in Council, 2 March 1687, after hearing Master Wardens and Assistants of the Fellowship of the Clockmakers' Company against the granting of a Patent to Edward Barlow for the making and managing of all Pulling Clocks and Watches, usually called repeating clocks; and ordering that no Patent be granted. 2 l.
  2. Observations upon a jewelled watch made by Ignatius Huggeford. This watch was produced before the Committee of the House of Commons, and confirmed them against granting the Patent applied for by Nicholas Facio, Peter Debaufree, and Jacob Debaufree. The watch had a stone fixed in the cock (*see* exhibit 45 in the company's museum). This paper gives a most interesting account of the maker, from which it appears that he flourished 1658–98. From the minutes of a special court of Assistants held 11 December 1704. 2 l.

933 – *continued*

3. Copy of a petition of Nicholas Facio, Gent., and Peter Debaufree, and Jacob Debaufree, Watchmakers to the House of Commons, 6 December 1704, praying for the continuance to them for a longer term of the sole use of their invention for jewelling clocks and watches. Proceedings in Parliament thereon, and petitions on the subject from the Clock and Watch Makers in and about the Cities of London and Westminster. 2 l.

(4–37.) Letters, petitions, etc. on the subject of Clay's patent for repeating watches, with copy of Letters Patent, etc.

4. 7 January 1716. Caveat. If any petition or order is referred to Mr Attorney Generall . . . please to give notice to Francis Speidell, Clerk to the Company.
5. Letter of Edw. Greene to Mr Speidell, 14 February 1716.
6. Letter of Edwd. Northy, 18 February 1716.
7. Edward Green to Mr Speidell, 13 March 1716.
8. Edward Green to Mr Speidell, 27 March 1717.
9. Copy of petition (signed 8 April 1717) from the Company to the King. 2 l.
10. Letter of Ch. Delafaye to Mr Quare, 6 June 1717.
11. Copy of the Company's petition to His Majesty (signed 24 July 1717) relative to Clay's patent.
12. 'Copy of Mr Clay's Invencon.' Letters Patent, dated July 1717, to grant patent for fourteen years. 4 l.
13. Copy of proceedings of the Privy Council on the petition of the Company to His Majesty (signed 8 April 1717), with copy of the petition.
14. Order of Lord Privy Seal deferring the hearing of the case from Monday 9 December to Monday 16 December 1717.
15. Rough draft of the Company's petition to the Council. 24 July 1717. 2 l.
16. Copy of Charles Clay's petition to the King. February 1716.
17. Copy of the Company's petition to the Lord Privy Seal. 1 August 1717. 2 l.
18. Copy of order, dated 20 December 1717, that no patent be granted to Charles Clay.
19. Report of the proceedings of the Company of Clockmakers in opposing Mr Clay's patent.
20. Copy of Charles Clay's petition. 2 l.
21. Reasons for not passing a patent for Charles Clay's pretended new invention.
22. Answers to the Company's pretended reasons. 2 l.
23. Reply to My Clay's answer.
24. Copy of the Attorney General's report. Brief for the Clockmakers' Company against a patent for Charles Clay's invention.
25. Order of Lord Privy Seal appointing 9 December to hear the case. 9 November 1717.
26. Copy of the order of Council, 15 July 1717, relating to Clay's patent.
27. Copy of the Company's petition to His Majesty, 8 April 1717, against Clay's patent.
28. Copy of the Company's petition to the Council to be heard by counsel, signed 24 July 1717.
29. Reasons for not passing Clay's patent.
30. Reply to Mr Clay's answer.
31. Further objections of the Clockmakers.
32. Copy of the Company's petition against Clay's patent.
33. Reasons for not granting a patent. 2 l.
34. Reasons for not granting a patent. 2 l.

933 – *continued*

35. Letter from Wm. Sharpe to Mr Speidell requesting him to come to Mr Beake to discuss the 'affair of the Clockmakers'. 29 December 1717.
36. Sharpe to Speidell. December 1717.
37. 'Wooddeson's letter about his bill'. December 1717.
38. Copy of Letters Patent granted by George II to Joseph Bosley, for improvements made in watches. 8 l.
39. Copy of Mr Bosley's petition for a patent, with Mr Murray's opinion thereon. January 1755. 2 l.
40. Extracts from Acts of Parliament for preventing frauds in gold and silver wares, etc. (Printed sheet.)
41. Letter from Thomas Lane, Clerk of the Goldsmiths' Company, upon the above subject. 7 May 1788. (Printed sheet.)
42. Report of the Committee appointed by the General Meeting of the Clock and Watch Makers of the Cities of London and Westminster. 3 December 1789. (Printed tract.)

(43–77.) Letters and opinions of the Members of the Trade, in answer to questions proposed to them by a Committee of the Company, on engraving the name of the makers upon watches and clocks and pirating the name of any maker upon either watches or clocks.

43. Mr Arnold
44. Mr Grant
45. Mr Joyce
46. Mr Morice
47. Mr Brockbank
48. Mr Bidlake
49. Mr G. Clark
50. Mr Clerke
51. Mr G. Clark
52. Mr Morice
53. Mr Barraud
54. Mr Jackson
55. Mr Smith
56. Mr Morice
57. Mr Clerke
58. Mr Savage
59. Mr Savage
60. Mr Barwise
61. Mr Earnshaw
62. Mr Grignon
63. Mr Grignon
64. Mr Grignon
65. Messrs Vulliamy and Son
66. Mr Chater
67. Mr Gordon
68. Mr Gordon
69. Mr Rogers
70. Mr Rogers
71. Mr Taylor
72. Mr Brockbank
73. A well-wisher to the trade
74. Mr Holmes
75. Mr Holmes
76. Mr Robson
77. Mr Holmes

78. Report of the Committee appointed by the Company upon the above question, with an appendix containing a copy of the questions submitted to the trade and a fair copy of the correspondence, opinions, etc. 20 l.

933– *continued*

79. Memorial of the Company to the Privy Council for Trade on the above subject, with draft regulations. 5 l.
80. Draft of a proposed Act of Parliament to regulate the importation and exportation of watches, and to encourage the manufacture thereof within the United Kingdom. 9 l.
81. Copy of a Bill for regulating the exportation, and putting an end to the importation, of clocks and watches, etc. 38 l.
82, 83. Rough sketch of a Bill for the above purpose. 7 l.
84. Extracts from the Company's records respecting the pirating of makers' names and the use of fictitious names. 4 July 1808. 2 l.
85. Memorial of the Master, Wardens, and Court of Assistants to the Lords of the Council for Trade. 1809. 4 l.
86. Reply of the Goldsmiths' Company to the Memorial of the Clockmakers' Company. 28 October 1812. 2 l.
87. Statement of the number of gold and silver watch-cases marked at Goldsmiths' Hall 1791–97.

(88–133.) Letters, opinions, reports, etc., with reference to the marking of gold and silver watch-cases, bows, pendants, etc.
88. Letters of Chas. Smith to H. Potter. 20 February 1812.
89. Resolution of a Committee of the Clock and Watch trade held Thursday 12 March 1812.
90. Mr Richmond to G. Atkins. July 1812.
91. John Thwaites to the Master of the Clockmakers' Company.
92. Abstract of conference between the Goldsmiths' and Clockmakers' Companies. 7 October 1812.
93. Further documents relative to the above.
94. Clerk of the Clockmakers' Company to the Goldsmiths' Company. 10 November 1812.
95. Thos. Lane to George Atkins. 1 December 1812.
96. Rough minutes of conference with the Goldsmiths' Company held 8 December 1812. 2 l.
97. Memorial of certain watch-case makers to the Clockmakers' Company. 29 December 1812. 5 signatures.
98. Memorial of certain watch-case makers to the Clockmakers' Company. 29 December 1812. 9 signatures.
99. Memorial of watch-pendant makers.
100. G. Smith and W. Collier to the Court of the Clockmakers' Company. 18 January 1813.
101. J. Jackson to the Court of the Clockmakers' Company. 31 December 1812.
102. Notice (5 January 1813) by the Goldsmiths' Company as to the standard of gold and silver watch-cases sent to their Hall. (Printed sheet.)
103. Notice of the Goldsmiths' Company as to the standard of watch-pendants sent to their Hall. 15 January 1810.
104. Thos. Lane to the Master and Wardens of the Clockmakers' Company. 5 January 1813.
105. Counsel's opinion respecting further order issued by the Goldsmiths' Company.
106. Report of Committee of the Clockmakers' Company appointed 13 August 1812, in consequence of abuses in the marking of gold and silver watch-cases.
107. Resolutions of meeting of watch-case makers held 20 January 1813.
108. Rough notes at meeting of case-makers.
109. Conference of case-makers with Clockmakers' Committee held 12 January 1813.
110. Conference at Goldsmiths' Hall held 14 January 1813.

933 – *continued*

111. Requisitions delivered to the Goldsmiths' Company. 14 January 1813.
112. Resolutions of the Goldsmiths Company. 16 January 1813.
113. Rough minutes taken at Goldsmiths' Hall. 16 January 1813.
114. Copy of letter sent to the Goldsmiths' Company by the Clerk of the Clockmakers' Company. 26 January 1813.
115. Messrs Comtesse and Humbert to the Goldsmiths' Company. 19 January 1813.
116. Messrs Comtesse and Humbert to the Goldsmiths' Company. 26 January 1813.
117. Tho. Lane to George Atkins. 28 January 1813.
118. Copy of letter of Vulliamy and Sons to the Goldsmiths' Company. 3 February 1813.
119. Memorial of watch-case makers to the Clockmakers' Company. February 1813.
120. Thos. Lane to Vulliamy and Sons. 5 February 1813.
121. Memorial from case-makers to the Goldsmiths' Company. 6 February 1813.
122. Geo. Atkins to Thos. Lane. 1 March 1813.
123. Third report of Committee on watch-cases of inferior make. 1 March 1813.
124. Thos. Lane to Geo. Atkins. 17 March 1813.
125. Goldsmiths' order of Court. 17 March 1813.
126. Joseph Glenny to Mr Rogers. 22 March 1813.
127. Mr Rogers to Joseph Glenny. 22 March 1813.
128. Notice of the Goldsmiths' Company relative to standard of gold and silver pendants. 25 March 1813. (Printed.)
129. Draft clauses for an Act of Parliament relative to gold and silver pendants.
130. Statement by Mr Leeming.
131. Copy of petition to Parliament from the Clockmakers' Company. 25 February 1814. 5 l.
132. Confession of G. C. Maining to having pirated the name of Mr Barraud. 9 September 1818. (Printed sheet.)
133. Board of Trade to Mr Potter. 23 June 1812.
134. Letter from the Secretary of the Customs to the Company about marking foreign watches. 30 June 1812.
135. Letter from the Goldsmiths' Company to the Lords of Trade about country Hall-Marks upon watch-cases, etc. 19 June 1830.
136. Draft of a memorial from the Clockmakers' Company to the Treasury on the above subject. 13 September 1830.
137. Rough draft of the same.
138. Memorial to the Treasury not to allow clock movements to be exported. 5 March 1830.
139. Letter from the Right Hon. Spring Rice to the Company as to the importation of foreign clocks, watches, etc. 2 March 1832.
140. Copy of an advertisement upon the above subject. (Printed cutting.)
141, 142. Calculations of the number of watches imported without paying duty, 1829–32.
143. Copy of a memorial from the Company to the Board of Trade, asking them to take steps for the protection of the trade.

(144–161.) Letters, chiefly to Mr S. E. Atkins, Clerk of the Company, about marking foreign clocks and watches with the names of English makers, etc. 1839–42.

933 – *continued*

144. Alex. Smart to Mr Atkins. 3 January 1839.
145. B. L. Vulliamy to Mr Atkins. 7 January 1839.
146. The Secretary, Customs House, to Mr Atkins. 26 February 1839.
147. C. A. Pettermand to Mr Vulliamy. 3 January 1842.
148. J. Tennant to Mr Vulliamy. 29 January 1842.
149. Copy of letter from G. Clark to E. C. Branbridge. 29 January 1842.
150. Vulliamy to Mr Tennent, MP. 2 February 1842.
151. Atkins to Messrs Christie. 3 February 1842.
152. Messrs Christie to Atkins. 5 February 1842.
153. Prospectus of proposed watch-makers' company for manufacture by machinery. July 1842. (Printed tract.)
154. Copy of memorial of the Clockmakers' Company to the Treasury. 7 February 1842. 2 l.
155. Mr Pemberton to the Clockmakers' Company. 26 July 1842.
156. Copy of letter from Clark of the Clockmakers' Company to the *Times*. 13 September 1841.
157. Copy of anonymous advertisement in reply to the above letter.
158. Copy of letter to the *Times* in further reply. 14 September 1841.
159. Mr Troup to Mr Atkins. 21 September 1841.
160. Editor of the *Town* to Mr Atkins. 24 September 1841.
161. Mr Troup to Mr Atkins. 7 October 1841.

934 Titles of patents relating to clocks, watches, chronometers, etc., arranged in chronological order. 1661–1857. MS 3940A

935 A folio volume containing deeds and documents relating to charities, gifts to the Company for the poor, and financial matters. 1678–1817. 66 items; 7 vellum skins. MS 3941

Contents

1. Bond of Sir Robert Viner, Knt, under his hand, for repayment of £100 lent by the Company to him, being an assignment upon the Exchequer for £6 yearly from Lady Day 1678.
2. Assignment by Jane Goodwin, widow and executrix of Thomas Goodwin, assignee of Sir Robert Viner, Knt and Bart, of a yearly annuity of £3 to the Master Wardens and Fellowship of the Company. 18 January 1706.
3. Letters of Administration under the seal of the Prerogative Court of Canterbury to Francis Speidell, Clerk of the Company, to receive the above annuity on behalf of the Company from the estate of the late Jane Goodwin, executor of Thomas Goodwin, dated 31 March 1708.
4. Assignment from Francis Speidell to the Master, Wardens and Fellowship of the Company of the said annuity of £3, dated 10 November 1708.
5. Order of the Court of Assistants, dated 14 January 1705, referring to the above.
6. Official copy of the last Will, with probate, of Thomas Goodwin, Clerk of the Company, dated 13 June 1694.
7. Deed of Gift from Edward East of £100 to the Master, Wardens and Fellowship of the Company, in trust, to pay to five freemen, or their widows, twenty shillings annually, dated 20 June 1693. Signed by Edward East.

935 – *continued*

8. Deed of Gift from Henry Jones of £100 to the Master, Wardens and Fellowship of the Company, in trust, to pay to five poor freemen, or their widows, twenty shillings annually, dated 20 June 1693. Signed by Henry Jones.
9. Deed of Gift, dated 1 September 1701, from Charles Gretton of £50 to the Master, Wardens and Fellowship of Clockmakers, to pay yearly the sum of fifty shillings to apprentice the sons of deceased Freemen of the Company to the trade of Watch or Clockmaking. Signed by Charles Gretton. Endorsement, altering and amending the gift, dated 4 July 1715, and signed by Charles Gretton and the Master and Wardens.
10–20. Three receipts for Bank of England Stock, 22 June 1697 to 15 May 1702. With receipts for interest to 1710.
21. Extract from the last will and testament of Samuel Wilson, leaving money to be lent to young tradesmen, dated 17 October 1760. 3 l.
22. Extract from the will of Devereux Bowley, leaving £500 4 per cent bank annuities to the poor of the Company, dated 17 July 1772.
23, 24. Extract from the will of William James Frodsham, leaving £1,000 3 per cent bank annuities to the poor of the Company. August 1850. 3 l.
25, 26. Letter from Joseph Fenn, enclosing extract from the will of his late uncle, Samuel Fenn, dated 10 February 1816, leaving £200 bank stock to the poor of the Company. 1821. 4 l.
27. Letter from Nicholas Carlisle, Secretary to the Charity Commissioners, asking for a return of all charities connected with the Company. 25 September 1820. 2 l.
28. Order from the Charity Commissioners for the attendance of the Clerk of the Company and the production of deeds and other documents relating to the charities of the Company. 24 July 1821.
29, 30. Letter from Nicholas Carlisle and accompanying copy of the Commissioners' Report upon the charities of the Company. 24 July 1822.
31–39. Further formal correspondence between the Charity Commissioners and the Clockmakers' Company as to the Company's charities. 4 February 1854 to 28 March 1860.
40. Order of the Recorder of London to compel persons carrying on the trade of Watch and Clock makers to become free of the Clockmakers' Company. 4 August 1641.
41. Informations against persons using the art of watch and clock making without having served their apprenticeship. 1654. 5 l.
42. Letter addressed to the Court of the Company, asking for redress of the grievances suffered by the trade, signed by twenty members of the trade. 1656. 2 l.
43. Heads of ordinances by the Court of Assistants of the Company as to the employment of foreigners and non-freemen in the art of watchmaking. Ordered to be printed.
44. Draft of public advertisement announcing the Company's intention to put into execution the laws enforcing penalties for bad workmanship. 19 December 1777.
45. A statement of the number of apprentices bound 1694–1748, copied from the Orphan's book. 2 l.
46. A list of watch and clock makers who keep shops within the City of London, and are free of the Clockmakers'

935 – *continued*

Company, and a list of those who are not free. *c* 1773. With other statistics of freemen and shopkeepers. 8 l.

47. Memorial from the Livery and Freemen of the Company to the Court of Assistants, against non-freemen exercising the craft of watchmaking. Signed by thirty-two leading members of the trade. 1 February 1802. 2 l.

48. Reply of the Court of Assistants to the above memorial.

49. Forfeits for non-appearance or late attendance at meetings of the Company.

50. Printed appeal by the Managing Committee of Trades against the abolition of the apprenticeship system. 8 April 1813. 4to sh.

51. Printed list of subscriptions received in London and from the country, 13 May 1812 to 6 August 1813(?), by the above Committee.

52. Printed summons to a Court of Common Council on 22 November 1813, to consider (*inter alia*) the question of subjecting persons to penalties for exercising trades to which they have not served an apprenticeship. Folio sh.

53. Printed statement of a Committee to promote a petition to Parliament in favour of retaining the system of apprenticeship. 29 November 1813. 4to sh.

54. Printed request to cities and towns throughout the country to support the above appeal to Parliament, with form of petition for that purpose. 4pp folio.

55. Resolutions in favour of the above petition passed at a meeting of master manufacturers and tradesmen held at Freemasons' Tavern 14 January 1814. Printed. 4pp folio.

56. Copy of memorial of the Spectacle Makers' Company against the claim of the Clockmakers' Company to exercise control over makers of mathematical instruments. 17 February 1815. 2 l.

57. Decision of the Chamberlain of London on the above point at issue between the Companies. 25 March 1815.

58. Description of the Common Seal of the Worshipful Company of Spectacle Makers. Midsummer 1810.

59. Letter from Mr H. Woodthorpe, Town Clerk, notifying a meeting of the Court of Aldermen to consider the above matters in dispute between the Clockmakers' Company and the Spectacle Makers' Company. 22 October 1817.

60. Letter from the Clerk of the Spectacle Makers' Company. 23 June 1817. 2 l.

61. Printed abstract of an Act of Common Council for regulating the Company of Clockmakers, passed 15 October 1765. Folio sh.

62, 63. Formal notices to attend, and correspondence respecting, meetings in connection with the above dispute. October–November 1817. 6 l.

64. Draft report of a Committee of the Clockmakers' Company upon the dispute with the Company of Spectacle Makers. 2 l.

65. Fair copy of the report from the above Committee signed by six members. 25 November 1817. 2 l.

66. Brief dated list of documents in the controversy.

936 A folio volume containing copies of the charter, bye-laws, acts of Common Council and original documents and papers relating to the establishment and regulating of the Company; also grant of livery, etc. 1631–1817. 52 items. MS 3942

936 – *continued*

Contents

1. Copy of the Charter of Incorporation granted to the Company, dated 22 August, 7th Charles I, 1631. 9 l.

2. Order to the Company from the Committee for Corporations to deliver the Company's charter to be examined. Signed Daniel Blagrave and dated 21 December 1652. 2 l.

3. Copy of an order of the above Committee referring the Charter to John Farwell Esq., Counsel to the Commonwealth, for examination. Signed by Isaac Pennington and four others. 2 l.

4. Order directing the Charter to be returned to the Company. 27 January 1652. 2 l.

5. Letter from Ahasuerus Fromanteel about his journeymen and his son's apprentices. 3 March 1656. *See* plate 25.

6. Six heads of 'Agrievances' of the Company in general. 8 September 1656.

7. Proposals by members of the Company concerning the management of its affairs. 8 September 1656.

8. Copy of a petition to the Lord Mayor, signed by thirty-three freemen of the Company, complaining of the action of the Court of Assistants in matters relating to the trade. 1656. 2 l.

9. Order of the Lord Mayor directing that Thomas Loomes should keep only two apprentices instead of five. 25 February 1656.

10. Petition of certain freemen of the Company to the Lord Mayor in support of the proceedings of the Court of Assistants. Twelve signatures, five of them cancelled.

11. Another copy of the above petition with fourteen signatures.

12. Another petition of certain freemen of the Company to the Lord Mayor for the redress of grievances. 2 l.

13. An answer to the above petition (No. 12) of some of the Company to the Lord Mayor. 2 l.

14. Copy of a petition from the Master, Wardens and Court of Assistants of the Company to the Court of Common Council, and a draft for an Act of Common Council which they submitted for approval. Read in Common Council *c* July 1698. 5 l.

15. Official copy of the Act of Common Council for regulating the Company. 15 October 1765. 2 l.

16. Another copy of the above Act. 4 l.

17. Report of a Committee appointed by the Company to examine the Charter and Bye-Laws of the Company, and to obtain Counsel's opinion as to the powers of the Company in the following respects: 1. to compel freemen of the Company to take up their Livery; 2. to levy quarterage upon freemen of the Company, clockmakers who are Freemen of other Companies, and clockmakers who are non-freemen, but reside within the City or ten miles thereof; 3. to compel clockmakers who are free of another Company to become freemen of the Clockmakers' Company, and also clockmakers who are non-freemen to become Members of the Company. November 1795. 4 l.

18. Proceedings at a meeting (held 26 February 1802) of the freemen and Livery of the Company who had signed a memorial to the Court of Assistants in December 1801. 2 l.

19. Case of the Company, with the opinion of Sergeant Adair. 10 January 1796. 10 l.

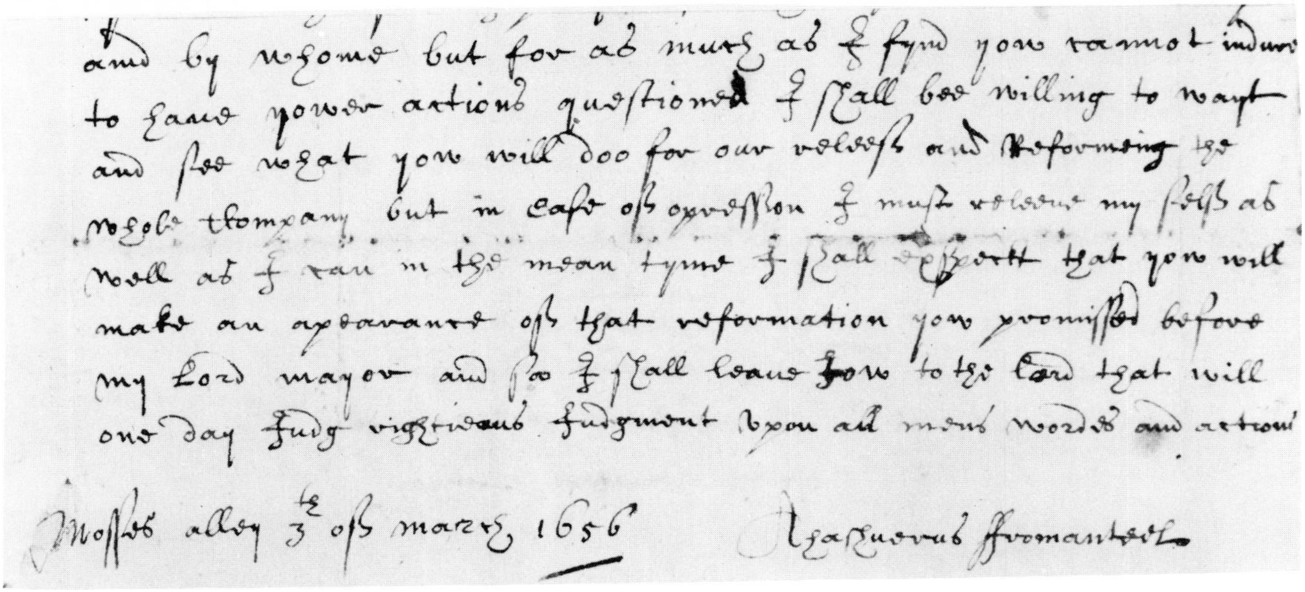

PLATE 25 Last page of a holograph letter from A. Fromanteel to the Company, refuting in strong terms charges against him and his son for keeping an unlawful number of apprentices.

'. . . but for as much as I fynd you cannot indure to have yower actions questioned I shall be willing to wayt and see what you will doo for our releef and reforming the whole company but in case of opression I must releeve my self as well as I can in the mean tyme I shall expectt that you will make an apearance of that reformation you promised before my Lord Mayor and soo I shall leave you to the lord that will one day judg righteous judgment upon all mens words and actions

Mosses alley 3rd of March 1656   Ahashaerus Fromanteel

(No. 936(5))

936 – *continued*

20. Case and opinion of Sergeant Merewether. 3 March 1832. 8 l.
21. Case and opinion of J. Mirehouse. 19 February 1831. 8 l.
22. Report of a Committee appointed to prepare a classified catalogue of all books, papers, and documents belonging to the Company. 7 January 1817. 2 l.
23. Abstract of the powers of the Company, its officers and their duties, fees payable, meetings of the Court of Assistants, etc. 13 l.
24. Report of a Committee appointed by the Court of Aldermen on the petition of the Glass-sellers' Company for a Livery. 8 May 1712. 2 l.
25. Petition of the Master Wardens and Assistants of the Clockmakers' Company to the Court of Aldermen for a grant of Livery.
26. Case of the Company, for counsel, about the Livery, 1749. 2 l.
27. Copy of letter of Master and Wardens requesting the attendance of Aldermen at the Court of Aldermen on 27 June 1749, when the report of the Committee as to a grant of a Livery to the Company was to be considered.
28. Draft of petition to the Court of Aldermen for the grant of a Livery.
29. Case and opinion of Mr Wilbraham with reference to a grant of Livery. 11 May 1750. 3 l.

936 – *continued*

30. Case and opinion of Mr Lloyd upon the above subject. 23 April 1750. 4 l.
31. Report and Order of the Court of Aldermen for granting a Livery to the Company, 1 July 1766. 4 l.
32, 33. Copies of petitions from the Company and its members to the Lord Mayor and Court of Aldermen for a grant of a Livery; the latter petition is signed by the Members of the Company, 1766.
34. Report and Order of the Court of Aldermen for increasing the Livery of the Company to 200. 25 June 1810. 2 l.
35. Report of the Committee of the Court of Aldermen, and order thereon increasing the Livery to 250. 11 April 1826. 4 l.
    Orders in the suit of the Company against W. J. Burrowes to compel him to take up his Livery. February–May 1797.
36. Notes on the powers of the Company over its members and strangers. 3 l.
37. Information against William James Burrowes for refusing to take up his Livery, filed 14 February 1797. 32 l.
38. Case and opinion of J. Mirehouse concerning the powers of the Company for compelling freemen of the craft to take up their Livery. 30 June 1830. 5 l.

(39–47.) Original letters about taking up the Livery.

936 – *continued*

39. J. Barraud to G. Atkins. 7 March 1814.
40. J. Rake to G. Atkins. 8 October 1814.
41. J. Starling to the Court of Assistants. 10 October 1814.
42. W. Moon to the Master. 12 October 1814.
43. J. W. Smith to G. Atkins. 25 October 1814.
44. I. Rogers and H. Clarke to G. Atkins. 28 February 1814.
45. P. T. Lemaitre to the Master. 6 May 1816.
46. P. T. Lemaitre to the Master. 3 June 1816.
47. W. Mansell to J. Thwaites. 2 December 1816.
48. Memorial of G. Clerke, W. Harris, James Rawlins, P. T. Lemaitre, E. Griffiths, and T. Humphries to the Master, Wardens, and Court of Assistants as to the management of the affairs of the Company, presented 7 April 1817. 2 l.
   Copy of the same. (Printed sheet.)
49. Reply to the above memorial, 23 May 1817, stating 'that there is nothing to warrant the claims advanced'.
50. Further memorial of the individuals named under No. 48, *ante*, with others. 25 August 1817. 2 l.
   Printed copy of the same, with reply from the Clerk to the Company, dated 16 September 1817.
51. Letter from G. Clerke to W. Robson, Master, on the subject of the above memorial (No. 48). 26 August 1817.
52. Letter from G. Clerke to George Atkins, Clerk to the Company, on the same subject. 26 August 1817.

937 A folio volume containing a collection of documents and papers chiefly relating to other companies making clocks and watches. 1672–1860. 103 items.
MS 3943

Contents

1. Copy of letter from B. L. Vulliamy to A. Ross, Surveyor General of the Customs, on the duty on foreign watches. 15 April 1842.
2, 3. Reply to the above, and copy. 16 April 1842.
4. Note from Mr Macgregor of the Board of Trade to Mr Vulliamy. 27 May 1842.
5. Copy of letter from Mr Vulliamy to Mr Macgregor about the importation of foreign clocks and watches. 1 June 1842.
6. Letter from Mr W. J. Frodsham to Mr Vulliamy about the British Watch and Clock Making Company. 25 October 1842.
7. Copy of Mr Vulliamy's reply to the above. 31 October 1842.
8. Copy of letter to the Editor of the *Morning Herald* from eight City chronometer-making firms disavowing approval of Mr Ingold's method of producing watch movements in large quantities. 29 October 1842.
9–11. Printed circular and two prospectuses of the British Watch and Clockmaking Company. 1842–43.
12. Printed statement of the origin and progress of the above Company, presented to a meeting convened for the purpose of inquiring into its character and pretensions. 1843.
13. Printed statement in support of the Bill for establishing the above Company. 1 March 1843.
14. Printed statement in opposition to the above Bill. 1843.
15. Printed division-list of the House of Commons on the second reading of the above Bill. 31 March 1843.

937– *continued*

16. Copy of issue of the *Neuchâtel Gazette* containing an account of Ingoldt's patent for manufacturing watches. Thursday 13 April 1843.
17. Printed prospectus of the National Company for the manufacture of watches.
18. Printed prospectus of the Patent Chronometer-Watch and Clock Company (Philcox's patents). 1852.
19. Indenture from the Lords of the Treasury giving three standards of brass for measuring. 4 September 1671.
20. Order of Lord Mayor (Abney) for fining Mr Fromanteel on his refusal to serve as steward to the Clockmakers' Company. 7 May 1701(?).
21. Case of the Company of Clockmakers concerning the powers of the Company to select and fine stewards. 22 August 1607 to 30 September 1672. 2 l.
22. Case and opinion of E. Northey on seizure of watches from John Billie, a free clockmaker. 13 September 1699. 2 l.
23. Opinion of T. Garrard on the issue of summonses by the Company. 2 l.
24, 25. Decision of counsel on the engraving on watches, clocks, etc. 12 and 23 July 1734. 2 l.
26. Letter from the Court of Lord Mayor and Aldermen asking the Company for contributions towards maintaining the troops in the City during the late tumults. 19 July 1780.
27. Printed letter from the Lord Mayor (Plomer) and Common Council enclosing copy of letter from the Earl of Shelburne setting forth a proposal for augmenting the domestic forces of the nation. 22 May 1782.
28, 29. Letter from the Sheriffs to the Company (and reply) asking for a grant to assist the Society for the discharge of persons confined for small debts, in celebration of the Jubilee of George III. 20 August and November 1809.
30. Letter from Patent Searcher, London Docks, concerning the seizure of watches made by Jews under fictitious names. 11 August 1810.
31. Letter from Henry Clarke about a certificate being given by the Company to freemen. 8 October 1812.
32. Letter to the Company from the executors of the Master, Mr Harry Potter, announcing his death. 4 September 1813.
33. Letter from Henry Clarke to the Company laying before them some watches and movements for purchase. May 1814.
34, 35. Letters offering offices to be let to the Company. 14 April and 6 May 1814.
36. Letter from Charles Smith requesting freedom of the Company for William Gammon, who had been his apprentice. 3 September 1814.
37. Protest against proceedings of an especial Court of Assistants of the Company held Friday 25 February 1814. 6 l.
38. List of books etc. taken from the Company's chest. 12 January 1818. 2 l.
39. Particulars of eleven deeds. 1676–1740. 2 l.
40. List of articles in the Company's chest. 9 December 1817. 2 l.
41. Letter enclosing the resolution of the Committee appointed by the General Meeting of the Trade. 15 June 1822.
42–44. Letters concerning the Warehousing Bill before the House of Commons. June–October 1822.

937 – *continued*

45. Printed petition of the Clerkenwell masters and workmen to the House of Commons against the Warehousing Bill. 7 June 1822.
46. Copy of letter from Mr Thomas Reid of Edinburgh to Mr B. L. Vulliamy of London. 26 January 1821. 4 l.
47–49. Letters relating to a gift of a watch to the Company from the Honourable Mrs Damar. 7 July 1817 to 26 January 1818.
50. Letter from William Harris declining to present the resolution of the Company to the Duke of Sussex. 11 January 1817.
51. Copy of the above resolution.
52. Report of a Committee on the refusal of William Harris to present the above resolution. 3 February 1817. 2 l.
53. Memorial of the liverymen and freemen of the Company on the proposed presentation of the honorary freedom and livery to the Duke of Sussex. 3 February 1817. 2 l.
54, 55. Printed addresses on behalf of the distressed poor in the north of London, especially the poor clock and watchmakers of the parish of St Luke, Middlesex. December 1816, January 1817.
56. Copy of advertisement by Mr Fearn in the Sunday newspaper of 2 January 1832, regarding bronze clocks, etc.
57. Letter from Mr W. Auld presenting to the Company the engraved portrait of Mr Reid. 15 March 1831.
58, 59. Letters regarding the placing of the Company's arms in one of the windows of the Great Hall of Christ's Hospital. 10 and 13 March 1841.
60, 61. Letters from Charles Frodsham Esq presenting the Company with a portrait of his father. 29 June 1858.
62. Letter from Thomas Reid thanking the Company for his election as an honorary freeman. 6 December 1825.
63–65. Two letters and printed paper relating to the presentation of the honorary freedom of the Company to Sir Jamsetjee Jeejeebhoy. January 1855.
66. Letter from Cursetjee Jamsetjee acknowledging the receipt of the freedom of the Company. 31 March 1855.
67. Letter from Sir Jamsetjee Jeejeebhoy acknowledging the receipt of the freedom of the Company. 31 March 1855.
68. Letter from Cursetjee Jamsetjee enclosing £150 for the charitable fund of the Company from Sir Jamsetjee Jeejeebhoy. 26 May 1855.
69. Copy of letter of thanks from the Company for the above gift. 7 July 1855.
70, 71. Letters of thanks to the Company from Cursetjee Jamsetjee and Sir Jamsetjee Jeejeebhoy. 26 June 1855.
72, 73. Letters from Justice Halliburton relating to his admission as an honorary freeman of the Company. 9 May 1855; 10 February 1857.
74. Letter from R. Hartley Kennedy, Alderman, upon the investments of the Company's funds. 29 March 1855.
75. Letter from R. Hartley Kennedy, Alderman and Sheriff-elect, inviting the Company to attend him in the procession to Westminster. 28 September, 1 October 1855.
76. Memorial of the Company to the Queen on behalf of R. Hartley Kennedy, Alderman. 6 May 1858. 2 l.
77–81. Letters from R. Hartley Kennedy, Alderman, to S. E. Atkins, Clerk of the Clockmakers' Company. 10 April 1855 to 23 March 1858.

937 – *continued*

82. Printed memorial of the inhabitants of Newcastle-on-Tyne to the Queen relating to the affairs of R. Hartley Kennedy, Alderman. 1858.
83. Printed letter from R. Hartley Kennedy, Alderman, to his ward, resigning the office of Alderman on sentence of imprisonment. 2 March 1858.
84. Letter from R. Hartley Kennedy to Mr S. E. Atkins. 1860.
85–94. Reports of the Library Committee, with lists of books and specimens for the museum acquired by the Company and correspondence from 10 January 1814 to 5 October 1821.
95. Letter to the Company relating to the Charity Trusts Bill. 1 May 1846.
96. Printed circular letter relating to the Charity Trusts Bill.
97. Petition of the Company to the House of Lords against the Charity Trusts Bill.
98. Printed petition of the Clothworkers' Company to the House of Lords for exemption from the above Bill.
99. Printed extract from the *Times* relating to the above petition. 4 July 1845.
100. Printed petition of the Merchant Tailors' Company for exemption from the operation of the Charity Trusts Bill.
101. Notices of the House with reference to the Charity Trusts Bill. 14 May 1846.
102. Documents relating to the fixing of a clock in the tower of the new Royal Exchange. July 1843. 10 l.
103. Printed transcript of notes of charges against Anthony Myers for having six gold watches with forged marks of the Goldsmiths' Company, taken at the Mansion House. 9 May 1850.

938 A folio volume containing papers and correspondence relating to foreign importations. 1807–52. 93 items. MS 3944

Contents
1. Proposed alterations and additions to the Act of Parliament for enabling His Majesty to levy a tax on foreign clocks and watches. 2 l.
1*a*. Outline of a plan for marking foreign watches. 2 l.
2. Return to Parliament of the number and amount of licences granted for selling gold or silver plate in Great Britain for ten years, 1807–16. (Printed sheet.)

(3–17.) Petitions of distressed watchmakers of Coventry, London, Roxburgh, etc. to Parliament, and proceedings thereon.

3. Printed petition of distressed watchmakers of Coventry to Parliament. 17 June 1817. Folio. 1817
Also another counter petition. Folio. London, 1817.
4. Petitions of watchmakers, presented 17 June, referred to a Select Committee. (Printed extract.)
5. Petition of watchmakers of London, and petition of clock and watchmakers of Roxburgh, to Parliament. 4 July 1817. Folio. London, 1817.
(Nos 3–5 are extracts from the printed Votes and Proceedings of the House of Commons.)
6. Petition of the distressed watchmakers of Coventry to the House of Commons. Broadside. (Undated; London, 1817.)
7. Letter from Joseph Butterworth to George Atkins, 2 September 1817, with reply on 4 September.

938 – *continued*

8. Letter from Joseph Hogan. 26 February 1818.
9. Draft reply of George Atkins to Joseph Butterfield (No. 7). 27 February 1818.
10. Announcement of resolutions passed by the committee appointed by the workmen in the different branches of the watch trade to consider the distress they are suffering and its causes, to endeavour to point out practical remedies, and to adopt the best means in their power of obtaining them. Broadside. (Undated; London, 1817.)
11. Memorandum to Peter Moore Esq, MP. 9 March 1818.
12. Petition of watchmakers of Aberdeen to Parliament. 25 February 1818.
13. Petitions of watchmakers of Berwick and of watch makers of Montrose to Parliament. 6 February 1818. (Nos 12 and 13 are extracts from the printed Votes and Proceedings of the House of Commons.)
14. Report of the Committee appointed to prevent the illicit importation of foreign clocks and watches. 18 May 1818. 2 l.
15. Resolutions passed at a meeting of the committee appointed for carrying into effect the petition of clock and watchmakers, held at the Anchor Tavern, West Orchard (Coventry), on Thursday 26 February 1818. Broadside, Coventry, 1818.
16. Address to the trade, adopted at a meeting of the Watchmakers' Committee held at the Anchor Tavern, West Orchard (Coventry), on Wednesday 17 February 1819. Broadside. Coventry, 1819.
17. Resolutions passed at a general meeting of the Watchmakers, held at the Anchor Tavern (Coventry) on 15 March 1819. Broadside. Coventry, [1819].
18. Heads of the clauses in the Bill proposed by the Committee of the Watch and Clock Trade. 2 l.
19. Proposed alterations and additions to the Act of Parliament for enabling His Majesty to levy a duty on foreign clocks and watches. 3 l.
20. A Bill for more effectually discovering the longitude at sea, etc. 9 March 1818. Folio. 1818.
21. A Bill to regulate the manufacture of clocks and watches. 14 June 1819. Folio. 1819.
22. Memorial of the Company to the Treasury. 5 March 1830. 2 l.

(22–43.) Letters, returns, etc., concerning the stamping of all foreign watches, and levying a duty thereon, etc.

23. Letter from watchmakers of Plymouth and Devonport. 20 June 1833.
24. Letter from the Board of Trade. 20 July 1833.
25. On the Liverpool application. 21 July 1833. 2 l.
26. Regulations first proposed. 12 July 1833. 2 l.
27. Letter from the Board of Trade. 22 July 1833.
28. Memorial of the clock and watch manufacturers to the Lords of the Treasury. Printed.
29, 30. J. Troup to the Board of Trade. 22 July 1833. 4 l. Further letter. 24 July 1833.
31. Reply from the Board of Trade to Mr Troup. 6 August 1833.
32. Result of interviews with Lord Althorp (7 August) and Mr P. Thompson (16 August). Statement for the consideration of Mr P. Thompson and the Board of Trade. 3 l.
33. Regulations at present under the consideration of the Lords of the Treasury. 27 August 1833. 2 l.

938 – *continued*

34. Calculation of the number of watches imported without paying duty.
35. J. Troup to the Board of Trade. 27 August 1833.
36. Reply from the Board of Trade to Troup's letter. 3 September 1833.
37. Board of Trade to Troup. 12 September 1833.
38. Troup to the Commissioners of the Customs. 13 September 1833.
39. Reply from the Board of Customs to Troup. 4 October 1833.
40. Troup to the Board of Trade. 28 October 1833.
41. Mr Troup to Mr Atkins. 31 October 1833.
42. From Mr Troup. 4 November 1833.
43. Troup to the Lords of the Privy Council for Trade. 28 October 1833.
44. A return to Parliament of the number of metal clocks and watches, and of movements, etc., exported and imported since 1825; ordered to be printed 5 July 1833. Folio.
45. Advertisements cautioning the public against purchasing foreign watches with English makers' names fraudulently affixed to them. 1823. Newspaper cuttings.

(46–69.) Letters, etc., upon the illicit importation of clocks and watches, and other matters.

46. Mr Ross to Mr Vulliamy. 16 June 1841.
47. Mr Ross to Mr Vulliamy. 18 June 1841.
48–51. M. Viel to Mr Vulliamy. Letters in French, on the subject of marking gold watches in France, etc.
52. Mr Vulliamy to Mr Ross. 26 June 1841. 4 l.
53. Mr Pons to Mr Vulliamy. 16 July 1841.
54. Letter in French from M. Viel to Mr Vulliamy on the seizure of watches by the officers of the Customs.
55. George Atkins to B. L. Vulliamy, enclosing printed cuttings of the Clockmakers' Company's advertisements.
56. Petition of clock and watch manufacturers to the Lords of the Treasury. 23 December 1841. Printed.
57. Copy of letter from B. L. Vulliamy to Lord Wharncliffe. 24 December 1841. 2 l.
58. Copy of answer from the Lords of the Treasury to the memorial of the Company. 29 January 1842.
59. Memorial of the Company to the Treasury. 9 December 1841. Printed. Folio.
60. Copy of answer to the above memorial from the Lords of the Treasury. 29 January 1842.
61. From Mr Sharp. 7 May 1842.
62. Copy of letter, signed 'A Watchmaker', to the *Morning Herald*. 19 May 1842. 2 l.
63. Copy of letter sent by Mr Vulliamy to the *Morning Herald*. 21 May 1842. 2 l.
64. J. MacGregor to B. L. Vulliamy. 4 July 1842.
65. Mr Vulliamy to Mr MacGregor. 9 July 1842.
66. Description of the mode of marking watches in France.
67. Account of the regulations connected with the levying of the duty and assaying and marking the cases of foreign gold watches imported into France.
68. Copies of several letters of Vulliamy, Atkins, and others. 5 l.
68A. Duplicate of 59 *ante*.
69. Vulliamy to Atkins. 24 February 1845.

(70–77.) Letters, etc., on the seizure at the Customs of watch-dials, watches, etc.

938 – *continued*

70. Mr Scanlan to consult the Secretary of the Watch-makers' Company about the expediency of the exportation of watch dials. 23 July 1848.
71. Atkins to Vulliamy. 24 July 1845.
72. Atkins to Scanlan. 26 July 1842.
73. Vulliamy to Atkins. 6 August 1845.
74. Scanlan to Vulliamy. 2 August 1845.
75. Scanlan to Vulliamy. 26 July 1845.
76. Copy of letter from Vulliamy to Mr Scanlan. 6 August 1845. 2 l.
77. Mr Walford to the Clockmakers' Company. 20 December 1845.
78. Petition of the Company to the House of Commons concerning the seizure of watches, etc., by the Customs, and the sale thereof. 8 February 1849. 2 l.

(79–93.) Letters on the above petition.
79. Mr Wright to Mr Atkins. 23 January 1849.
80. Atkins to Vulliamy. 30 January 1849.
81. From F. B. Adams. 25 January 1849.
82. Vulliamy to Atkins. 27 January 1849.
83. Copy of advertisement in the *Times, Herald, Chronicle, Post,* and *Daily News.* 25 January 1849.
84. Atkins to Vulliamy. 29 January 1849.
85, 86. Vulliamy to Atkins, with enclosure. 1 February 1849.
87. Mr Parker to Mr Atkins. 8 February 1849.
88. Petition of the Clockmakers' Company. Printed. Folio.
89. Vulliamy to Atkins. 29 January 1849.
90. Sir G. Cornewall Lewis to the Clockmakers' Company. 19 August 1850.
91. Extract from the minutes of a Court of the Clock-makers' Company, held 13 January 1851. 2 l.
92. Memorial of the Clockmakers' Company concerning the importation of foreign clocks, watches, etc. 5 August 1850. 4 l.
93. Further memorial on the above subject. 1 April 1852. 8 l.

939 A folio volume containing documents and correspondence relating to taxes and import duties on clocks and watches. 1787–98. 32 items.   MS 3945

Contents
1, 2. Letters from Mr Cottrell to Mr Vulliamy. 9 December 1786, 24 February 1787.
3. Proposal to insist on the marking of foreign clocks and watches to ensure the payment of duty on them. 2 l.
4. Letter from Mr Upjohn with reference to the above proposal.
5. Statement of reasons why French watches and clocks are lower in price than the English, which makes the importation of foreign watches undesirable or which should render them liable to a heavy duty. 4 l.
6. Letter from Edward Tutet, Master of the Clockmakers' Company, relating to the above proposed duties. 16 January 1787.
7. Letter from Stephen Cottrell to Mr Vulliamy appointing a meeting with the Lords of the Committee of Council for Trade. 21 February 1787.
8. Copy of the questions delivered by Order of the Lords of the Committee of Council for Trade to Messrs Vulliamy, Upjohn, Jackson, and Potter, for their answer in writing. 2 l.

939 – *continued*

9. Copy of a printed bill for granting to George III certain duties on clocks and watches. 5 July 1797.
10. Manuscript amendments and alterations to the above. 11 l.
11. Address of the Court of Assistants of the Clock-makers' Company to the Right Honourable William Pitt, Chancellor of the Exchequer, with relation to the proposed duties on clocks and watches (No. 5). 6 July 1797.
12. Additional address to Mr Pitt, protesting against an annual tax on every person using a watch or clock, and also containing a statement with reference to the standard of gold used in the manufacture of clocks and watches. 2 l.
13, 14. Further statements made to Mr Pitt, relating to a new standard of gold. 3 l.
15. Copy of letter from George Rose on behalf of Mr Pitt, enclosing papers received from the Goldsmiths' Company with reference to the standard of gold. 14 July 1797.
16. Resolution of the Goldsmiths' Company with reference to a change in the standard of gold appointed by law. 13 July 1797.
17. Letter from Mr Pitt acknowledging the receipt of the above address (No. 11) of the Committee (Court of Assistants) of Watchmakers, and promising to repeal the duties on clocks and watches. 18 July 1797.
18. Memorial of the Clockmakers' Company to Mr Pitt, relating to the duty on clocks and watches. 28 November 1797. 2 l.
19. Number and weight of gold and silver watch-cases stamped at Goldsmiths' Hall in 1796 and 1797.
20. Petition of the Clockmakers' Company to the House of Commons against the Act of Parliament imposing a duty on the users of clocks and watches. 1798. 5 l.
21, 22. Notices of Mr Pitt's consent to receive a deputation from the Company. November to December 1797.
23. Copy of note to Mr G. Rose, MP, from the Master of the Company, asking him to deliver an enclosure to Mr Pitt. 16 December 1797.
24. Above mentioned enclosure, with reference to the tax on clocks and watches, from the Master of the Clockmakers' Company. December 1797.
25. Letter to the Company from the trade requesting them to oppose the proposed tax on clocks and watches. 5 July 1797.
26. Answer of the Master and Wardens of the Clock-makers' Company to the summons to attend a deputation to Mr Pitt. 6 July 1797.
27. Note appointing a day for the reception of the above deputation by Mr Pitt. 6 July 1797.
28. Note to the Master and Wardens of the Company of Clockmakers, enclosing a copy of the Bill for imposing a tax on clocks and watches. 6 July 1797.
29. Memorandum relating to the reception of the above deputation (No. 26) by Mr Pitt. 7 July 1797.
29a. Note to Mr Pitt enclosing a copy of the representation made to the Clockmakers' Company, relating to the duty on clocks and watches. 7 July 1797.
29b. Note from Mr Rose, requesting the attendance of one or two members of the Company. 8 July 1797.
30. Letter of thanks from the Company to Mr Pitt for laying their petition before the House of Commons. 22 July 1797.

939 – *continued*

31. Letter from Mr Pitt relating to a deputation. 18 December 1797.
32. Letter from a Committee of conference with the Goldsmiths' Company on matters concerning the watch and clock making trade. 15 March 1798.

940 Contemporary copy of the charter of incorporation, 1631, granted to the Company by Charles I.
MS 3946

941 Original bye-laws of the Company signed by Lord Coventry, Lord Keeper of the Great Seal, Sir Thomas Richardson, Chief Justice of the Court of King's Bench, and Sir Robert Hall, Chief Justice of the Court of Common Pleas. 2 January 1631/32.   MS 3946A

942 A folio volume containing papers chiefly relating to the payment of quarterage. 1700–1818. 23 items.
MS 3947

Contents

1, 2a. Printed copies of the oath of every freeman of the Company of Clockmakers.
2, 3. Cases of the Company of Clockmakers and opinions of counsel relating to the following: 1. the payment of quarterage by Abraham Fromanteel; 2. the manufacture of a silver watch by Nicholas Vanstripe on which he illegally engraved the name of P. Gretton. 31 January 1700. 6 l.
4. Attorney's (T. Benn) bill for services in obtaining a livery for the Company. 4 September 1766. 2 l.
5. Attorney's (R. Gatty) bill for services done for the Company from November 1795 to May 1797. 7 l.
6. Attorney's bill due to R. Gatty. October 1796.
7. Abstract of the Charter of Incorporation and Bye-laws of the Company of Clockmakers. 4 l.
8. Declaration of John Wilkes Esq, Chamberlain, against John Allen for carrying on the trade of a watchmaker without being made free of the Clockmakers' Company, with the opinion of William Lambe. 7 May 1787. 8 l.
9. Declaration of John Wilkes Esq, Chamberlain, against John Allen to the same effect as the above. 2 September 1786. 5 l.
10. Judgment of the Lord Mayor against John Allen and warrant for his committal. 15 June 1787.
11. Notes and opinion of William Lambe, Special Pleader, in the above case of Wilkes versus Allen. 7 May 1787.
12. Letter from James Freshfield relating to the non-payment of his quarterage. 19 September 1796. Order from the Court to proceed against him. 10 October 1796.
13. Letter from James Freshfield relating to the above. 19 September 1796.
14, 15. Notices of proceedings against Freshfield in the Court of Common Pleas. 19 November 1796.
16. Declaration that the above notices were served.
17. Declaration against James Freshfield for non-payment of quarterage, 1797, containing an account of the Clockmakers' Company, their charter, privileges, and powers. 9 l.
18. Instructions to the Attorney for proceeding in the above case. 6 February 1797.
19. Additional copy of the above declaration (No. 17). 15 l.

942 – *continued*

20. Petition from Joseph Bramley against being compelled to take up the freedom of the Clockmakers' Company. 31 January 1797. 2 l.
21. Order of the Court of the Company of Clockmakers to the beadle to summon freemen of the Company for neglecting to pay quarterage. 2 July 1705.
22. Report of the Committee on the Quarterage Act.
23. Report of B. L. Vulliamy, Renter Warden, upon members who have not paid their quarterage. 30 November 1818.

943 Charter of incorporation granted to the Company by Charles I. 22 August 1631. Three membranes with illuminated heraldic borders; membrane I with portrait of sovereign enthroned, in coronation robes. Great seal on original cord in tin capsule. In contemporary tooled charter box.   MS 6430

944 Ratification of bye-laws. 11 August 1632. Four membranes with ornamental initial on membrane I; three seals on original cords in ivory skippets.
With supplementary bye-law (No. 53) relating to the refusal of a freeman to serve on his election as a livery-man. Nineteenth century. One membrane; no seal.
Both documents kept in contemporary charter box.
MS 6431

945 Copy of the charter incorporating the Company, 1631, with the bye-laws, 1631–32; examined by Edward Tutet and Charles Howse. The Act of Common Council for regulating the Company, passed 15 October 1765, authenticated by the signature of Sir James Hodges, Town Clerk. Compiled *c* 1786.   MS 3948

946 The charter, 22 August 1631 (= 7 Chas. I), bye-laws, grant of arms, charitable bequests, and other official Company documents, concerning foundation and constitution. Compiled *c* 1828. On p 123 are the Company's arms in colour, on vellum.   MS 3949
On the cover is an engraved brass plate, with the Arms of the City of London and the Company, bearing the following inscription:

'Death could not cause my love to die:
My love doth live though dead am I.
The free guift of Richard Morgan to the Clockmakers of London. Symon Hackett, Master, 1647; Thomas Alcock, Onesiphorus Helden, wardens. I Droeshout sculp., 31st January, 167½'

See plate 26.

947 The charter and bye-laws, with several other matters connected with the constitution of the Company. Also a list of the Masters, 1632–1716; Wardens, 1632–1712; and Assistants, 1631–97.
Note inside cover: 'This Booke is all that I had of Mrs. Jane Goodwin, after her Husband's decease, for my Nine Years service in Assisting him in the Clerk-ship of the Clockmakers Company. The collection was made for his private use, and no ways belongs to the Company; When I dye it will be worth to my Successor (whomsoever he shall be) Twenty Guineas, which I charge them whose hands it shall fall into not to part with it under. Witnes my hand, this 20th day of February, Anno. Dni. 1717. Francis Speidell.'

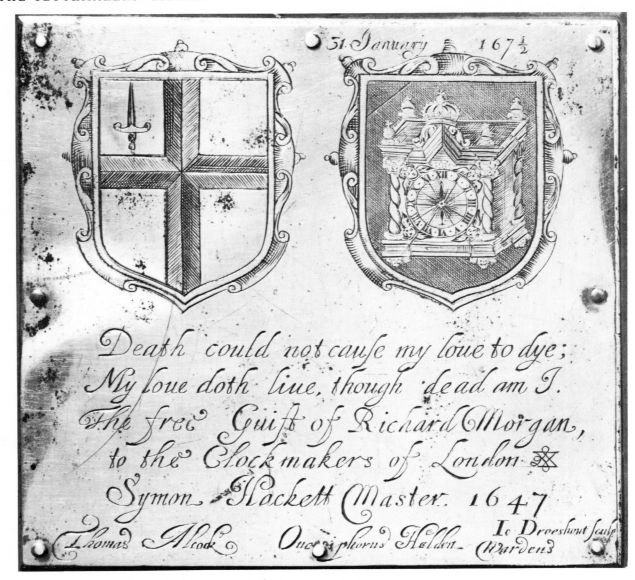

PLATE 26 An engraved brass plate on the cover of a book of documents connected with the early history of the Company, the arms being those of the City of London and the Clockmakers Company. Richard Morgan, the donor of the book, was a member of the Blacksmiths Company and in 1630 was a 'humble suitor' for obtaining the approval of the Sovereign for the incorporation, or official formation, of the Clockmakers Company. It would seem that he gave the book to the Company in 1647, and that the date '31 January 167½' was added in the year that the Company obtained the right to bear arms. By today's usage this date denotes 31 January 1672; until 1 January 1753 the civil, ecclesiastical and legal New Year's Day was 25 March, and to avoid confusion it is customary to give, for the intervening period, both the 'old style' and 'new style' dates, as here: 1671/2. (No. 946)

947 – *continued*

'1st April, 1745. – The Renter Warden was desired to give a guinea to Mr. Shuckburgh for a Book, now produced, which appeared to be of the hand-writing of Mr. Goodwin, a former clerk, containing copies of the Charter, Bye Laws, and other things relating to the Company.' [Court minutes].   MS 3950

948 A folio volume containing petitions to Parliament and other documents and correspondence relating to the importation, exportation and seizure of watches. 1717–1817.   83 items.   MS 3951

Contents

1. Petition to the House of Lords against a clause in the Act of Parliament against the running of prohibited goods, which relates to the exportation of clocks and watches. 12 March 1717.   2 l.
2. Petition to the House of Commons relating to the above.   2 l.
3. Memorial of the trade to the Company requesting a meeting to consider means for preventing the importation of foreign watches. 15 September 1780.   2 l.
4. Order of the Treasury with reference to the seizure of watches for export. 7 August 1789.
5. Printed copy of the Resolution of the Committee appointed to consider the distress suffered by workmen engaged in the watch trade.   Folio sh.
6. Printed proposal to alter the standard of gold from 22 carat to 18 carat.
7. Copy of a petition of the Goldsmiths' Company to the House of Lords against the above proposed Act of Parliament to prevent the running of prohibited goods. 10 March 1717.
8. Reasons of the Watchmakers for supporting the above Act.
9. Amended clause of the proposed Act of Parliament relating to the quality of the gold and silver to be used for ornamenting watches. 19 December 1718.
10. Clause to be inserted in the proposed Act of Parliament relating to the quality of the gold or silver in watches which are to be exported. 2 January 1718.
11. Minutes of the Court of the Company relating to the seizure of watches by the Customs officers, and a list of prices of certain watches. 26 November 1718.   2 l.
12. Draft of an Act against enticing artificers to emigrate. 1718.   6 l.
13. Attorney's bill for costs of obtaining a copy of the original order of King James II in connection with a patent.
14. Copy of the *London Gazette*, 27 December–30 December 1777, containing an advertisement of the Company forbidding watchmakers to make bad watches and engrave on them the names of good makers.
15. Letter from the Customs House to the Clerk of the Company with reference to the seizure of certain watches. 13 July 1790.
16. Heads of the Clauses in the Bill proposed by the Committee of the Clock and Watch Trade, with an account of the manner in which they were settled. 15 February 1811.   2 l.
17. Letter from the Customs House to Mr Atkins with reference to the seizure of watches. 18 June 1790.
18–20. Letters from members of the trade to the Company relating to the seizure of watches on their premises. August–September 1790.

948 – *continued*

21. Letter from the Secretary of the Customs summoning members of the Company to attend the Board with reference to the seizure of certain watches. 31 December 1789.
22, 23. Minutes of the proceedings of the Court of Assistants of the Company of Clockmakers at meetings held in February 1790 and February 1802.
24. Thirteen letters from L. Naylor giving notice of proceedings against the Customs Officers for the seizure of watches, etc., dated 7 November 1789.
25. Letter from the Office of Trade summoning members of the Clockmakers' Company to attend a meeting. 18 March 1808.
26. Letter from Alderman Shaw offering his services to the Company on the re-opening of Parliament. 22 January 1808.
27. Letter from the Treasury refusing to alter the method of inspecting watches for exportation. 1 April 1808.
28. Copy of a memorial, presented to the Customs, relating to the inspection of watches for export.
29. Questions submitted to members of the trade relating to the engraving of the maker's name on watches.
30. Letter from the Treasury relating to the mode of inspecting watches intended for exportation. 24 May 1808.
31. Report of the Committee of Customs to the Treasury concerning the inspection of goods for export.
32. Letter from Alderman Shaw with regard to a conference with the Court of the Company. 6 May 1809.
33. Letter from the Secretary of Customs with reference to the inspection of watches for exportation. 11 February 1809.
34. Printed statement by the Goldsmiths' Company, of reasons against the clause in a Bill for giving liberty to export clocks and watches containing gold or silver without declaring the quality of the precious metal. 1717?
35. Extract from the *Morning Advertiser* regarding the Bill in Parliament for regulating manufacture. 2 March 1811.
36. Minutes of a conference between a Committee of the Clockmakers' Company and a Committee of the Trade with regard to persons entitled to carry on the art of watchmaking.
37. Report of the Clerk of the Company on his interview with the Board of Excise. 24 October 1810.
38. Extracts from the Letters Patent granted to the Company by Charles I, dated 22 August 1632.   3 l.
39. Printed statement regarding the decay of the watch trade, with suggestions for its improvement.   Folio. 1812.
40. Report of a Committee to the Court of Assistants of the Company on a watch belonging to Sir Charles Flint. 10 January 1814.
41. Letter from J. Beckett informing the Company of the expulsion of M. Moreau from the kingdom by the Prince Regent on the 2 August 1813. 14 January 1814.
42. Letter from H. Clarke asking for the Minute-book of the Company for Freemen and Apprentices. May 1814.
43–45. Letters relating to the presentation of a petition to Parliament. 3–19 May 1814.
46. Letter of Thomas Day relating to the above petition. 30 June 1814.
47. Draft letter from the Company relating to the above petition.   2 l.

948 – *continued*

48. Letter of Justin T. Vulliamy asking for a copy of the above petition. 8 October 1814.
49. Draft report of the Committee appointed by the Court of the Company to make regulations to remedy the distressed state of the trade. 25 February 1814. 2 l.
50. Report of the Committee for the suppression of mal-practices in the trade. 29 April 1814.
51. Letter from the Duke of Buckingham permitting his watch to be brought by Mr Vulliamy for the inspection of the Company. 23 December 1814.
52. Letter from Mr Vulliamy to the Company. 20 July 1814.
53. Letter from the Duke of Newcastle concerning a watch made by Barwise. 1 March 1814.
53a. Petition of the Company to the House of Commons asking for remedies for the distressed state of the trade. 23 May 1814.
54. Letter from P. Moore to the above Committee (No. 49). 5 March 1818.
55. Printed copy of the resolutions passed at a meeting of the master manufacturers and tradesmen of London and Westminster held to consider the best means to preserve and promote the prosperity of their trade. Folio. 14 January 1814.
56. Printed minutes of the proceedings at a meeting of practical clock and watch makers and workmen of London and Westminster held 11 February 1814. Folio.
57. Printed address from the Committee of Practical Clock and Watch Makers to all practical artisans. 11 February 1814.
58. Letter from J. T. Vulliamy enclosing a report of the proceedings of the above Committee. 19 February 1814.
59. Printed letter announcing a general meeting and asking for support. Enclosure to the above. 14 February 1814.
60. Copy of the *London Gazette* for 1 March 1814, containing an announcement of a meeting of the Company for the purpose of considering a petition to Parliament.
61. Printed letter announcing a meeting of practical artisans. 2 March 1814.
62. Printed report of the Committee of the Trade after a third meeting on 1 March 1814. Folio.
63. Printed provisions of a proposed Act of Parliament to be entitled 'the Clock and Watchmakers Act'. Folio sh.
64. Printed summons to a special court of the Freemen of the Company, to be held 7 March 1814, to oppose the passing of any measure to the detriment of the welfare and protection of the Company and of the individual freemen.
65, 66. Printed petitions to Parliament to remedy the bad state of trade.
67. Printed letter relating to the engraving of the names of English makers on foreign clocks and watches. 1 June 1814.
68. Printed resolutions of a meeting of practical artisans interested in the British manufactory of clocks and watches, held 2 June 1814.
69. Printed letter transmitting the above resolutions.
70. Printed notice of a further meeting of artisans to be held 25 October 1814.
71. Report of the Company of the Committee for preventing the illicit introduction of foreign watches, after the

948 – *continued*

presentation of the petition to Parliament. 8 January 1816. 2 l.
72. Report of the above Committee to the Court of the Company. 31 December 1816.
73. Advertisement of the Company for insertion in the *Times* and the *Morning Advertiser*, with directions for freemen who are applicants for relief. 19 January 1817.
74. Printed circular of the Company, publishing the leading cause of the distress in the trade. 20 February 1817.
74a. Printed report on the destitute state of the working classes in the watch and clock trade, with a list of donations received.
75–77. Letters on the above subject. March 1817. 4 l.
78, 79. Letters to Lord Sidmouth, and his reply, on the above subject. April 1817.
80. Letter from the Treasury. April 1817.
81. Memorial to Lord Sidmouth, Secretary of State, on the distressed state of the trade. 21 April 1817. 4 l.
82, 83. Letter to and answer from Lord Sidmouth on the above, 1817.

949 A folio volume containing miscellaneous papers relating to the binding of apprentices, paying of quarterage, patents, inventions, and seizing of watches and movements, etc. 1699–1717. 14 items. MS 3952

Contents

1. Copy of the opinion of Mr Duncan Dee, one of the City Counsel and afterwards Common Serjeant, as to the binding of apprentices and persons using other trades. 22 February 1699.
2. Copy of the case and opinions of Mr Sam. Dodd and Con. Phipps. 31 January 1700. 4 l.
3. Case as to the seizing of watches and movements belonging to Mr John Billie. 1686–87.
4. Copy of the petition of John Hutchinson to the House of Commons for securing the property of a movement invented by him for the most exact measuring of time both in motion and at rest.
5. Copy of the petition of the Company of Clockmakers to the House of Commons against the above. 20 May 1712. Signed by twelve members of the Company.
6. The Clockmakers' reasons against Mr Hutchinson's pretended invention. (Printed.)
7. Reasons for Mr Hutchinson's Bill in answer to the Clockmakers' objections. (Printed.)
8. The Clockmakers' further reasons against Mr Hutchinson's Bill and printed reasons. (Printed.)
9. Further reasons for Mr Hutchinson's Bill, in answer to the Clockmakers' further objections. (Printed.)
10. Report of the Company's proceedings in order to oppose the passing of a Bill in Parliament in favour of the above Patent of Mr Hutchinson (No. 4). 7 July 1712. 2 l.
11. Instructions for the Company as to attending the Parliamentary Committee called to consider Hutchinson's proposed Bill. 30 May 1712.
12. Names of gentlemen serving on the Committee convened by Hutchinson to draft his proposed Bill.
13. Report of the proceedings of the Company in opposing Clay's patent. 14 January 1716. 7 l.
14. Order of the Lord Mayor (Sir Thomas Abney), 7 May 1701, upon Mr Abraham Fromanteel, on his refusal to serve in the office of Steward.

950 Copy of the bye-laws of 1631/32, preceded by index. 18th century.   MS 3953

951 Report of the committee appointed to obtain counsel's opinion on the powers contained in the charter etc. for compelling clockmakers, freemen of other companies, residing within the City or within ten miles thereof, to become members of this company. 1 February 1796.   MS 3954

952 Copy of the Charter of 1631. Mid-18th century.
                                                      MS 3955

953 Brief notes on the history of the Company. 2 November 1778 to 18 January 1790. Indexed. MS 3956

954 A list of the freemen, denoting those admitted to, or excused from serving on, the livery, c 1767–1813.
                                                      MS 3957

955 A list of the freemen who pay quarterage, as on the books, but who are not on the livery, with notes of addresses, trades, and financial status. 1811. MS 3958

956 A list of 223 freemen who pay quarterage, arranged alphabetically, 1811–17. With trades and some addresses.   MS 3959

957 List of freemen, 1811–97. Compiled by Henry Charles Overall, Clerk of the Company. The names are written on small slips of paper and pasted down in chronological order under each letter.   MS 3960

958 A list formed by Mr Benjamin Vulliamy, in 1782, of 286 persons carrying on trade as clock and watch-makers, arranged alphabetically. With addresses.
                                                      MS 3961

959 Topographical list of clock and watchmakers, with addresses, in London, with a short list of members of the Company resident outside London and in America, Gibraltar, Antigua, Guernsey, Jamaica, and Barbados. c 1813. Possibly compiled by Henry Clarke, citizen and Clockmaker.   MS 3962

960 A list of watch-case, pendant and glass makers, joint finishers, springers and line gilders and coverers; arranged alphabetically, with the names (in most cases) of the persons to whom they were apprenticed. Early 19th century.   MS 3963

961 A folio volume containing memoranda, descriptions, observations and correspondence relating to a variety of matters, mostly mechanical, collected by Alexander Cumming 1766–1812. 35 items. MS 3964

Contents
1. Memorandum on Lord Bute's small organ, giving some account of its mechanism. 29 June 1777.
2. Description of a globular clock 'that shows at one view the mean time in all places that are delineated on the Terrestial Globe, with the difference of time in any two places, Sun's place in the ecliptic, and relative position in regard to the Earth', with remarks by A. Cumming. 3 l.
3. Memorandum for the machine for measuring the velocity or pressure of the winds (with diagram).
4. Scheme for showing the strength of the wind by its pressure on the surface of mercury or other fluid. Diagram (signed A.C.).

961 – *continued*
5. A scheme for showing the motions of the sun, moon, etc.
6. Account of the action of a timekeeper, by A. Cumming. 13 August 1771.
7, 8. Description and drawing of the mechanism of the above.
9. Two letters, and remarks, on Cumming's 'Essay on Clockwork'. Cutting from the *Gentleman's Magazine*, June 1767, pp 301–303.
10. Comparative observations of the barometer for ascertaining heights.
11. Observations on the barometer at Snowdon and Bangor.
12. Observations on the barometer at Luton Park and London, 9–19 September 1770.
13. Comparative observations on the barometer at Luton and London.
14–16. Experiments made with the barometer at Luton, 7 September 1773. 3 l.
17. Observations made on the barometer in Bond Street, 12 December 1773.
18. Remarks on the quantity of water raised by the wheel and buckets, and by the pump, at the farm at Luton Park.
19. Preparatory experiments to ascertain the best sizes of ropes, and the most advantageous velocities of the rope, for raising water by the new hydraulic machine, made at Windsor by order of His Majesty, 25 January 1783.
20. Further remarks on the hydraulic machine at Windsor. 25 January 1783.
21. Experiments made with the new hydraulic engine, Belmont Castle, August and September 1783.
22. A notebook in the handwriting of Alexander Cumming. 19 l.
    Pp 1–10 give data (some personal) of what occurred at the meeting in 1763 of the special commissioners appointed by the Board of Longitude to hear John Harrison's explanation of the mechanism of his longitude watch, H.4.
    Pp 11–19 contain Cumming's remarks on his essays concerned with the pendulum and other mechanical matters.
    See also **976–978** *post.*
23. Upon the raising of weights. 10 November 1768. 30 l.
24. Review of the 'Dissertation on the influence of gravitation considered as a mechanic power, by Alex. Cumming', a printed cutting from the *British Critic*, September 1805, pp 276–279, with letter of Mr Cumming to the editor in reply (March 1806, pp 332–336).
25. Remarks on an astronomical clock (with figure). 2 l.
26. To find how much the barometer will be affected by heat.
27. Printed cutting, apparently by A. Cumming, on the subject of pendulums.
28. Properties of the magic alarm, by means of which many pleasing and surprising tricks may be played in the manner of Comus.
29. Scheme by Professor Rassel, of Edinburgh, for illustrating the centrifugal force of whirling bodies (with diagram).
30. Method of making glass globules of great magnifying powers, from Dela Torre, 1776. 2 l.
31. To make an electrical machine (with diagram).

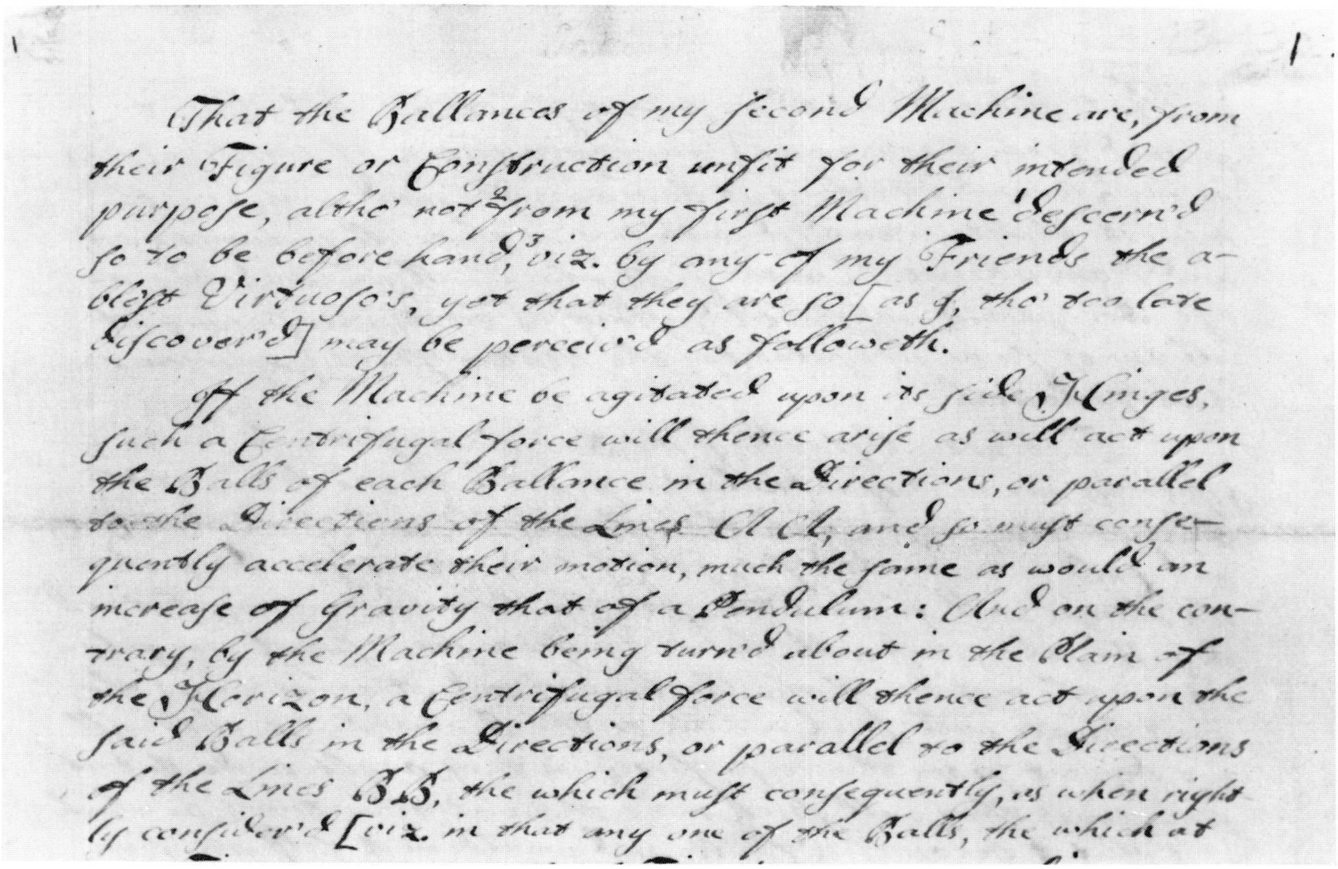
That the Ballances of my Second Machine are, from
their Figure or Construction unfit for their intended
purpose, altho' not from my first Machine deserv'd
so to be before hand, viz. by any of my Friends the a-
blest Virtuoso's, yet that they are so [as is, tho' too late
discover'd] may be perceiv'd as followeth.
If the Machine be agitated upon its side Hinges,
such a Centrifugal force will thence arise as will act upon
the Balls of each Ballance in the Directions, or parallel
to the Directions of the Lines Cl Cl, and so must consequently accelerate their motion, much the same as would an
increase of Gravity that of a Pendulum: And on the con-
trary, by the Machine being turn'd about in the Plain of
the Horizon, a Centrifugal force will thence act upon the
said Balls in the Directions, or parallel to the Directions
of the Lines BB, the which must consequently, as when right-
ly consider'd [viz. in that any one of the Balls, the which at

PLATE 27 The title and the opening eleven lines of an essay written by John Harrison *c* 1740–41: 'That the Ballances of my Second Machine are, from their Figure or Construction unfit for their intended purpose'. In this essay Harrison explains why it was necessary for him to discard his second longitude timekeeper, H.2, which had bar-shaped balances and four balance springs, and replace it with a new timekeeper, H.3, which would have circular balances and only one balance spring. This essay may have been a draft for a very similar essay (see No. 973, items 5–7). (No. 973)

961 – *continued*

31*a*. Recipe for paste.
32. Process for preparing a composition for covering flat roofs.
33. Report of the arbitrators appointed to settle the price of the clock made by Mr William Hardie for the Royal Observatory, Greenwich. 26 March 1812.
34. Letter of Alex. Cumming relating to carriage wheels, dated 2 October 1804. 3 l.
34*a*, 35. Calculations by A. Cumming and J. South (Sir James South, FRS?) to determine the Longitude of Kensington. *c* 1800.

962 Libary committee. Book of receipts and expenditure. 1814–29. MS 3965

963 Library committee. Loan issue book. 1819–42. MS 3966

964 Library committee. Minute book. 2 July 1814 to 12 December 1836. MS 3967

965 Library committee. Reports and books added. 1814–19. MS 3968

966 A table or index of several petitions and orders of the Court of Aldermen about obtaining the Clockmakers' charter (including tables of the principal points contained in the charter and ordinances of the company), 1629–33. Compiled *c* 1808. MS 3969

967 Grant of arms to the Company, dated 31 January 1671/72, by Sir Edward Walker Kt, Garter King of arms, in pursuance of the charter of incorporation granted by Charles II. With signature and seal of office. The seal is reappended by new cords. The tray of the original seal box, covered with gilt tooled leather, is shown. 1 skin vellum; illuminated coat of arms. MS 3970

968 Sundry papers of 1816–17 dealing with Court matters and charitable awards. MS3971

969 Scrapbook containing letters connected with the everyday running of the Company, including the museum and library, livery dinners, etc. 1832–1930. MS 3988

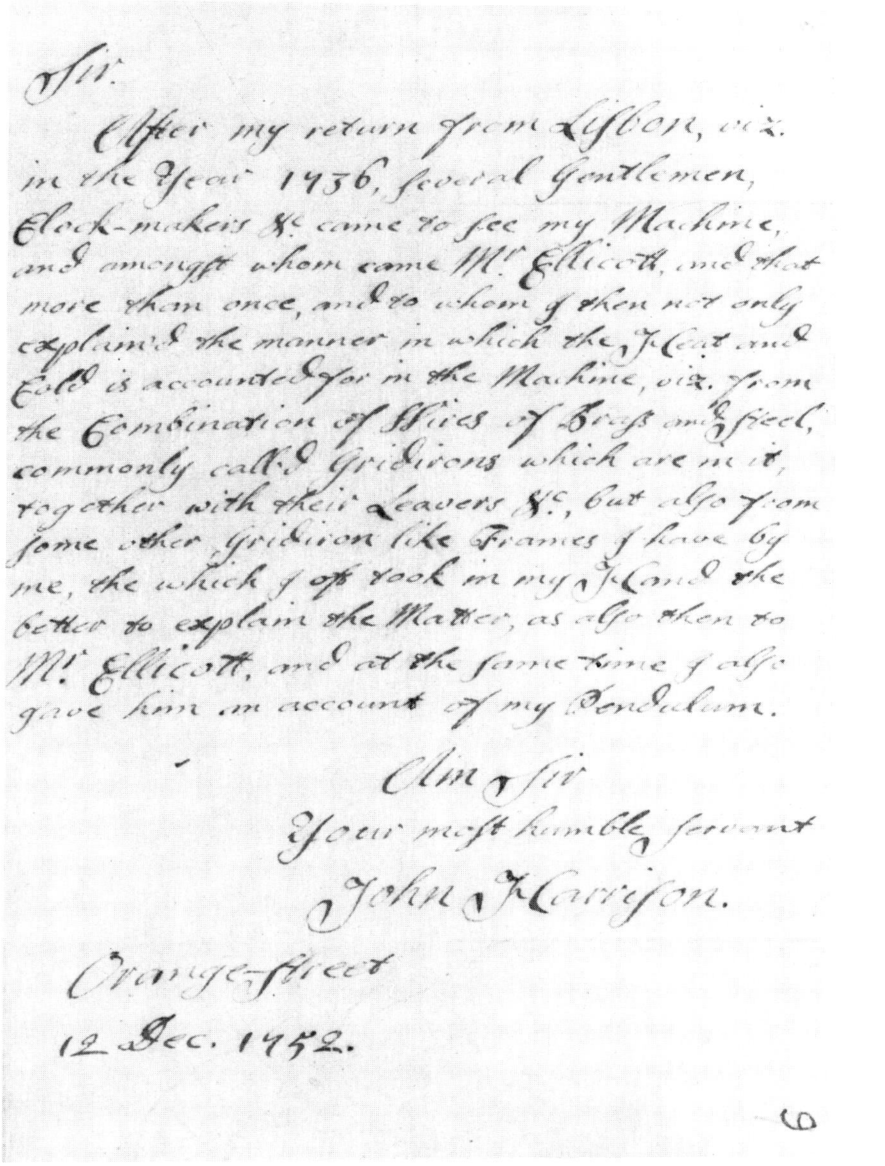

Sir.

After my return from Lisbon, viz.
in the Year 1736, several Gentlemen,
Clock-makers &c came to see my Machine,
and amongst whom came Mr Ellicott, and that
more than once, and to whom I then not only
explain'd the manner in which the Heat and
Cold is accounted for in the Machine, viz. from
the Combination of Wires of Brass and Steel,
commonly call'd Gridirons which are in it,
together with their Leavers &c, but also from
some other Gridiron like Frames I have by
me, the which I oft took in my Hand the
better to explain the Matter, as also then to
Mr Ellicott, and at the same time I also
give him an account of my Pendulum.

                    I'm Sir
              Your most humble servant
                John Harrison.

Orange-street

12 Dec. 1752.

PLATE 28 Holograph letter, dated 12 December 1752, from John Harrison to James Short, FRS, the optician, concerning Harrison's first marine timekeeper, H.1, and its gridiron temperature compensation. Short has added his comments at the end of the letter. (No. 973)

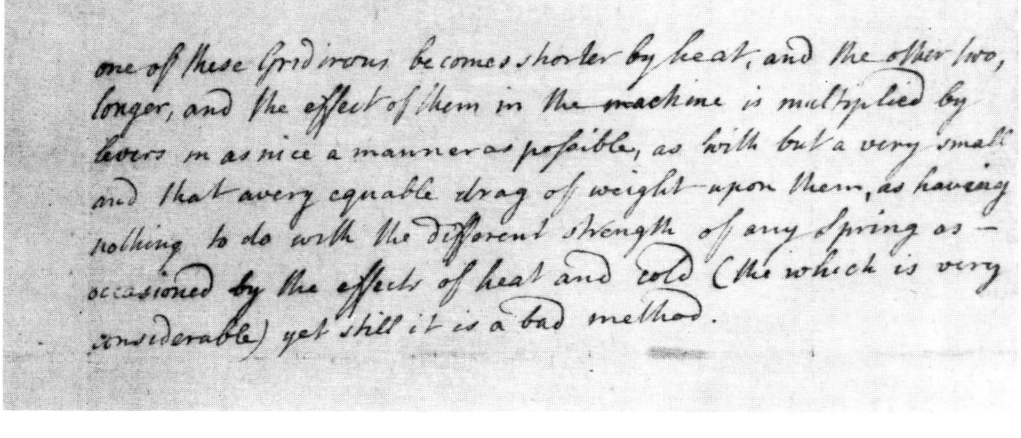

one of these Gridirons becomes shorter by heat, and the other two,
longer, and the effect of them in the machine is multiplied by
levers in as nice a manner as possible, as with but a very small
and that avery equable drag off weight upon them, as having
nothing to do with the different strength of any spring as —
occasioned by the effects of heat and cold (the which is very
considerable) yet still it is a bad method.

95

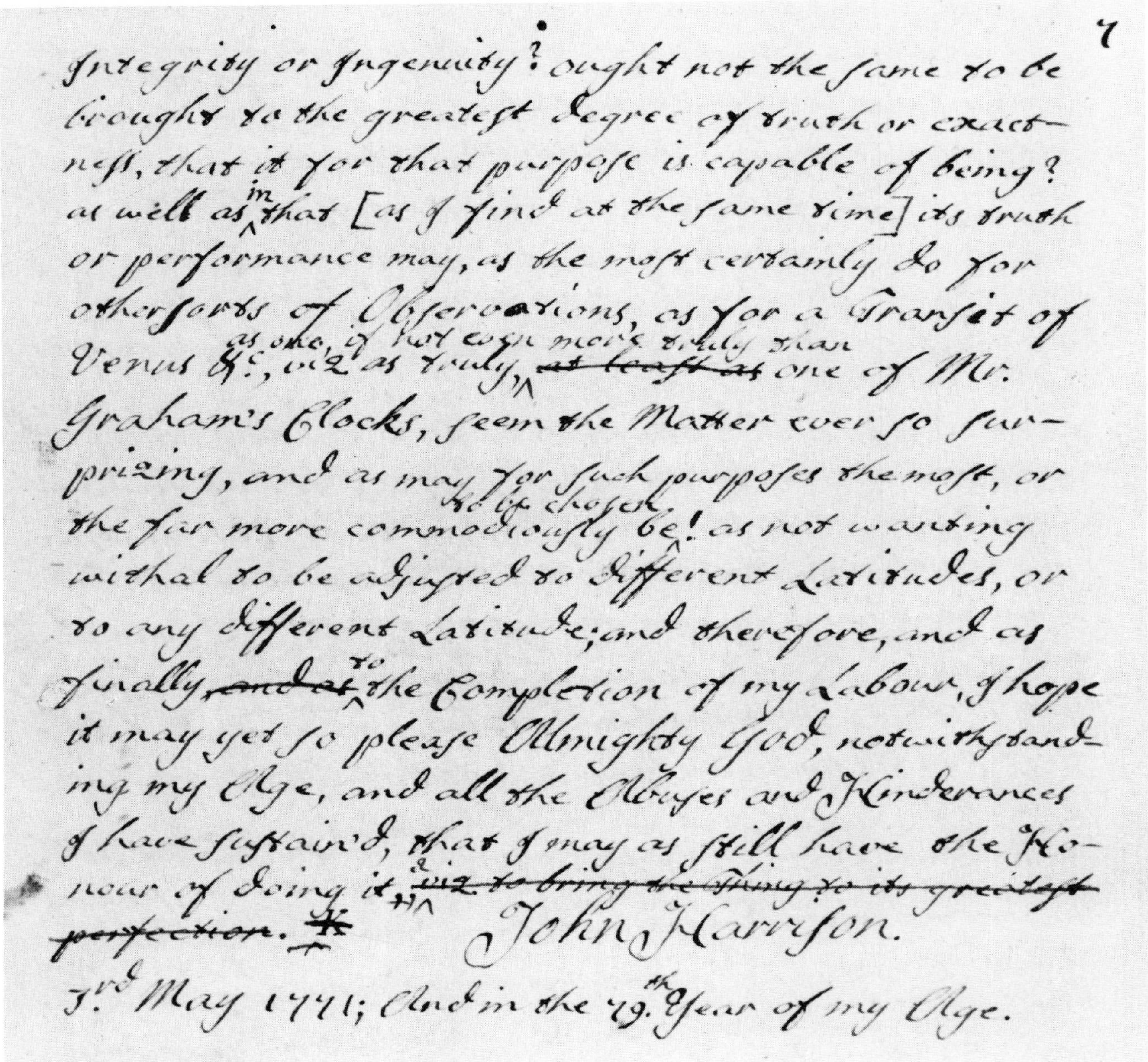

Integrity or Ingenuity? ought not the same to be brought to the greatest degree of truth or exactness, that it for that purpose is capable of being? as well as in *that [as I find at the same time] its truth or performance may, as the most certainly do for other sorts of Observations, as for a Transit of Venus &c., viz as truly,* as one, if not even more truly than ~~at least as~~ *one of Mr. Graham's Clocks, seem the Matter ever so surprizing, and as may for such purposes the most, or* to be chosen *the far more commodiously be! as not wanting withal to be adjusted to different Latitudes, or to any different Latitude; and therefore, and as* finally ~~and at~~ to *the Completion of my Labour, I hope it may yet so please Almighty God, notwithstanding my Age, and all the Abuses and Hinderences I have sustain'd, that I may as still have the Honour of doing it* viz ~~to bring the thing to its greatest perfection.~~ **John Harrison.**

3rd May 1771; And in the 79th Year of my Age.

PLATE 29 The final page of a long essay, written by John Harrison in 1771, entitled 'Some account of the Pallats &c. of my Second made Watch for the Longitude' (H.5). In the last five lines before his signature Harrison expresses his feelings: '. . . I hope it may yet so please Almighty God, not withstanding my age, and all the Abuses and Hinderences I have sustained, that I may still have the honour of doing it.' He is referring to his plan to alter the shape of the curved backs to the diamond verge pallets of his second longitude watch, H.5, which he considered would then enable H.5 to perform 'as truly as one, if not even more truly, than one of Mr Graham's clocks, seem the matter ever so surprising.' (No. 973)

970 Clerks' letter books, 1808–56 and 1879–1921.
Vol 1. 1808–56   Vol 3. 1903–19
     2. 1879–1903   4. 1919–21
MS 10554

971 List of freemen, 1631–1896. Compiled alphabetically (with additions) from a MS list made by H. C. Overall, former Clerk of the Company, by Charles Atkins. c 1900. Photocopy.   MS 11568

Harrison (John), 1693–1776: MSS and printed sources
972 Holograph manuscript dated 7 April 1763, including two pages of diagrams.
In three parts: pp 1–102, 'An explanation of my watch or timekeeper for the longitude . . .'; pp 103–119, 'A description of the nature or phenomenon of ballances as found from experience in my 3ᵈ machine; or the solution of a seemingly paradox therein'; pp 120–146, additions to the preceding two parts.   MS 3972/1

973 Various essays, remarks, and calculations by John Harrison and his son William, including a copy of the latter's will. c 1740–1814. John Harrison describes the fundamental errors in his longitude timekeeper, H.2, and explains why he built H.3. In a paper, dated 3 May 1773, he lays down his final calculations for the curved backs of his diamond watch pallets. (A full analysis of the contents is inserted in the volume.)
See plates 27–29.   MS 3972/2

974 Mechanical notes and drawings compiled by Harrison and his son William, c 1726–72, comprising information on Harrison's five longitude timekeepers as well as on his 'lesser watch'. With grasshopper escapement diagrams and turret clock data. (A full analysis of the contents is inserted in the volume.)
See plates 30–33.   MS 3972/3

975 Journal, 1761–66, relating to the testing of John Harrison's chronometer for the determining of longitude at sea in accordance with Stat. 12 Anne, c 15. Possibly compiled by Walter Williams, c 1766. 1 volume. Photocopy.   MS 3972A
Williams was friend and legal adviser to William Harrison (son of John): *see* H. Quill, *John Harrison, the Man who found Longitude*, 1966, pp 83–84. The journal contains accounts of John and William Harrison's dealings with the Board of Longitude, the Admiralty, the Astronomer Royal, etc.; of John's petitioning to Parliament for the payment of his prize, and the actual testing of the Longitude Watch H.4 on voyages to Jamaica and Barbados.

976 A folio volume containing papers, documents, correspondence, pamphlets, newspaper cuttings, Acts of Parliament, etc. concerning John Harrison. They were collected by Alexander Cumming as a result of his appointment in 1763 as one of the Special Commissioners authorized by the Act 3 Geo. III c XIV to hear and adjudicate on Harrison's expected explanation of the mechanism of his longitude timekeeper, H.4. 1763–74. 25 items.   MS 3973

Contents
1. Draft of a letter from Andrew Dickie, watchmaker, to the Earl of Morton, asking to be excused attending Harrison's expected explanations of his longitude watch, H.4, in 1763. 1 l.

976 – *continued*
2. Minutes of the first meeting of the Special Commissioners appointed by Act 3 Geo. III c XIV to hear Harrison's explanations of his longitude timekeeper, H.4. These minutes record their views on how Harrison's explanations should be made. 13 April 1763. 2 l.
3. Copy of John Harrison's letter to the Commissioners, in which he objects to their requirements for his explanations. 20 April 1763. 2 l.
4. Minutes of a meeting of the Commissioners at which they decided on a reply to Harrison's letter. 23 April 1763. 2 l.
5. Copy of Harrison's letter to the Commissioners saying that he cannot agree to their requirements. 2 May 1763. 2 l.
6. Letter from John Harrison to Mr A. L. Cammin (Alexander Cumming) stating his readiness to explain his timekeeper. A. Cumming has added a draft of his reply. 23 June 1763. 1 l.
See plate 34.
7. Letter from the Earl of Morton to Mr Cumming summoning him to a meeting at the Admiralty. 30 June 1763. 1 p.
8. Summary by A. Cumming of the proposals that had been put to Harrison and the latter's replies. 13 April 1763. 1 l.
See also **961**, No. 22, p. 3.
9. Record by A. Cumming of the further proposals that were put to Harrison and his replies. 23 April 1763. 1 l.
9a. Queries by A. Cumming concerning John Harrison's unique escapement used in his longitude timekeeper. 6 l.
10. List of seventeen queries drawn up by A. Cumming in an attempt to clarify the meaning of Act 3 Geo. III c XIV. 6 July 1763. 4 l.
10a. A copy of the above. Unsigned but of the same date.
11. Signed statement by A. Cumming concerning his reservations before agreeing to certify that Harrison had fulfilled the requirements of Act 3 Geo. III c. XIV. 6 July 1763. 2 pp.
11a. Copy of the above, unsigned. 6 July 1763. 2 l.
12. Minutes of the meeting of the Commissioners at which they decided that Harrison's proposals did not fulfil the meaning of Act 3 Geo. III c XIV. 7 July 1763. 2 l.
13. Some particulars relative to the Discovery of the Longitude . . . list of the present commissioners. 39p. Printed pamphlet. 8vo. London, 1765.
14. Remarks on a Pamphlet lately published by the Rev Mr Maskelyne under the Authority of the Board of Longitude. By John Harrison. 34p. Printed pamphlet. 8vo London, 1767. (*See* **415** *ante*.) These 'Remarks' refer to the official publication by the Rev N. Maskelyne, *An Account of the Going of Mr John Harrison's Watch* . . . (*see* **567** *ante*).
15. Minutes of the proceedings of the Commissioners appointed by Act of Parliament for the discovery of the longitude at sea, at their meetings on 25, 28 and 30 May and 13 June 1765. (Printed.) 4to. (London?) 1765.
16. A succint account of the proceedings relative to the discovery of the longitude at sea, by means of artificial time keepers, particularly Mr Harrison's . . . Extract from the *Annual Register*, pp 113–133, 1765. (Printed.) 8vo. London, 1765.

continued on page **108**

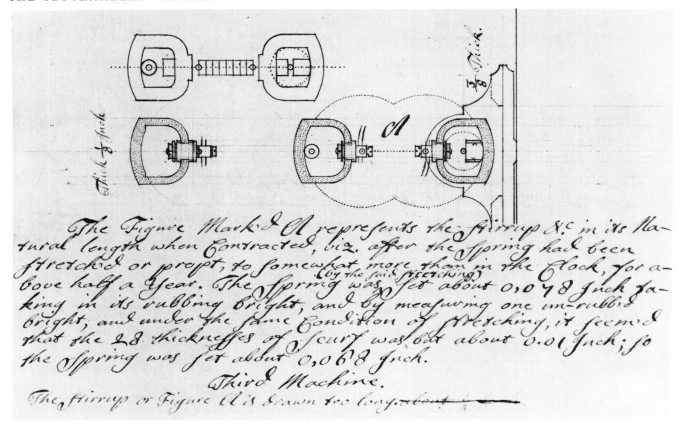

The Figure Mark'd A represents the stirrup &c. in its Natural length when Contracted, viz. after the spring had been stretched or prest, to somewhat more than in the Clock, for above half a Year. The spring was (by the said stretching) set about 0,078 Inch taking in its rubbing bright, and by measuring one un-rubb'd bright, and under the same Condition of stretching, it seem'd that the 2 8 thicknesses of scurf was but about 0.01 Inch; so the spring was set about 0,068 Inch.

Third Machine.

The stirrup or Figure A is drawn too long. about

Third Machine,

The lower Pevet of the stirrup was requir'd to be smaller, viz. than as here (on the other side) describ'd, so its whole Diameter is but 0,3/16 + Inch; but both the Pevets [for the future] may better be somewhat smaller still, but with still letting the Diameter of the lower be to that of the upper as 3 to 2, or there abouts; Not but that the lower Pevet might be as small as the other if so requir'd, the Matter being that the smaller each Pevet, or either one Pevet is, the slower greater Vibrations are render'd with respect to lesser.

PLATE 30 A descriptive drawing (with verso) made by John Harrison at some time between 1741 and 1760 of a 'stirrup' device designed for use in his third longitude timekeeper, H.3, in an attempt to obtain isochronism from the two interconnected circular balances and the single balance spring. From examination of H.3 it is clear that Harrison experimented with various devices in an attempt to obtain this isochronism, and it is believed that this drawing represents a device subsequently discarded and replaced by his saddle-piece. The latter is still in position in H.3 and has been described and illustrated by Commander R. T. Gould, in the *Horological Journal*, April 1932 (see No. 451). (No. 974)

a b   Note, the distance between the two Lines a, b, is right in this Draught, but is somewhat too great in the Draughts to which this belongs: And it is to be observed that one of the Pillars must be plac'd a little farther from the end of the Ballance Spring. ~~But it is to be noted, see below~~

Rad. 4½ Inch.

But it is to be noted, that what I thought of gaining, as in this Draught &c. viz: from the Ballance being transfer'd to the other side of a Watch I afterwards considered would be nothing, or at least very immaterial; hence, as in common the most proper.

PLATE 31   John Harrison's drawing of his 'lesser watch', mentioned by him to the Board of Longitude on 19 June 1755. The diameter of the watch plates in the actual drawing is 53 mm. It is not known whether this watch was ever completed. (No. 974)

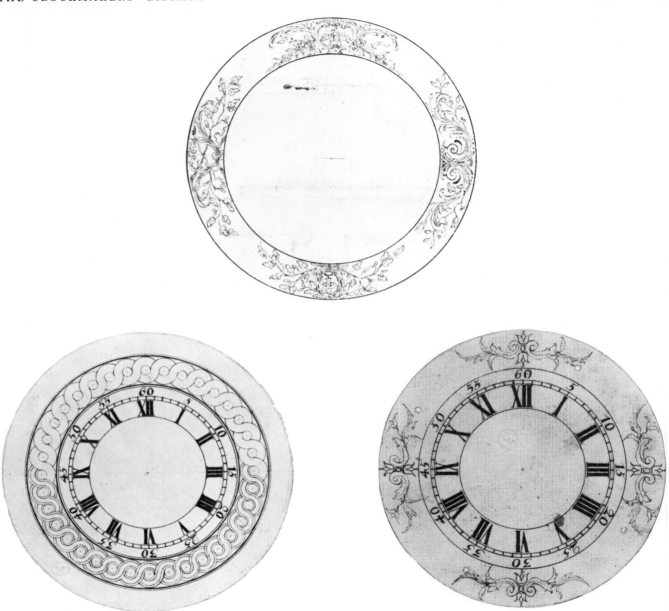

PLATE 32   Three designs for large enamel watch dials. They were presumably
drawn by John Harrison, but the manuscript note is not in his usual hand. (No. 974)

...let the dotted line Mark'd a [with what pertains thereto] be $\frac{1}{10}$ Inch nearer to the Pyrometer; and let the stud mark'd b [as at one end thereof] be about half that quantity nearer to the side of the Watch.

March 31. 1772.

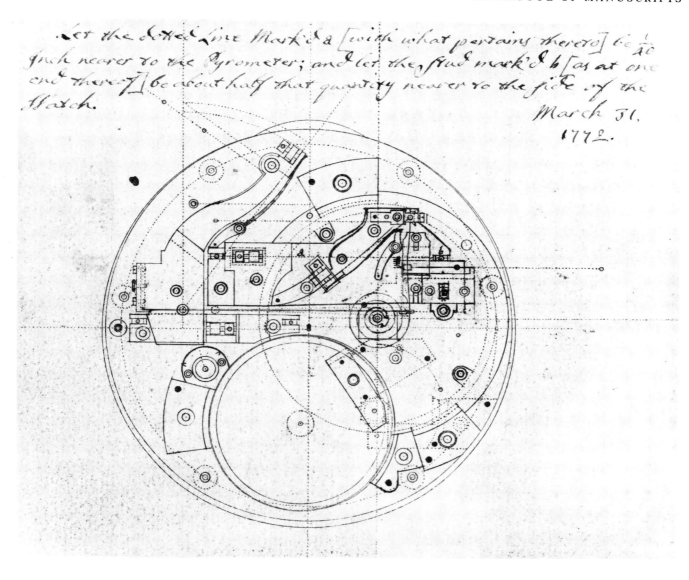

PLATE 33 A drawing (enlarged) by John Harrison of the mechanism of a watch that cannot be identified because, from the outline shape of the various parts, it does not represent H.4 or H.5. The drawing shows a cycloid pin which Harrison had fitted to H.4 (but not to H.5, completed in 1770). The drawing may have been finished on 31 March 1772, so that neat copies of H.4 or H.5 could be made, as was required at that time by the Board of Longitude before they would give Harrison the final portion (£10,000) of the £20,000 longitude award. In the drawing, the diameter of the watch plate is 99 mm, which is 4 mm greater than the diameter of that shown in the somewhat similar engraving published with the official description of the mechanism of H.4: *The Principles of Mr Harrison's Timekeeper*, 1767 (see No 205). (No. 974)

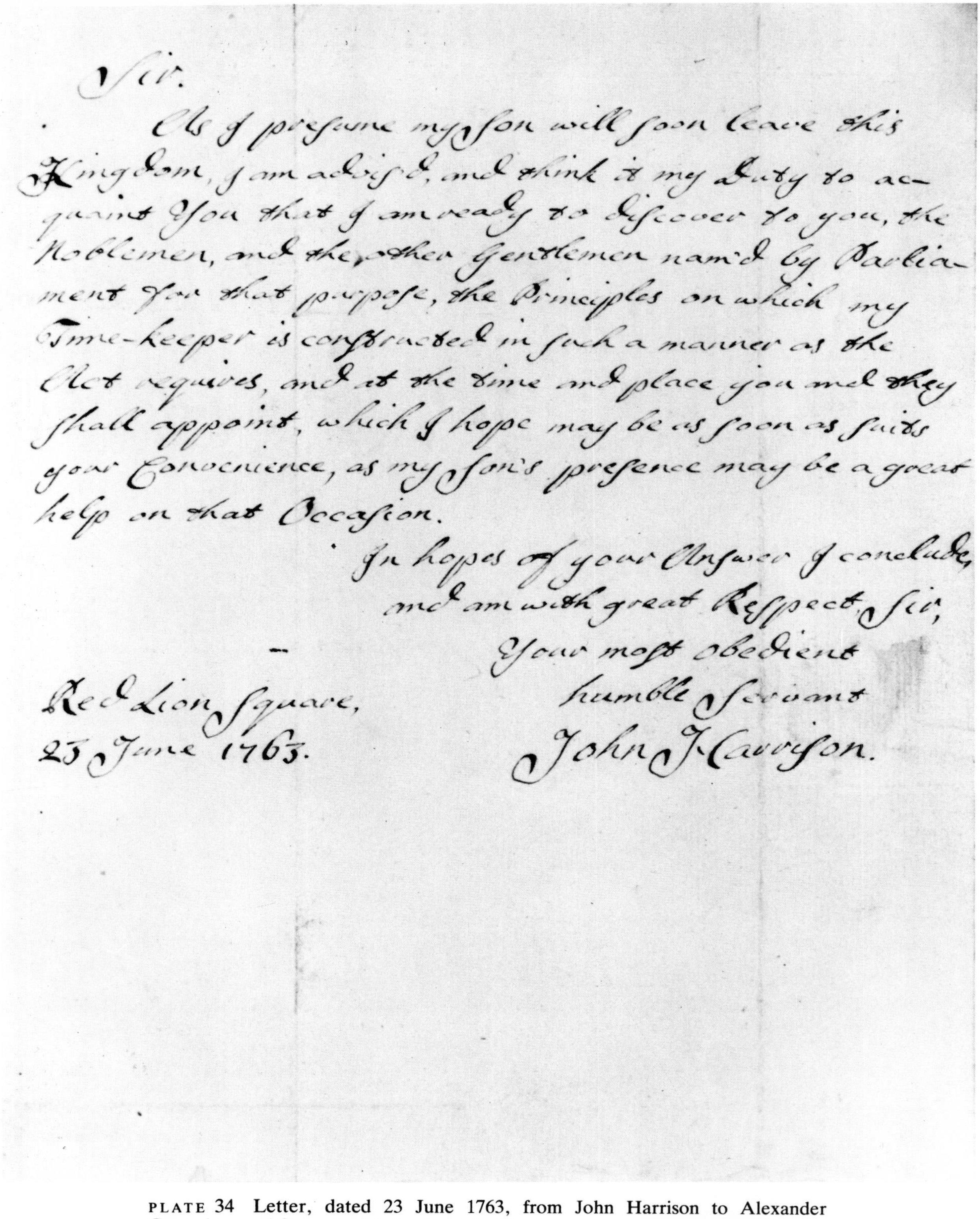

Sir:

As I presume my son will soon leave this Kingdom, I am advis'd, and think it my duty to acquaint you that I am ready to discover to you, the Noblemen, and the other Gentlemen nam'd by Parliament for that purpose, the Principles on which my Time-keeper is constructed in such a manner as the Act requires, and at the time and place you and they shall appoint, which I hope may be as soon as suits your Convenience, as my son's presence may be a great help on that Occasion.

In hopes of your Answer I conclude, and am with great Respect, Sir;
Your most obedient
humble servant

John Harrison.

Red Lion Square,
23 June 1763.

PLATE 34 Letter, dated 23 June 1763, from John Harrison to Alexander Cumming, and Cumming's letter in reply. Harrison was apprehensive for the safety of his son William during the forthcoming voyage to Barbados on the second trial of the longitude watch, H.4. To avoid the necessity of this voyage Harrison, in his letter to Cumming, offers to divulge the mechanical secrets of the Board of Longitude. Cumming's reply is guarded. (No. 976 (6))

Copy of the answer

Sir

I have this day received your letter of yesterday wherein you inform me that young Mr Harrison will probably soon leave this Kingdom; and that you are ready, before he goes to Discover the principles on which your Time keeper is Constructed in such a manner as the Act requires.

In Answer to which, I am ready to sign such certificate as the Act requires, So soon as you put it in my power so to do; in terms of the Act. And I shall most cheerfully attend any meetings of the Commissioners in order to consider of such means as you may suggest for rendering the Discovery easier to you and satisfactory to us; Or by which you can be put in possession of the £5000 and the intention of the Parliament in granting it may be fully answered. I am Respectfully Sir

June 24th 1763

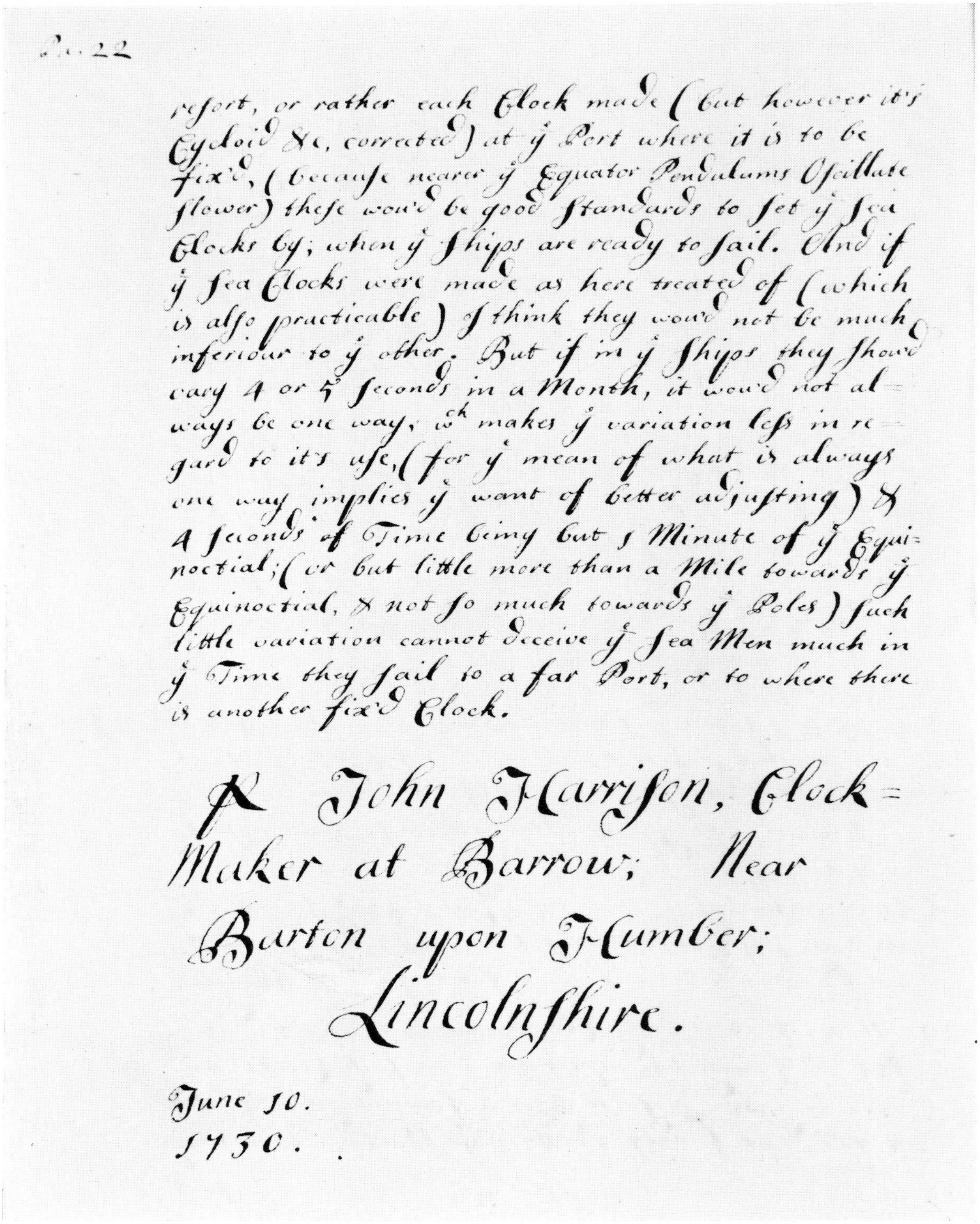

p. 22

resort, or rather each Clock made (but however it's Cycloid &c, corrected) at y Port where it is to be fix'd, (because nearer y Equator Pendulums Oscillate slower) these wou'd be good standards to set y Sea Clocks by; when y Ships are ready to sail. And if y Sea Clocks were made as here treated of (which is also practicable) I think they wou'd not be much inferiour to y other. But if in y Ships they shou'd vary 4 or 5 seconds in a Month, it wou'd not always be one way, wᶜʰ makes y variation less in regard to it's use, (for y mean of what is always one way implies y want of better adjusting) & 4 seconds of Time being but 1 Minute of y Equinoctial; (or but little more than a Mile towards y Equinoctial, & not so much towards y Poles) such little variation cannot deceive y Sea Men much in y Time they sail to a far Port, or to where there is another fix'd Clock.

℞ John Harrison, Clock=
Maker at Barrow, Near
Barton upon Humber,
Lincolnshire.

June 10.
1730.

PLATE 35 The final page of an illustrated holograph document, dated 10 June 1770, by John Harrison, consisting of twenty-three pages and six illustrations. The document ends with a strikingly full indication of its authorship. The symbol which precedes 'John' is the contraction which was commonly used as an abbreviation for the Latin *per*, or by. It is believed that Harrison took this document to London in 1730 when he journeyed there to explain to the Astronomer Royal (Dr Halley) and George Graham his revolutionary ideas for making very accurate clocks for use on land or at sea. For two of the illustrations, see Plate 36. (No. 977)

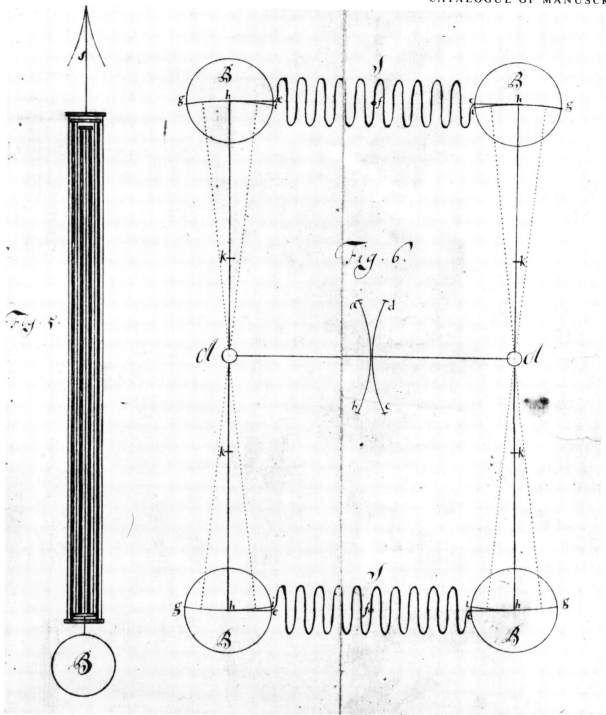

PLATE 36 Page of diagrams from the holograph document by John Harrison illustrated in Plate 35. On the left: a gridiron pendulum suspended between cycloid cheeks, as used by Harrison in his precision long case clocks. On the right: a drawing of the two inter-connected bar-shaped balances, with their balance springs, which Harrison apparently intended to fit when building his first longitude timekeeper, or 'sea-clock', now known as H.1. In this document Harrison has described the balance springs as 'worm springs', and he has certainly drawn them serpentine in outline, but it is not known if he intended them to be, in practice, helical or cylindrical springs, such as those that are now fitted to H.1. The original springs were found to be corroded away when, in 1920, H.1 was first restored by Commander R. T. Gould. (No. 977)

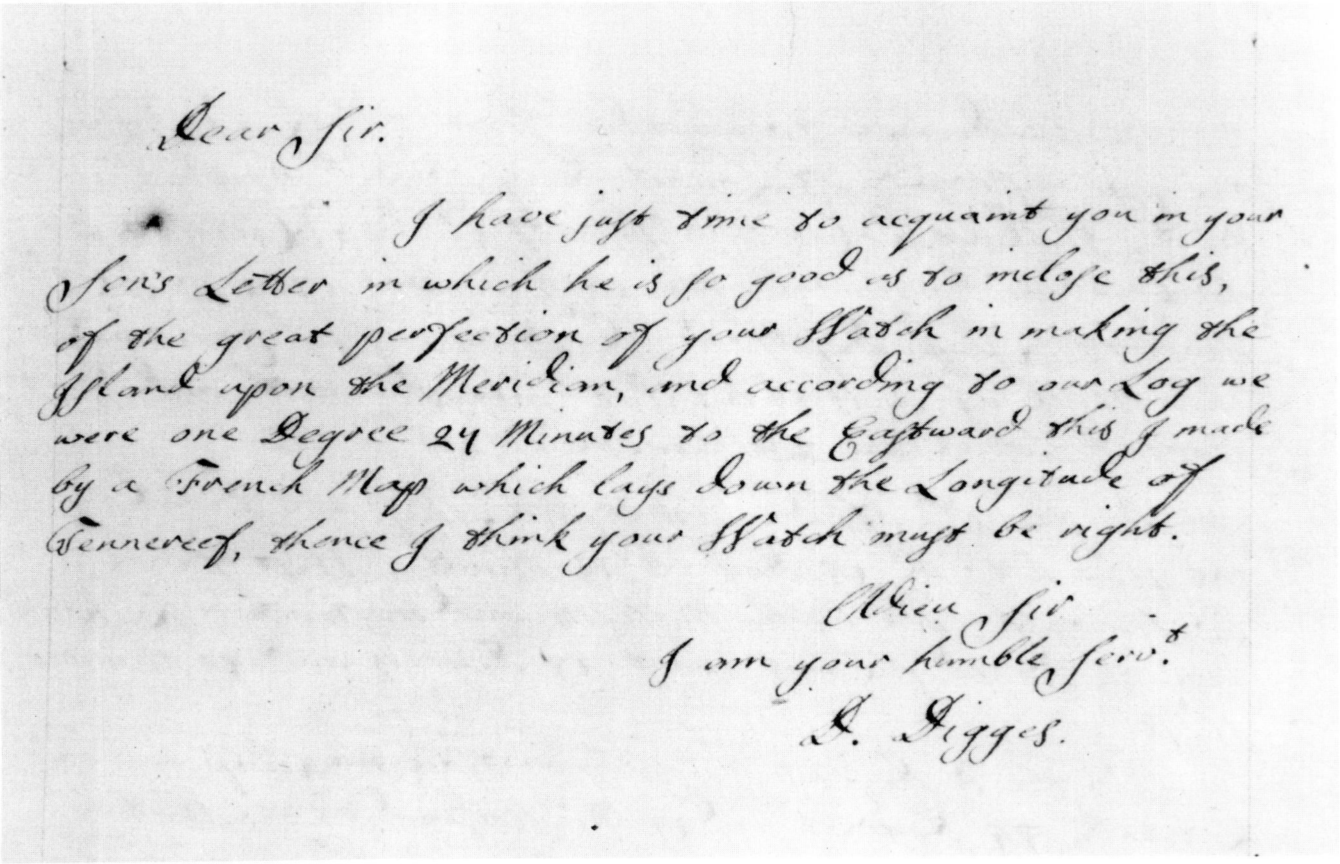

Dear Sir.

I have just time to acquaint you in your Son's Letter in which he is so good as to inclose this, of the great perfection of your Watch in making the Island upon the Meridian, and according to our Log we were one Degree 24 Minutes to the Eastward this I made by a French Map which lays down the Longitude of Tennereef, thence I think your Watch must be right.

Adieu Sir

I am your humble Serv.t

D. Digges.

PLATE 37 John Harrison's copies of two letters written to him in December 1761 by Captain D. Digges, of HMS *Deptford*, on the arrival of the ship at Madeira, while carrying William Harrison and the longitude watch H.4 to the West Indies on its first trial at sea. Captain Digges gives high praise to the accuracy of the watch, which had greatly aided precise navigation. (No. 979)

In obedience to an order from the Right Hon.ble the Commissioners of Longitude appointed by Parliament; William Harrison son of John Harrison set sail from Portsmouth the 18 November 1761 in His Majesty's ship Deptford — Digges Esq. Commander on a trial of a Watch: Put into Plymouth, and departed thence the 29 November.

On the 6th of December the ship was found by the Watch to be 15 degrees 19 Minutes West from Portsmouth; but by the Master's and most other Reckonings on board she was about 15 degrees and 30 Minutes West.

On the 8 December by observation the ship was in Latitude 35 degrees and 17 Minutes, and by the Watch 15 degrees 17 Minutes West of Portsmouth; so that, according to the Longitude as formerly determined of Porto Santo one of the Madeiras the ship continuing the same Course that Island must be seen the next Morning.

Captain Digges depending more on the Watch than the ship's Reckoning did not alter his Course, and at 7 the next Morning the Land of Porto Santo was seen.

William Harrison in his Letter to his Father Mentions that his Majesty's ship Beaver sailed from Portsmouth 10 days before the Deptford bound for Madeira, but the Deptford got to Madeira 3 days before the Beaver; that the Beaver was in the Latitude of those Islands above a fortnight before the Deptford — The reason was that by the Reckonings on board the Beaver they were a good deal to the East, tho' in reality they were to the West. This proceeded from their having no other than the common method of ascertaining the Longitude at Sea.

Copy of D. Digges's Esq. Letter to John Harrison Dated the 18 December 1761.

976 – *continued*

17. Remarks on the best manner of constructing watches, deduced from an examination of a pendulum clock. By Alex. Cumming. 7 April 1763.   8 l. These remarks were compiled by Cumming before hearing, as a Special Commissioner, John Harrison's hoped-for explanation of the mechanism of his longitude watch, H.4. Cumming wrote this paper as a precaution against any future accusation of plagiarism of Harrison's secrets.

18. The Case of Mr John Harrison. (Printed.) Undated, but late 1766.   2 l. This was one of the broadsheets issued by John Harrison to obtain public support in his fight to obtain the second portion of the £20,000 longitude prize. (*See also* **979** *post*, which includes another copy and also a later edition dated 1770.)

19. A succinct Account of the Proceedings relative to the Discovery of the Longitude, from the year 1714 to the present time (1765) . . . Extract from *The Monthly Review*, July 1765. (Printed.) 8vo. London, 1765. This is a summary of two pamphlets of anonymous authorship but probably written by James Short FRS in 1763 (*see* **410** *ante*) and in 1765 (*see* **414** *ante*).

19a. A review of John Harrison's book *A Description concerning such Mechanism* . . . , 1775. Extract from *The Monthly Review*, October 1775, pp 320–329. (Printed.) 8vo. London, 1775. (*See* **412** *ante*.) With MS annotations by Alexander Cumming.

20. Small notebook in the handwriting of Alexander Cumming containing five main items, *a–e*:

    a. Copy of the correspondence that passed between the Rev John Michell (Woodwardian Professor at Cambridge) and the Rev William Ludlam (Professor of Mathematics, Cambridge), resulting from the former's essays on horological matters. 1766–67.   12 l.

    b. Copy of letter written by John Harrison to the Earl of Morton eulogizing his longitude watch (H.4) and its performance in 1761 on a sea voyage to Jamaica. 24 December 1762.   5 p.

    c. Copy of letter from James Short to the Earl of Morton in which he gives great support to the excellence of John Harrison's longitude watch, H.4. 7 June 1763.   2 l.

    d. The Rev Mr John Michell's account of Mr Harrison's Timekeeper submitted to the Commissioners of Longitude 12 September 1765.   3 l. This account refers to John Harrison's explanations in 1765 of the mechanism of his longitude timekeeper, H.4, at which the Rev. Michell was present. Michell's account appeared also in printed form in *The Monthly Review*, October 1775, pp 328–329, and signed J. M. (*see* No. 19a.).

976 – *continued*

    e. Ten newspaper cuttings covering the years 1765–68 and mainly expressing contemporary criticism of the completeness of the published explanations (*see* **205** *ante*) of John Harrison's longitude timekeeper, H.4.

21. Stat. 13 Anne. Cap. 14. 1714. (Also in **669** *ante*.)
22. Stat. 8 George II. 1735.
23. Stat. 2 George III. Cap. 18. 1762. (Also in **671** *ante*.)
24. Stat. 5 George III. Cap. 20. 1765. (Also in **673** *ante*.)
25. Stat. 14 George III. Cap. 66. 1774. (Also in **674** *ante*.) This Act repealed all previous statutes concerning the longitude at sea and laid down entirely new and severe conditions for the award of further longitude prizes of up to £10,000.

977 Holograph manuscript describing and illustrating Harrison's basic designs and calculations for the construction of his precision long-case clocks of *c* 1726, and for his proposed portable longitude timekeeper or 'sea-clock'. Signed 'John Harrison, Clockmaker at Barrow, near Barton upon Humber, Lincolnshire. June 10 1730'. 23p, including 2p of ink diagrams. A copy of this document was printed in the *Horological Journal*, July 1950, pp 448–450, and August 1950, pp 504–506. *See* plates 35, 36.   MS 6026/1

978 The same. A photocopy.   MS 6026/1A

979 Statements, letters, printed documents, etc. connected with the trials at sea of Harrison's timekeepers. Several of the letters are from William Harrison, who gives a personal account of the attempts made by his father and himself to win the £20,000 longitude prize. 1750–73. (A full analysis of the contents is inserted in the volume.)   MS 6026/2
See plates 37–40.

980 Typed copy of the above.   MS 6026/2A

981 Letters relating to the dispersal of the John Harrison relics. 1836–76.   MS 6026A

This correspondence passed between Mrs Elizabeth Wright, granddaughter of John Harrison, and the Patent Office Museum in 1868, when she wished to sell the family relics which had been in the care of her father, Sir John Barton, and her step-brother, W. H. Barton, at the Royal Mint. The Patent Office had not the funds to buy the relics for the nation, but gave active assistance to Mrs Wright in disposing of them to Robert Napier, of West Shandon, Scotland. The relics included the Harrison regulator clock (now owned by the Royal Astronomical Society), the longitude watch H.5, the James Harrison long case clock of the Clockmakers' Company, a portrait of John Harrison in oils, and many documents.

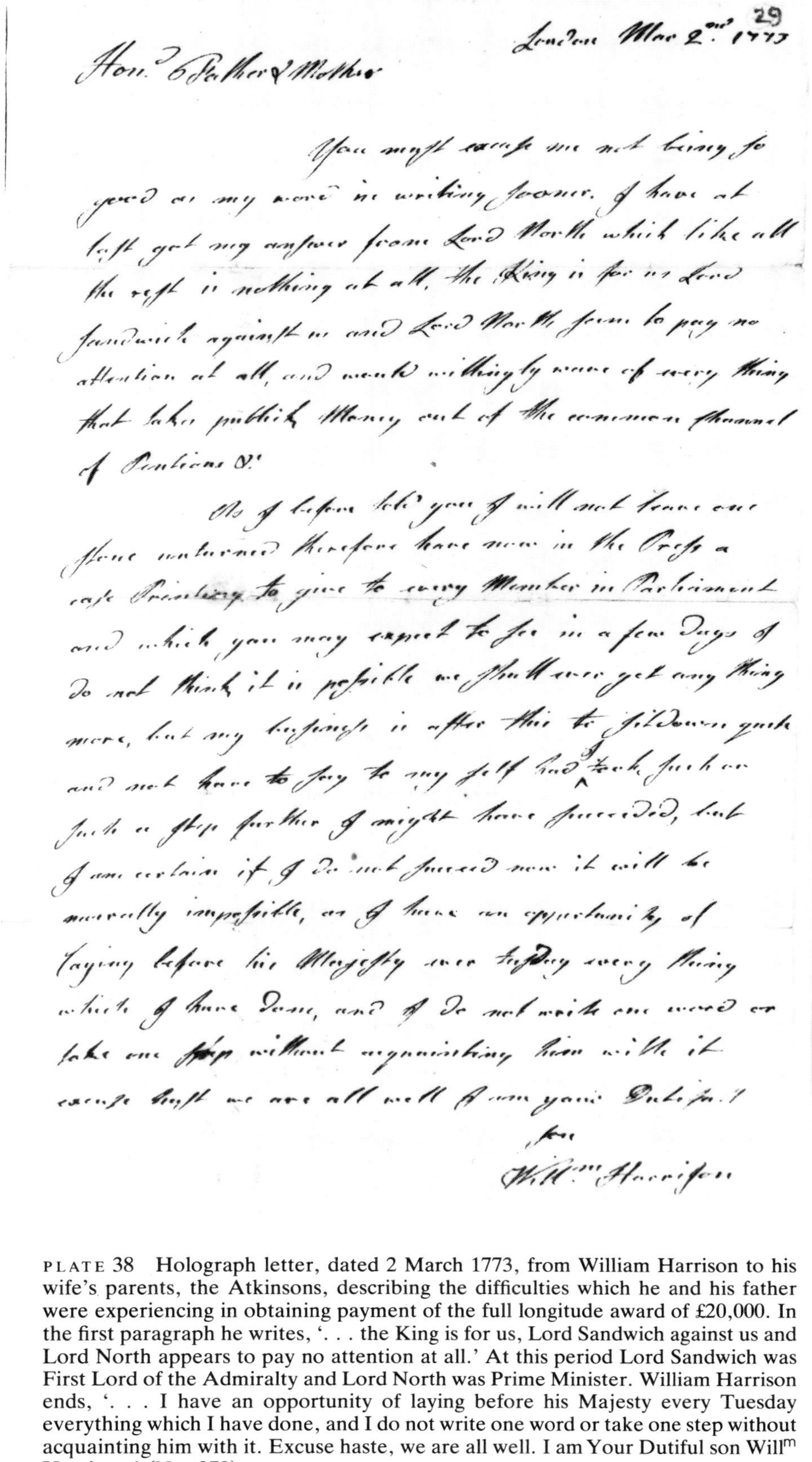
29

London Mar 2nd 1773

Hond Father & Mother

You must excuse me not being so good as my word in writing sooner. I have at last got my answer from Lord North which like all the rest is nothing at all, the King is for us Lord Sandwich against us and Lord North seems to pay no attention at all, and would willingly wave of every thing that takes publick Money out of the common channel of Pensions &c.

As I before told you I will not leave one stone unturned therefore have now in the Press a case Printing to give to every Member in Parliament and which you may expect to see in a few Days I do not think it is possible we shall ever get any thing more, but my business is after this to sitdown quite and not have to say to my self had I took such or such a step further I might have succeeded, but I am certain if I do not succeed now it will be morally impossible, as I have an opportunity of laying before his Majesty every tuesday every thing which I have done, and I do not write one word or take one step without acquainting him with it excuse hast we are all well I am your Dutiful Son

Willm Harrison

PLATE 38 Holograph letter, dated 2 March 1773, from William Harrison to his wife's parents, the Atkinsons, describing the difficulties which he and his father were experiencing in obtaining payment of the full longitude award of £20,000. In the first paragraph he writes, '. . . the King is for us, Lord Sandwich against us and Lord North appears to pay no attention at all.' At this period Lord Sandwich was First Lord of the Admiralty and Lord North was Prime Minister. William Harrison ends, '. . . I have an opportunity of laying before his Majesty every Tuesday everything which I have done, and I do not write one word or take one step without acquainting him with it. Excuse haste, we are all well. I am Your Dutiful son Willm Harrison.' (No. 979)

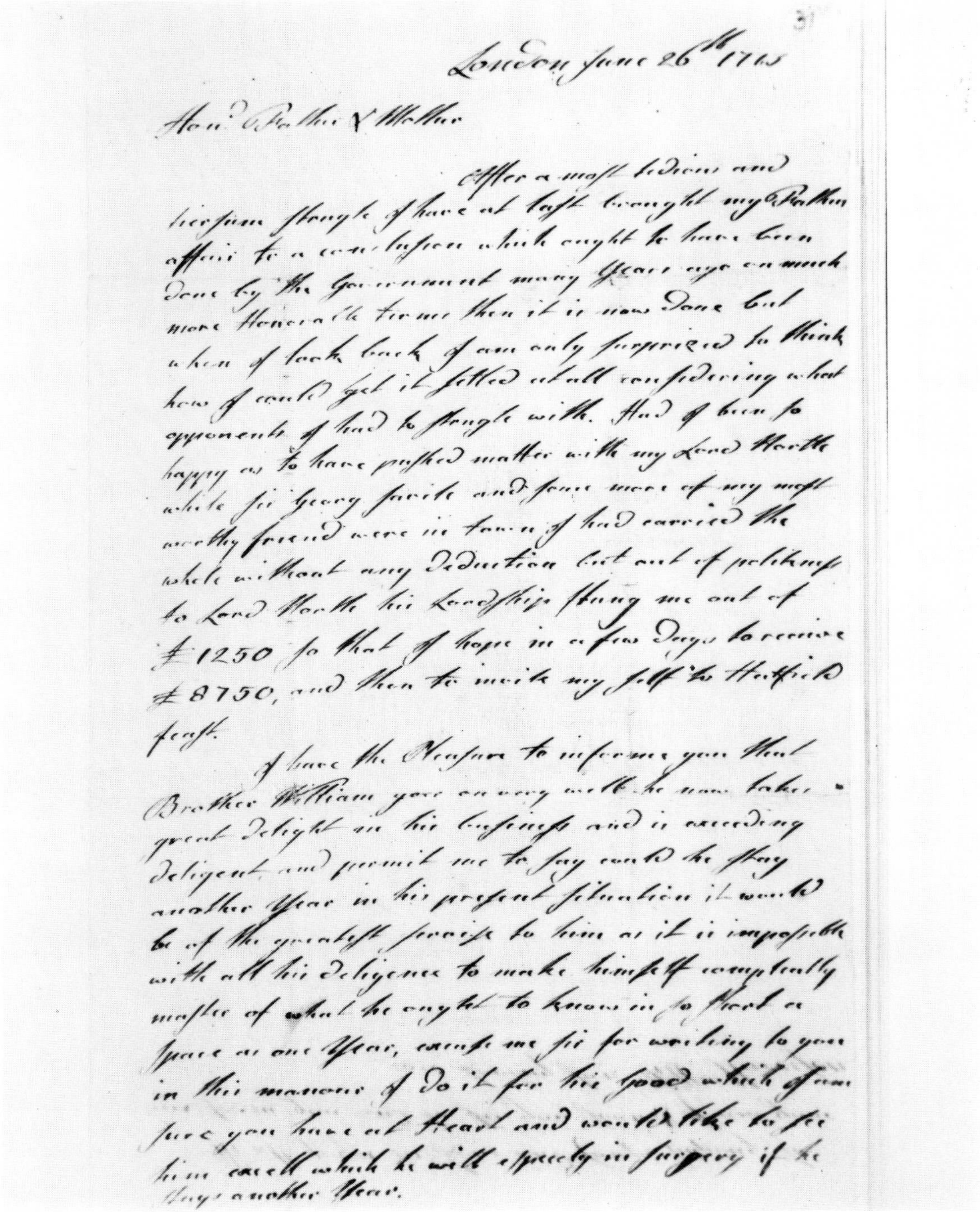

London June 26th 1773

Hond Father & Mother

After a most tedious and tiresome strugle I have at last brought my Fathers affair to a conclusion which ought to have been Done by the Government many Years ago on much more Honorable terms then it is now Done but when I look back I am only surprized to think how I could get it settled at all considering what opponents I had to strugle with. Had I been so happy as to have pushed matter with my Lord North while Sir George Savile and some more of my most worthy friend were in town I had carried the whole without any Deduction but out of politeness to Lord North his Lordship stung me out of £1250 so that I hope in a few Days to receive £8750, and then to invite my self to Hatfield feast.

I have the Pleasure to inform you that Brother William goes on very well he now takes a great Delight in his business and is exceeding deligent and permit me to say could he stay another Year in his present situation it would be of the greatest service to him as it is impossible with all his deligence to make himself compleatly master of what he ought to know in so short a space as one Year, excuse me sir for writing to you in this manner I do it for his good which I am sure you have at Heart and would like to see him excell which he will especially in surgery if he stays another Year.

PLATE 39 Holograph letter, dated 26 June 1773, from William Harrison to his wife's parents, the Atkinsons, after Parliament had granted his father the final sum of £8,750, bringing his total longitude award to £18,750. The letter commences 'After a most tedious and tiresome strugle I have at last brought my Father's affair to a conclusion. . . .' Further on, when referring to Lord North, he adds, '. . . his Lordship stung me out of £1,250, so that I hope in a few days to receive £8,750 and then invite myself to Hatfield feast.' (The Atkinsons lived at Hatfield, Yorkshire.) (No. 979)

THE
CASE
OF
Mr. *JOHN HARRISON.*

IN 1714 a Petition of feveral Merchants and others was prefented to Parliament, praying that a publick Reward might be offered for any Method of afcertaining the Longitude at Sea: A Committee was appointed in Purfuance thereof, at which Sir *Ifaac Newton*, and other Men of Eminence, were ordered to attend; and Sir *Ifaac* (enumerating the probable Methods of effecting the defired Purpofe) placed an exact Time-Keeper at the Head of his Lift — *Vide Journals of the Houfe of Commons, Vol.* 17, *Page* 677.———An Act was accordingly paffed the fame Year, being the 12th of Queen *Anne*, giving a Reward of

10,000 £. To the Author of any Method whereby a Ship fhall actually fail under the Direction of Commiffioners appointed, from *Great Britain*, to the *Weft Indies*, without lofing her Longitude more than a Degree.

15,000 £. IF fuch Ship keeps her Longitude to Two Thirds of a Degree.

20,000 £. If to Half a Degree.

IN 1726, Mr. *John Harrifon* compleated a Pendulum Clock, which did not err above a Second of Time in a Month, and which continues at this Hour to go with the fame Exactnefs, although it has never been cleaned or repaired, nor its Motion ever fince ftopped, except twice, when it was removed from one Houfe to another.

IN 1735 he finifhed a Machine, in which the fame Principles were adapted to the Motion of a Ship, which in 1736 was tryed by Direction of the firft Lord of the Admiralty, in a Voyage to *Lifbon* and back, and found to anfwer. From that Time, till the Year 1761, he continued to improve the Invention, and had then made four Time-Keepers adapted for Ufe at Sea, all founded on the fame Principles, but different in Size and Conftruction, the laft being only five Inches in Diameter.

IN

PLATE 40 *The Case of Mr. John Harrison.* A propaganda broadsheet issued by John Harrison as part of his attempt to obtain the full £20,000 longitude prize. This particular 'Case' was issued in late 1766 and consists of four pages. Other editions of the 'Case' were issued in 1770 (see No. 979 (39, 43)) and 1773. The annotation in the margin, 'N.B. This is at W^t Shandon', was made by Robert Napier, of West Shandon, Scotland (see No. 981), and refers to the clock that he once owned and which is now exhibit no. 553 in the Company's Museum. (No. 979)

MISCELLANEOUS DOCUMENTS

982 Deeds relating to William Harrison, FRS (1728–1815). 1783–1814.   MS 9074

Contents

Invention by William Harrison and William Atherton of Clerkenwell of a new cotton spinning machine. 30 September 1783.

Marriage settlement of William Frodsham, witnessed by William Harrison. 13 January 1785.

Sale by William Harrison of his share in the Holywell Twist Co. to Daniel Whittaker of Manchester. 20 May 1791.

Declaration of trust of John Harrison, deceased, William Harrison being the sole surviving trustee. 19 January 1786.

Deed by which William Harrison obtained judgment for £17,000 against the late Daniel Whittaker. 17 April 1794.

Copy of William Harrison's will (dated 14 May 1814), with probate (dated 3 July 1815). (Another copy of this will is in **973** *ante* pp 33–336.)

983 Clarke (Henry), compiler. Historical facts showing the rise and progress of the Clockmakers' Company; with a list of all the clockmakers (both freemen and foreigners, aliens, and outliers) in the City of London. Dated 26 June 1662, arranged under localities. *c* 1813.   MS 3974

984 Abstracts of and index to the journals of the ordinances, orders and public acts; precedents (1632–1816) which are to be found in the journals of the Clockmakers' Company concerning the exercise by that company of the rule and divers branches, arts and trades connected in and with the charter of incorporation and bye-laws. 1813–16.   MS 3975

985 Abstracts from the bye-laws and ordinances of the Clockmakers' Company. *c* 1813. Compiled by Henry Clarke, citizen and Clockmaker.   MS 3976

986 Directory of clock and watchmakers, also of workmen and shopkeepers carrying on any type of trade in any respect. Dated London 4 November 1813.   MS 3977

987 Alphabetical list of streets in the parish of St Marylebone, with their lengths. 1825? Compiled by Henry Clarke, citizen and Clockmaker.   MS 3978

988 Vulliamy (Benjamin Lewis). Two calculations: 1. Rate of going of a clock made by Vulliamy for Lowther Castle for the Earl of Lonsdale, from 9 November 1813 to 17 August 1814. 2. Rate of going of a clock made by Vulliamy for Colombo, by order of the Lords of the Treasury, from 1 October 1814 to 17 April 1815.   MS 3979

989 Instructions by B. L. Vulliamy for fixing in its place a turret clock made by him for Colombo. March 1815.   MS 3980

990 Howells (W.). Twelve original ink drawings of clock and watch escapements by W. Howells, with brief descriptions. Compiled *c* 1815. Added at the end in a different hand is an illustrated explanation, possibly written by H. Sully, of Howells's longitude clock of 1724.   MS 3981

1. Remontoire escapement for a watch. Folios 1, 11.
2. Cylinder escapement. Folios 1v, 12.
3. Breguet detached lever escapement. Folios 2, 13.
4. Remontoire escapement for a watch. Folios 3, 14.
5. Frictional rest escapement with two pallets and one wheel for a clock. Folios 3, 15.
6. Mudge's lever escapement for a watch. Folios 4, 4v, 16.
7. Duplex escapement. Dated 1815. Folios 5, 5v, 17.
8. J. Arnold's spring detent. Folios 6, 6v, 18.
9. Earnshaw's spring detent. Folios 6v, 19.
10. Spring detent escapement with duplex escape wheel. Folios 10, 20.
11. Howells's double detached escapement with two escape wheels. Folios 8, 8v, 9, 21.
12. Earnshaw's and Arnold's compensated balances. Folios 10, 10v, 12.
13. Explanation, possibly in Sully's handwriting, of H. Sully's longitude timekeeper. Signed 'Sully, Versailles, June the 29th. 1724'. 5 l. 1 plate (folios 23–27). This letter is quoted in **812** *ante*; it is clear that Sully sent it to George Graham FRS, as the latter's reply is also quoted. This document, although signed 'Sully', does not appear to be in a handwriting of the early 18th century and it may be a 19th-century copy. The clock described is Item No. 668 in the Clockmakers Museum.

991 An anonymous handwritten book, carefully compiled, probably by a dealer who has copied out items on clocks, watches, etc., from books, magazines, etc. There are a few personal remarks. Included is a list of horological works in several languages. Prefixed are two portraits of George Graham and John Harrison, and two drawings. London, 1821. 28p.   MS 3982

992 Holmes (John). Copies of letters, on the subject of turret clocks, that passed between John Holmes (watchmaker of London), Mr John Smeaton (engineer), and the Rev W. Ludlam (Professor of Mathematics, Cambridge), when Holmes was awarded the contract for providing a turret clock for Greenwich Hospital. The clock was subsequently made by Thwaites, to Holmes's design. 1779–80. (This MS was presented to the Clockmakers' Company by Thomas Reid in a letter to B. L. Vulliamy dated 26 January 1821, which is prefixed to the volume. The letters were also included as Appendix A in T. Reid's *Treatise*; see **726** *ante*.)   MS 3983

993 Account of John Smith, clockmaker, taken from *Antitrinitarian Biography* by Robert Wallace, FGS, London, 1850.   MS 3984

994 Copy from the *Journal of the House of Commons* of a report, dated 29 April 1793, from the select committee of the House of Commons upon the position of Thomas Mudge concerning his timekeeper for estimating longitude. *c* 1821.   MS 3985

995 Brief account of the present and ancient state of China and its inhabitants. Written in the form of letters. 1753? *Anon.*   MS 3986

996 Atkins (Samuel Elliott). Catalogue of specimens of ancient watchwork, belonging to the Clock Makers Company, 1849. ('This catalogue of ancient watchwork, etc., compiled, and the information connected therewith gleaned from the records of the Company by S. E. Atkins, the Clerk of the Company, in the year 1849, there being no previous catalogue in existence relative to the various specimens of the art belonging to the Company.') With additions to 1874.

MS 3987 and 3987A

997 Two lists of books on clock and watch work, belonging to (1.) Mr Arnold and (2.) 'F. P. Jun.' 1 January 1814. Bound with tracts: *L'Horlogerie*, vol 1.

MS 3988A

998 Two items: 1. workman's ticket to Benjamin Vulliamy concerning a watch dial, enamel on gold, with seconds, 28 March 1778; 2. watch tax receipt for 1/10½, dated 30 April 1798.

MS 3988B

999 Late 17th century clockmakers' workshop notebook. 2 vols. Vol 1, 1690–1746. Vol 2, 1690. MS 6619
Vol 1 contains workshop entries made at various dates, 1690–1746, by several individuals and collected by (probably) Humfrey Hadley (d.1770), clockmaker of Birmingham.
Vol 2 contains MS extracts on spherical projection from *Cursus Mathematicus*, by William Leybourn, 1690.
In addition, there are some explanatory notes by Col H. Quill (compiled in 1968) on the origins of the notebook, together with an index and translations of some of the more indecipherable pages, including a photocopy of the relevant pages of *Cursus Mathematicus*.
See plate 41.

THWAITES AND REED; CLOCKMAKERS: BUSINESS ARCHIVES

*1000 Thwaites and Reed, formerly Ainsworth Thwaites & Co., of Rosomon Street, Clerkenwell, now of 15 Bowling Green Lane, London, E.C.1. MS 6788
Day Books. 1780–1955. 26 vols.

Vol 1. 1780–87	Vol 14. 1899–1904
2. 1788–98	15. 1905–07
3. 1799–1804	16. 1907–12
4. 1804–10	17. 1912–17
5. 1810–27	18. 1917–21
6. 1827–44	19. 1921–24
7. 1844–57	20. 1924–28
8. 1857–65	21. 1928–31
9. 1865–75	22. 1931–36
10. 1875–84	23. 1936–40
11. 1884–90	24. 1940–45
12. 1890–95	25. 1945–50
13. 1895–99	26. 1950–55

1001 Rough day books. 1804–30. 3 vols. MS 6789
Vol 1. 1804–15   Vol 3. 1827–38
2. 1816–26

1002 Rough day book, 1881, and weekly receipts, 1882–85.

MS 9197

1003 Journal and day book. 1809–25.

MS 6790

1004 Journal. 1872–76.

MS 9196

1005 Ledgers. 1789–1902. 9 vols.   MS 6791

Vol 1. 1780–1801	Vol 6. 1875–81
2. 1802–13	7. 1881–90
3. 1813–27	8. 1891–1902
4. 1827–59	9. 1902–13
5. 1859–74	

(Vol 1 is imperfect. For the index of Vol 4, *see* **1007** *post.*)

1006 Ledger: the company in account with the London Joint Bank (continued from MS 6791/8, p 349.) 1902–07. 1 vol.   MS 6791A

1007 Index to MS 6791/4.   MS 6791B

1008 'Private Ledger,' containing trading, and profit and loss accounts. 1902–21. Indexed.   MS 6791C

1009 Workmen's time and materials books. 1812–53. 2 vols.   MS 6792
Vol 1. 1812–25   Vol 2. 1826–53

1010 Workmen's time and material books, new series. 1882–1919 and 1951–58. 4 vols. Indexed. MS 6792A
Vol 1. 1882–92   Vol 3. 1902–14
2. 1892–1902   4. 1914–19 and 1951–58

1011 Shop ledgers. 1821–96. 2 vols.   MS 6793
Vol 1. 1821–44   Vol 2. 1845–76

1012 Estimate book. 1802–49.   MS 6794

1013 Order books. 1843–81. 3 vols.   MS 6795
Vol 1. 1843–51   Vol 3. 1869–81
2. 1851–69

1014 Order books, new series. 1907–45. 45 vols.
MS 6795A

Vol 1. April–Sept. 1907
2. Sept.–Dec. 1907
3. Jan.–May 1908
4. May–Nov. 1908
5. Nov. 1908–June 1909
6. June–Dec. 1909
7. Dec. 1909–July 1910
8. July 1910–April 1911
9. April 1911–Jan. 1912
10. Jan.–Sept. 1912
11. Sept. 1912–June 1913
12. June 1913–March 1914
13. March–Dec. 1914
14. Dec. 1914–Aug. 1915
15. Aug. 1915–April 1916
16. April–Dec. 1916
17. Dec. 1916–Sept. 1917
18. Sept. 1917–June 1918
19. June 1918–May 1919
20. May–Nov. 1919
21. Nov. 1919–June 1920
22. June 1920–April 1921
23. April–Nov. 1921
24. Nov. 1921–Oct. 1922
25. Oct. 1922–Oct. 1923
26. Oct. 1923–Aug. 1924
27. Aug. 1924–July 1925
28. July 1925–April 1926
29. April 1926–March 1927
30. March 1927–Feb. 1928
31. Feb. 1928–Jan. 1929
32. Jan. 1929–Jan. 1930

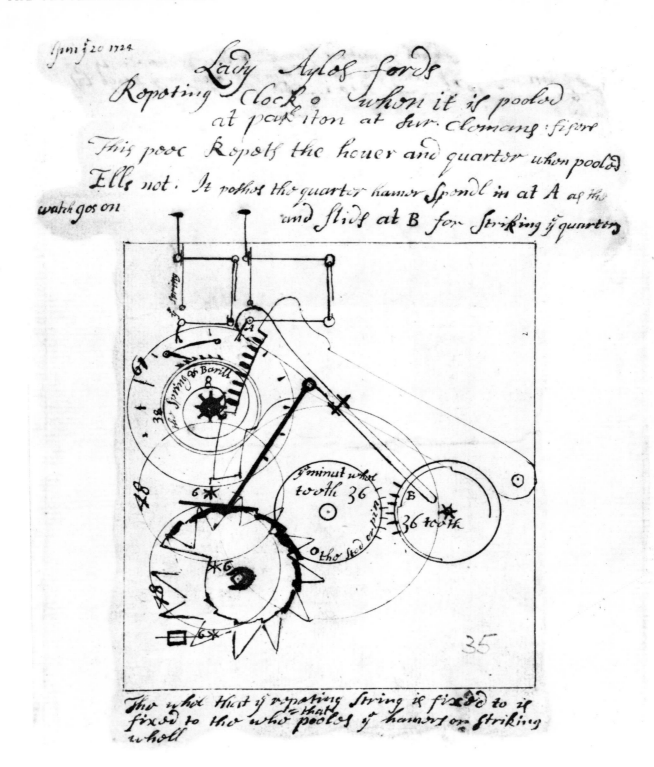

PLATE 41   A late seventeenth-century clockmaker's workshop notebook, vol 1, page 38B. Many of the entries are in quaint phonetic spelling: 'June 20 1724 Lady Aylesfords Repeting clock when it is pooled at Pakiton at Sur Clemans Fisers. This pool Repets the houer and quarter when pooled. Ells not. It poshes the quarter hamer spendl in at A as the watch goes on and slids at B for striking the quarters.' Sir Clement Fisher designed Lord Aylesford's second house in Packington Park. In the last sentence, 'watch' means the going part of the clock. (No. 999)

1014 – *continued*

    33. Jan.–Dec. 1930
    34. Dec. 1930–Nov. 1931
    35. Nov. 1931–Oct. 1932
    36. Oct. 1932–Oct. 1933
    37. Oct. 1933–Sept. 1934
    38. Sept. 1934–Sept. 1935
    39. Sept. 1935–Sept. 1936
    40. Sept. 1936–Oct. 1937
    41. Oct. 1937–Jan. 1939
    42. Jan. 1939–June 1940
    43. July 1940–March 1942
    44. March 1942–Sept. 1943
    45. Sept. 1943–May 1945

1015   Jobbing and order books. 1867–1900. 6 vols.
                                                MS 9195

Vol 1. 1867–74	Vol 4. 1879–82
2. 1873–79	5. 1898–99
3. 1874–88	6. 1899–1900

(Vols 1. and 3. were begun at both ends, backs inverted.)

1016   Wages books. 1828–84. 5 vols.   MS 6796

Vol 1. 1828–40	Vol 4. 1866–75
2. 1840–51	5. 1875–84
3. 1851–66	

1017   Wages books, new series. 1925–31. 5 vols.
                                             MS 6796A

Vol 1. 1925–26	Vol 4. 1929–30
2. 1926–27	5. 1930–31
3. 1927–29	

1018   Cash books. 1812–75 and 1881–1900. 15 vols.
                                             MS 6797

Vol 1. 1812–27	Vol 9. 1865–70
2. 1827–40	10. 1870–75
3. 1840–44	11. 1881–90
4. 1844–47	12. 1890–92
5. 1847–50	13. 1892–95
6. 1850–54	14. 1895–97
7. 1854–59	15. 1897–1900
8. 1859–65	

1019   Cash books, new series. 1911–51. 5 vols.
                                             MS 6797A

Vol 1. 1911–15	Vol 4. 1929–38
2. 1915–22	5. 1938–51
3. 1922–29	

1020   Weekly cash account books. 1890–1907. (Incomplete.) 3 vols.   MS 6797B

Vol 1. 1890–95	Vol 3. 1905–07
2. 1895–1900	

1021   Journals. 1890–99. 2 vols.   MS 6798

Vol 1. 1890–93	Vol 2. 1894–99

1022   Stock book. 1814–55.   MS 6799

1023   Accounts (mostly annual) of stock and 'book debts.' 1904–54. 4 vols.   MS 6799A

Vol 1. 1904–23	Vol 3. 1925–48
2. 1905–26	4. 1928–54

1024   Maintenance work and repair account books (rough). 1822–47. 2 vols.   MS 6800

Vol 1. 1822–29   Vol 2. 1830–47

(The beginning of vol 2 is damaged at the top.)

1025   Small-shop book. 1874–80.   MS 6801

1026   Rough order book. 1895–96.   MS 6802

1027   Rough order book, 1880–81; with workmen's time and expense account on out-jobs, 1880–86. Begun at both ends (back inverted).   MS 9198

1028   Rough work account book. 1866–72. MS 6803

1029   Petty cash books. 1862–68, 1890–97, 1903–07. 3 vols.   MS 6804

1030   Banking books. 1886–93, 1896–1907. 6 vols.
                                           MS 6805

Vol 1. 1886–93	Vol 4. 1901–03
2. 1896–98	5. 1903–05
3. 1898–1901	6. 1905–07

1031   Bank books. 1911–54. 8 vols.   MS 6805A

Vol 1. 1911–16	Vol 5. 1931–35
2. 1916–21	6. 1935–40
3. 1921–26	7. 1940–45
4. 1926–31	8. 1945–54

1032   Copy letter books. 1919–20. 4 vols. Indexed.
                                           MS 6806

    Vol 1. Feb.–July 1919
        2. Aug.–Dec. 1919
        3. Dec. 1919–May 1920
        4. May–Nov. 1920

1033   Spare parts issue (to workmen) books. 1842–1912. 2 vols.   MS 6807

Vol 1. 1842–61   Vol 2. 1861–1912

1034   Copy invoice books. 1917–20. 4 vols. Indexed.
                                           MS 6808

    Vol 1. Oct. 1917–Jan. 1919
        2. Oct. 1918–Dec. 1919
        3. Dec. 1919–Oct. 1920
        4. Sept.–Dec. 1920

1035   Holograph letter from Thomas Mudge, jnr, horologist and maker of chronometers to the Royal Navy, to George John Spencer, second Earl Spencer, First Lord of the Admiralty, chiefly relating to the claim for the government award for time-keepers advanced by his father, Thomas Mudge, snr. Dated 12 June 1795.
                                           MS 9473

1036   Specification for enrolment in the Court of Chancery by John Arnold, citizen and clockmaker, of Adelphi, Strand, upon a patent, dated 2 May 1782, of 'a new escapement and also a balance to compensate the effects arising from heat and cold in pocket chronometers or watches and for incurvating the two ends of the helical spring to render the expansion and contraction of the spring perfectly concentric . . .' 31 August, 1782. (*See Antiquarian Horology*, September 1966, pp 125–126.)
See plate 42.   MS 9473A

1037   Counterpart lease by the Cutlers' Company to the Clockmakers' Company of the Courtroom of the former's hall in Cloak Lane for meetings for 1¼ years. 7 July 1707.   MS 10501

1038   Records of two suits in the Court of Common Pleas: 1., Clockmakers' Company v. John Coward; 2., The Company v. Thomas Richards for non-payment of quarterage. 1796–97.   MS 10502

PLATE 42   John Arnold's specification. This specification forms part of Arnold's Patent No. 1329, taken out in May 1782. It illustrates and describes briefly the epicycloidal teeth of his escape wheels, also the terminal curves of his helical balance springs, and three forms of his temperature compensation devices (the last mentioned all being illustrated in a combined drawing of a balance). (No. 1036)

DESBOIS (DANIEL) AND SONS, CLOCK AND WATCHMAKERS: BUSINESS ARCHIVES

1039 Day books. 1855–1916. 11 vols. MS 14284

Vol 1. 1855–60	Vol 7. 1883–88
2. 1861–65	8. 1889–94
3. 1866–69	9. 1895–1901
4. 1870–73	10. 1901–07
5. 1874–78	11. 1908–16
6. 1878–82	

1040 Ledgers, 1853–1945. 13 vols. MS 14285

Vol 1. 1853–59	Vol 8. 1891–1900
2. 1860–64	9. 1900–09
3. 1865–69	10. 1910–1919
4. 1869–73	11. 1919–28
5. 1874–78	12. 1928–35
6. 1878–82	13. 1936–45
7. 1882–91	

MISCELLANEOUS DOCUMENTS

1041 Two stock books of a clock and watchmaker, recording manufacturing costs, retail prices and sales, 1847–1902. 2 vols. (These stock books may relate to the firm of William Connell and successors; see the envelope pasted inside the front cover of Vol 2.)
MS 14373

Vol 1. 1847–63	Vol 2. 1872–1902

1042 Account book of an unidentified clock and watchmaker, recording costs of components and payments to workmen, 1862–99. (Possibly part of the records of the firm of William Connell.) MS 14374

1043 Turner (William), successively of 167 and 173 Fenchurch Street, chronometer and watchmaker, fl. 1825–40. Jobbing or work day book, 1 January 1834 to 17 June 1839, giving names of customers or owners, makes of watches and their numbers, specifications of repairs required, and cost. The last three pages, covering the period 8 November 1839 to 1 February 1841, are headed 'Jobs from Mr Birch, Tenterden.' William Birch, watchmaker, succeeded Turner at 173 Fenchurch Street c 1840. See MS 14470. MS 14469

1044 Birch (William), 1815–1905, watchmaker, of 173 Fenchurch Street, and successors. Watch books, recording the number of the rough Birch movements, thereafter finishing work carried out, workmen's names, and the sums paid to them (in code, deciphered on the front fly of Vol 1). 1840–1920. 5 vols. MS 14470

Vol 1. 1840–48	Vol 4. 1889–1906
2. 1848–58	5. 1907–20
3. 1859–88	

(Vol 5 is mainly blank.)

V. KULLBERG, WATCH AND CHRONOMETER MAKER: BUSINESS ARCHIVES

V. Kullberg; of 105 Liverpool Road, Islington (before 1869 known as 12 Cloudesly Terrace).

1045 Manufacturing books. 1868–1943. 8 vols. (Incomplete.)
MS 14537

Vol 1. 1868–73 (Nos 740–1408, 1423–1789)
2. 1870–81 (Nos 1790–2613)
3. 1873–87 (Nos 2614–3618)

1045 – *continued*

4. 1877–91 (Nos 3619–5124)
5. 1890–97 (Nos 5125–6258)
6. 1897–1904 (Nos 6259–7476)
7. 1912–21 (Nos 8477–9478)
8. 1920–32 (Nos 9479–9978, with additions to 1943)

1046 Order books, containing specifications, abridged correspondence and some estimates. 1870–1939. 8 vols. (Incomplete.) MS 14538

Vol 1. 1870–84
2. 1884–90
3. 1890–94 (with additions to 1899)
4. 1900–07 (with additions to 1914)
5. 1906–14 (with additions to 1920)
6. 1913–19 (with additions to 1927)
7. 1920–28 (with additions to 1934)
8. 1928–36 (with additions to 1943)

(All volumes indexed under customers' names.)

1047 Ledgers, 1857–92. 4 vols. MS 14539

Vol 1. 1857–92	Vol 3. 1866–75
2. 1862–77	4. 1875–92

1048 Shop day books. 1890–1946. 3 vols. MS 14540

Vol 1. 1890–1904	Vol 3. 1929–46
2. 1904–29	

1049 Workshop repair instruction books, 1 47. 6 vols. (Incomplete.) MS 541

Vol 1. 1917–26	Vol 4. 1938–42
2. 1926–29	5. 1942–44
3. 1937–47	6. 1944–47

(Vol 3 is a fair copy of Vols 4–6.)

1050 Journal. 1931–40. 1 vol. MS 14542

1051 Out-letter books. 1871–1927. 8 vols. (Incomplete.) MS 14543

Vol 1. 1871–92	Vol 5. 1911–16
2. 1892–96	6. 1916–21
3. 1903–08	7. 1921–25
4. 1908–11	8. 1925–27

1052 Register of in-letters. 1873–94. 1 vol.
MS 14544

1053 Cash book. 1893–1904. 1 vol. MS 14545

1054 Stock list, including costs of parts, values of watches/chronometers Nos 3951–4108. 1885–87. 1 vol.
MS 14546

1055 Stock list, 1905–30, and payments to workers, 1890–92. 1 vol. MS 14547

1056 Stock book, 1897–1911. 1 vol. (Overlaps with MS 14547.) MS 14548

1057 Notes on watches Nos 516–1593. 1865–69. 1 vol. (Overlaps with MS 14537, Vol 1, but is rougher and less detailed.) MS 14549

1058 Repair instruction and estimate books. 1896–1928. 8 vols. (Incomplete.) MS 14550

Vol 1. 1896–98	Vol 5. 1907–09
2. 1898–1900	6. 1915–18
3. 1900–03	7. 1918–20
4. 1903–07	8. 1920–28

1059 Repair notebooks (?). Undated; late 19th to early 20th century. 5 vols. (Details indecipherable, possibly in code.)   MS 14551

1060 Carbon copies of instructions to outside repairers. 1920–47. 24 vols. (Incomplete.) MS 14552

Vol 1. Sept.–Nov. 1920
2. Jan.–April 1921
3. Aug.–Nov. 1921
4. Nov. 1921–March 1922
5. March–June 1922
6. June–Oct. 1922
7. Aug.–Dec. 1923
8. Dec. 1923–Aug. 1924
9. Oct. 1926–Jan. 1927
10. Jan.–April 1927
11. April–July 1927
12. July 1927–Feb. 1928
13. Nov. 1927–Feb. 1928
14. Feb.–July 1931
15. Dec. 1931–July 1932
16. July 1933–March 1934
17. March–Aug. 1934
18. Aug. 1934–Feb. 1935
19. March–July 1935
20. Aug.–Dec. 1935
21. Dec. 1935–May 1936
22. May 1936–Jan. 1937
23. July 1937–Jan. 1938
24. Oct. 1943–Feb. 1947

1061 Outside repairers' and suppliers' order and running account books, 1904–35. 18 vols. MS 14553

Vol 1. Geo. Abbott, 61 Sandford Ave., Wood Green, 1924–35
2. Ganival and Callard, 27 Alfred St, City Rd, 1918–35
3. H. Harris, 9 Spenser St, 1904–16
4. Kew Observatory, Teddington, Mdx, 1905 (fragment)
5. John Ottway, 178 St John St, London, E.C., 1911–18
6. P. Pendleton, 21 Hope St, Prescott, Lancs., 1914–34
7. J. Preston and Sons, 19 Eccleston St, Prescott, 1906–12
8. J. Preston and Sons, 43 St Helen's Rd, Prescott, 1912–35
9. E. Sills, 21 Foyle Rd, Tottenham, 1918–35
10. W. H. Steer, 25 Allesley Old Rd, Coventry
11. J. Travers, 7 Spencer Sq., Ramsgate, 1918–21
12. As above, 1935
13. J. Warwick, 10 Shirley Rd, Stratford, E.15, 1930–32
14. F. Willis, 30 Richmond Cres., Barnsbury, N.1., 1919–35
15. Woods and Sons, 54 Spencer St, E.C., 1907–10
16. As above, 1911–16
17. As above, 1916–29
18. As above, 1929–35

1062 Address books. Undated; late 19th to early 20th century. 2 vols.   MS 14554

MISCELLANEOUS DOCUMENTS

1063 E. Sills, watch and chronometer finisher, 21 Foyle Road, Tottenham. Job order books, 1901–43. 2 vols. (Part of the Kullberg archive.)   MS 14555

1064 Notes on watch repair with a covering letter to Professor David Torrens (former owner of the Kullberg archive). 1935. 1 vol. (The letter is signed 'Ralph', with no surname.)   MS 14556

1065 Lecture notes, examination questions and extracts from books relating to watchmaking. (Possibly compiled by Heinrich Otto, 1875–1966.) c 1910–14? 7 vols.   MS 14557

Vol 1. Instructions for dismantling chronometers
2. Notes (in German) for a series of lectures
3. Examination questions with comments (in German)
4. Extracts from *Uber den freien Ankergang, Journal der Uhrmacherkunst*, 24 January 1877, p 21.
5–7. Notes from *Manuel pratique sur le spiral règlant des chronomètres et des montres*, by M. Phillips, Paris, 1865.

(For Otto's obituary see *Antiquarian Horology*, No. 3, Vol 5, p 96.)

1066 Joseph Preston and Sons, watch, clock and chronometer makers, of Prescott, Lancashire. Business archives. Volume containing descriptions of parts and their manufacturers, with prices; arranged alphabetically by manufacturers. Undated; c 1890–95. (The identification of Preston is conjectured from the handwriting, cf. MS 14560 *post*.)   MS 14558

1067 Pass book for Parr's Bank, 1907–12. MS 14559 (Part of the Kullberg archive.)

1068 J. Barnsdale and Son, clockmakers, of 18 Brunswick Place, City Road, London, E.C. Business archives. Order and repair books, 1881–1921. 2 vols. Arranged by customers and indexed.   MS 14784
    Vol 1. 1881–1921   Vol 2. 1894–1920
(Stanley Barnsdale, the last owner of this firm, died in 1973.)

1069 C. Lupton, watchmaker, of 3 Newman's Court, Cornhill, London, E.C. (prior to 1876 of St Michael's Alley, Cornhill). Marine chronometer rating book, giving maker's name, chronometer number, owner's name and name of his vessel. 1850–72 (mainly 1850–51). (Believed to have been kept by Lupton while he was working for P. Hilton Barraud, chronometer maker, of 41 Cornhill.)
(Part of the Barnsdale archive.)   MS 14785

***1070** Buckley (Francis). List of lost watches of London watchmakers, 1763–1804, giving numbers and dates of loss, compiled from contemporary newspapers; with list of Liverpool horologists in the 17th and 18th centuries compiled from directories, poll books, wills and newspapers. c 1930.   MS 2921

***1071** Buckley (Francis) and Buckley (George Bent). Alphabetical list of references to 18th-century newspaper advertisements relating to watchmakers, clockmakers and members of allied trades in London. Compiled c 1934. 2 vols.   MS 3338

*1072 Buckley (Francis) and Buckley (George Bent). List of British clockmakers working outside London, compiled mainly from newspapers and directories of the 18th century, and including foreign makers whose watches were lost in England. Compiled 1937. 2 vols.
MS 3355

1073 Hobson (Charles), high-class clock restorer of Portland Road, Hove, Sussex. Photocopies of workshop notes and diagrams relating to repairs carried out by Hobson on clocks by notable makers. *c* 1940–68. 23 envelopes.
MS 14917

   1. Thomas Taylor
   2. Robert Sly
   3. Jason Cox, John Shelton
   4. Charles Clay, Charles Gretton, Fabian Robins
   5. Thomas Tompion, Joseph Knibb, — ? Ellicott
   6. George Graham
   7. Paul Beauvais
   8. Daniel Delander
   9. Joseph Windmills
  10. George Tyler, James McCabe
  11. Francis Robinson
  12. Thomas Potts
  13. Christopher Pinchbeck
  14. Charles Goode
  15. —? Grimaldi
  16. James Hassenius, Daniel Le Count
  17. Henry Jones
  18. John Knibb, Jonathan Lowndes
  19. —? Knibb
  20. Joseph Knibb.
  21. Richard Peckover
  22. —? Fromanteel
  23. Unidentified

1074 Hobson (Charles). Photocopies of workshop notes and diagrams. *c* 1940–68. 4 envelopes. MS 14918
   1. Setting up a deadbeat
   2. Clock trains (letter from W. Beckman to Hobson, 1945)
   3. French polishing wood
   4. Pin barrels for music

1075 Photograph (with photocopy) and photocopy of another photograph (not included) of Charles Hobson in his workshop; with photograph of two winders by Thomas Tompion. 1951–68.
MS 14919

1076 Quill (Colonel Humphrey). Explanation in typescript of the repeating and striking mechanism found in

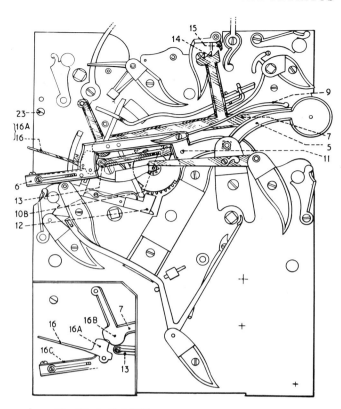

PLATE 43 One of the fifteen line drawings by E. A. Ayres which illustrate a step-by-step description of the repeating and striking mechanism found in some clocks by Thomas Tompion and George Graham. (No. 1076)

the clocks of Thomas Tompion and George Graham, with 15 diagrams (and photographic copies thereof) by E. A. Ayres and three photographs of the internal mechanism of an original Tompion clock and a Graham clock in the British Museum. 1969.
MS14921
See plate 43.

1077 Jump family, clockmakers. A scrapbook of letters, photographs, royal warrants, etc., connected with the family of Jump, of 93 Mount Street and elsewhere in London, 1785–1926.
MS 15189

INDEX TO THE CATALOGUE
OF MANUSCRIPTS

Figures in brackets indicate items listed under the catalogue numbers which precede them.

CONCORDANCE

OF GUILDHALL LIBRARY MANUSCRIPT NUMBERS AND CATALOGUE NUMBERS

The following table is provided for those who wish to identify in this catalogue a manuscript known to them by its Guildhall Library number only.

Guildhall Library MS no.	Catalogue no.	Guildhall Library MS no.	Catalogue no.
2710	902	3944	938
2711	903	3945	939
2712	904	3946	940
2713	905	3946A	941
2714	906	3947	942
2715	907	3948	945
2716	908	3949	946
2717	909	3950	947
2718	910	3951	948
2719	911	3952	949
2719A	912	3953	950
2719B	913	3954	951
2720	914	3955	952
2721	915	3956	953
2722	916	3957	954
2723	917	3958	955
2724	918	3959	956
2725	920	3960	957
2726	921	3961	958
2727	922	3962	959
2728	923	3963	960
2729	924	3964	961
2730	925	3965	962
2731	926	3966	963
2732	927	3967	964
2733	928	3968	965
2734	929	3969	966
2735	930	3970	967
2921	1070	3971	968
3334	931	3972	972–75
3338	1071	3973	976
3355	1072	3974	983
3939	932	3975	984
3940	933	3976	985
3940A	934	3977	986
3941	935	3978	987
3942	936	3979	988
3943	937	3980	989

Guildhall Library MS no.	Catalogue no.	Guildhall Library MS no.	Catalogue no.
3981	990	9195	1015
3982	991	9196	1004
3983	992	9197	1002
3984	993	9198	1027
3985	994	9473	1035
3986	995	9473A	1036
3987	996	10501	1037
3988	997	10502	1038
3988B	998	10554	970
6026	977–81	11568	971
6430	943	14284	1039
6431	944	14285	1040
6436	919	14373	1041
6619	999	14374	1042
6788	1000	14469	1043
6789	1001	14470	1044
6790	1003	14537	1045
6791	1005	14538	1046
6791A	1006	14539	1047
6791B	1007	14540	1048
6791C	1008	14541	1049
6792	1009	14542	1050
6792A	1010	14543	1051
6793	1011	14544	1052
6794	1012	14545	1053
6795	1013	14546	1054
6795A	1014	14547	1055
6796	1016	14548	1056
6796A	1017	14549	1057
6797	1018	14550	1058
6797A	1019	14551	1059
6797B	1020	14552	1060
6798	1021	14553	1061
6799	1022	14554	1062
6799A	1023	14555	1063
6800	1024	14556	1064
6801	1025	14557	1065
6802	1026	14558	1066
6803	1028	14459	1067
6804	1029	14784	1068
6805	1030	14785	1069
6805A	1031	14917	1073
6806	1032	14918	1074
6807	1033	14919	1075
6808	1034	14921	1076
9074	982	15189	1078

CATALOGUE OF PORTRAITS

On the Guildhall Art Gallery Register

1078 Atkins, George. Wax.

1079 Cumming, Alexander. Oils.
See plate 44.

1080 Grant, John. Master, 1838–39. Oils.

1081 Gray, Benjamin. Oils.

1082 Harrison, John. Enamel paste; by James Tassie.
See plate 45.

1083 Mudge, Thomas. Oils. By Nathaniel Dance.
See plate 46.

PLATE 44   Alexander Cumming (*c* 1732–1814). Portrait in oils by S. Drummond, ARA. Alexander Cumming was a celebrated Scottish clockmaker who worked in London for most of his adult life. He was a Fellow of the Royal Society of Scotland. In 1766 he wrote *The Elements of Clock and Watch-work*, of which his personal annotated copy is No. 220 in this book. He made two long case clocks (one is in Buckingham Palace) that record barometric pressure throughout the year and were provided with spring-driven, gravity escapements very similar to that made subsequently by John Grant (see exhibit no. 569 in the Company's Museum). Grant, who died in 1810, was Cumming's nephew, apprentice and successor. In 1763, Cumming was appointed a member of the special Committee of the Board of Longitude to hear John Harrison's explanation of the mechanism of his longitude watch, H.4 (see Nos 195 and 196). He was made an Honorary Freeman of the Company in 1781. (No. 1079)

PLATE 45   John Harrison (1693–1776). Portrait in enamel paste by James Tassie. John Harrison has been described by G. H. Baillie as 'the most remarkable man in the history of horology'. The Company is very fortunate in possessing in their library many original documents and drawings made by or connected with John Harrison, all of which bear on his life-long struggle to obtain the £20,000 longitude award. Also in this collection are unique examples of his clocks, watches and other important items. The provenance of many of these relics can be traced back without a break to John Harrison himself mainly by means of the letters of his great-grand-daughter, Mrs Wright (see No. 981). (No. 1082)

PLATE 46 Thomas Mudge (1715–94). Portrait in oils by Nathaniel Dance. Recently, a similar but larger portrait has come to light; it is owned by a descendant of the Mudge family. The Company also possesses a portrait of Thomas Mudge's father, the Reverend Zachariah Mudge (No. 1084). Thomas Mudge possessed exceptional manual skill as well as inventive ability. His invention in 1769 of the detached lever escapement was of great importance; in a developed form, this device is still used today in almost all watches and small clocks. In later life, Mudge concentrated on developing marine chronometers, and in 1793 his success was rewarded by a grant of £3,000 by the House of Commons. He became a Freeman of the Company in 1738 and a Liveryman in 1766. His son, Thomas Mudge Junior, made great efforts to obtain adequate recognition for his father and wrote three books (Nos 600–602) describing Mudge's special devices and attesting to the efficiency of his timekeepers. For a memoir of the Mudge family by S. R. Flint, see No. 328. (No. 1083)

PLATE 47 John Ellicott, FRS (1706–1772). Mezzotint by R. Dunkarton after the portrait by Nathaniel Dance. Although John Ellicott was a clock and watchmaker of great standing, he was more naturally a thinker and experimenter. He is especially remembered for his design of a compensated pendulum, which in 1751 was adjudged by Professor Bliss (afterwards Astronomer Royal) to be superior to the mercury pendulum of George Graham or the gridiron of John Harrison. Ellicott wrote two works on pendulums (see Nos 296–297), and is mentioned by John Harrison as having examined his gridiron compensation in his first marine time-keeper, H.1, in 1736 (see No. 973 (9)). John Ellicott was made a Fellow of the Royal Society in 1738. (No. 1099).

PLATE 48 William James Frodsham, FRS (1778–1850). Lithograph by Ada Cole after a painting by an unknown artist. Frodsham started the successful watch and chronometer firm of Parkinson and Frodsham which flourished from 1801 to 1947. He was Master of the Clockmakers Company in 1836 and again in 1837, and conferred lasting benefit by leaving in his will £1,000 to the poor of the Company, to be distributed as the 'Parkinson and Frodsham Charity', the name of Parkinson being included in memory of his old business partner. (No. 1101)

1084 Mudge, Rev Zachariah. Oils. By Lucy Deebonison, after Sir Joshua Reynolds.

1085 Nelthropp, Henry Leonard. Master, 1893–94. Oils.

1086 Vulliamy, Benjamin, Oils.

1087 Vulliamy, Benjamin Lewis. Wax.
See Frontispiece.

1088 Vulliamy, Francis Justin. Oils.

In the Guildhall Print Room Collection

1089 Arnold, John. Mezzotint. By R. Davy, after Susan Esther Reid.

1090 Atkins, Samuel Elliott. Photograph.

1091 Barnsdale, W. Photograph.

1092 Breguet, Abraham Louis. Lithograph. By Langlume, after A. Chayal.

1093 Carter, James, FRAS. Four times Master. Photograph in colour.

1094 Clarke, Henry. Photograph.

1095 Clarke, Henry Hyde. Soft-ground etching.

1096 Cumming, Alexander, FRS. Stipple engraving. By S. Drummond.

1097 Dent, Edward J. Lithograph. By C. Baugnut, 1853.

1098 Earnshaw, Thomas. Mezzotint. By S. Bellin, after Archer-Shee.

1099 Ellicott, John. Mezzotint. By R. Dunkarton, after Nathaniel Dance.
See plate 47.

1100 Ferguson, James. Mezzotint. After J. Townsend.

1101 Frodsham, William James. Lithograph. By Ada Cole, after a painting.
(*See* **937**, Nos 60–61, *ante* and plate 48.)

1102 Graham, George. Mezzotint. By J. Faber, after T. Hudson.
(*See* **991** *ante*.)

1103 Grant, John. Mezzotint. By Ryley.

1104 Grant, John. Photograph. By Maull and Co.

1105 Harrison, John. Engraving. By P. L. Tassaert, after T. Kind, 1768.
(*See* **991** *ante.*)

1106 Hartley-Kennedy, R. Lithograph. By Viner, after a photograph.

1107 Janvier, Antide. Lithograph.

1108 Jejeebhoy, Sir Jamsetjee, Bart, CSI. Three photographs.

1109 Le Roy, Julian. Engraving. By Moitte, after Perroneau.

1110 Mudge, Thomas. Mezzotint. By C. Townley, after Nathaniel Dance, 1772.

1111 Pinchbeck, Christopher. Mezzotint. By I. Faber, after Isaac Wood.

1112 Reid, Thomas. Engraving. By C. Thomson, after Sir Thomas Lawrence.
(*See* **937**, No 57, *ante* and plate 49.)

1113 Rogers, Isaac. Photograph; enlarged, after a miniature.

1114 Tompion, Thomas. Mezzotint. By John Smith, after Sir Godfrey Kneller.

1115 Tompion, Thomas. Miniature; a modern copy (*c* 1900) on thin card of a contemporary miniature, the sitter shown half length, facing right, looking front, and holding a watch in his left hand.

1116 Willis, Francis. Mezzotint. By W. Ward, after H. Sass.

PLATE 49 Thomas Reid (1746–1831). Engraving by Charles Thomson after a portrait by Sir Thomas Lawrence. Thomas Reid was a celebrated Edinburgh clock and watchmaker who wrote a *Treatise on Clock and Watch making*, which ran into seven editions and also a pirated edition in the United States (see No. 726). For some correspondence connected with Reid, see No. 937 (46, 57, 62). Reid also presented to the Company a file of letters that had passed between John Holmes, Professor W. Ludlam and John Smeaton (see No. 992). (No. 1112)

CATALOGUE OF PRINTS, DRAWINGS, PAINTINGS (other than Portraits) AND PHOTOGRAPHS

On the Guildhall Art Gallery Register

1117 Table, with articles of vertu, including a watch. Oil painting. Attributed to Peter Roestraten.

1118 Collection of fifteen engravings by Bartolozzi, P. W. Tomkins, Marcuard, G. W. Ryland and J. M. Delattre. (Kept with the Print Room Collection.)

In the Guildhall Print Room Collection

1119 Vera Effigies ac descriptio astronomici horologii Argentinensis in summo Templo extructi. Anno Christi MDLXXIV. (The Strasbourg cathedral clock, with Latin verses by Nicodemus Frischlinus.) Line engraving. 27 × 20cm.

1120 Horologium Astronomicum Argentoratense. (The Strasbourg cathedral clock, with description in French.) Line engraving. 60 × 42cm.

1121 Horologium Astronomicum Argentoratense. (The Strasbourg cathedral clock, with Latin verses by M. Georg Calaminus.) Woodcut. 55 × 37cm.

1122 Eigentliche Fürbildung und Beschreibung dess Künstreichen astronomischen . . . Uhrwerks zu Strazburg in Münster. (The Strasbourg cathedral clock, with description in German, probably by Johann Fischart.) Line engraving. By Isaac Brunn. 50 × 32cm.

1123 Eigentliche Fürbildung und Beschreibung dess newen Künstlichen Astronomischen Uhrwercks zu Strassburg in Münster diss 1574 Jahr vollendet zusehen. (The Strasbourg cathedral clock, with German verses.) Woodcut. 54 × 36cm.

1124 L'Horloge de Strasbourg. Line engraving. 21 × 13cm.

1125 A true figure of the famous clock of Strasbourg. Line engraving. 21 × 11cm.

1126 (The Strasbourg cathedral clock.) Line engraving. 6 × 4cm.

1127 Description de l'horloge que Messieurs les Comtes de Lyon ont fait faire dans l'église de St Jean . . . 1660. (With a description.) Line engraving. By Thourneysor, after Cordie. 49 × 36cm.

1128 L'Horloge de l'Eglise St Jean à Lion. Line engraving. 52 × 21cm.

1129 A village fair with a clock in the church tower. Woodcut. By H. S. Beham of Nürnberg. 34 × 28cm.

1130 Design for a clock. Line engraving, by J. C. Philips, 1721.

1131 An astromicall and crono-logicall clock, shewing all the most usefull parts of an Almanack. Line engraving. By Jos. Naylor, 1751. 59 × 37cm.

1132 A new and accurate geographical clock, shewing the time of day and night at most of the principal places of the world . . . Line engraving. By John Gibson, published by T. Kitchin, 1761. 42 × 39cm.

1133 The microcosm. (An astronomical clock with portraits of Sir Isaac Newton and Henry Bridges, its designer.) Line engraving. By R. Sheppard. 59 × 44cm. *See* plate 50.

1134 Three Italian designs for clocks. Line engravings, each *c* 44 × 25cm

1135 Musical clock by Jacob Lovelace, jnr (*c* 1695–1755). Lithograph. By Hackett, 1833. 52 × 37cm. (*See Antiquarian Horology*, vol 5, pp 78–85). *See* plate 51.

1136 Clock by Thomas Tompion in the Pump Room, Bath. Photograph. 29 × 17cm.

1137 Plan of church clock for Mr Raphael made by Brockbank and Atkins. Pen drawing. 53 × 66cm.

1138 The very extraordinary sun dial facing the market place at Settle . . . Yorkshire. Line engraving. By S. Buck and I. Feary, 1778. 42 × 53cm.

1139 A table for easily regulating clocks and watches. Ornamental design enclosing calendar showing apparent time at noon G.M.T. throughout the year. Line engraving. By E. Thorowgood, 1752. 33 × 24cm.

1140 Tomb of John Harrison in Hampstead churchyard. Photograph, *c* 1880. 19.5 × 24.5cm.

1141 Gnomonic chart of the north polar region. Circular, 60cm diam.

1142 Chart of Prince Regent Inlet area. 44 × 98cm.

1143 Brass sundial formerly owned by Governor John Endicott of Massachusetts. Photograph. 21 × 19cm.

1144 Illuminated Vote of Thanks to the Company from the Clock and Watchmakers' Asylum, 1883. 47 × 37cm.

1145 A perspective view of the altitude and azimuth instrument recently erected at the Royal Observatory, Greenwich. Steel engraving, from the *Illustrated London News*, September 1847. 45 × 35cm.

PLATE 50 *The Microcosm.* Print by Henry Bridges, *c* 1730. This print shows the elaborate astronomical clock which, together with its several moving scenes as well as an organ, was known as the 'Microcosm' or 'Little World'. Its maker, who lived at Waltham Abbey, sold the clock to E. Davies in 1740. During 1756 the clock was on exhibition in New York and Boston. Later the 'Microcosm' went to France and was largely destroyed, probably during the French Revolution. The clock mechanism, with its astronomical dial, is now in the British Museum. The cipher, or monogram, in the margin of this plate is that of B. L. Vulliamy, who donated the original print to the Company. (No. 1133)

PLATE 51 The Lovelace clock. Lithograph by Hackett, 1833. The description printed at the foot of this print is not entirely accurate. The clock was probably made between 1720 and 1740 at Exeter, and was so arresting in appearance and in mechanical construction that it was exhibited for money on several occasions. It was badly damaged when Liverpool Museum was bombed in the Second World War, but the dial, works and other parts are now on exhibition once more. A full illustrated description of the clock is given in *Antiquarian Horology*, June 1966 (see No. 18). (No. 1135)

1146 A self-moving wheel, with explanation. Line engraving, 1749. 39 × 33cm.

1147 The Master's badge and chain of the Clockmakers' Company. Two photographs, 1963. Each 20 × 24cm.

1148 Three photographs relating to the Knibb clock, 1964. Each 28 × 24cm.

1149 Silver tobacco box (1789?), made by Hester Bateman and bearing the arms of the Clockmakers' company. Photograph, 1957.

1150 Album of photographs of the ceremonial unveiling of a memorial plaque on the birth-place of Thomas Tompion at Ickfield Green, Bedfordshire, on 12 June 1952, together with three pamphlets connected with the ceremony.

1151 Collection of over 1250 watch papers, with typed index of makers' names. Three boxes and index.
See **137** *ante* and plate 52.

PLATE 52   Specimens from the collection of over 1250 watch papers (No. 1151)